SECRETS OF
SUCCESSFUL
PUBLIC RELATIONS

SECRETS OF SUCCESSFUL PUBLIC RELATIONS

An Insider's Guide to the Strategies and Techniques That Work Today

Charles S. Phillips

Prentice-Hall, Inc.
Englewood Cliffs, New Jersey

Prentice-Hall International, Inc., *London*
Prentice-Hall of Australia, Pty. Ltd., *Sydney*
Prentice-Hall Canada, Inc., *Toronto*
Prentice-Hall of India Private Ltd., *New Delhi*
Prentice-Hall of Japan, Inc., *Tokyo*
Prentice-Hall of Southeast Asia Pte. Ltd., *Singapore*
Whitehall Books, Ltd., Wellington, *New Zealand*
Editora Prentice-Hall do Brasil Ltda., *Rio de Janeiro*
Prentice-Hall Hispanoamericana, S.A., *Mexico*

© 1985 by

PRENTICE-HALL, INC.
Englewood Cliffs, N.J.

Library of Congress Cataloging in Publication Data

Phillips, Charles S.
  Secrets of successful public relations.

  Includes index.
  1. Public relations—Handbooks, manuals, etc.
I. Title.
HD59.P45 1985   659.2   85-6426

ISBN 0-13-798661-0

Printed in the United States of America

To my love, Phyllis I. Phillips.

To our brood: Kip and Doug
     Chip, Gina, "C. J." and Jerry
     Cliff
     Little Monte

To "Black Magic" and "Drambuie," and to the woman next door who does not like retrievers.

To the kids who stop by: Wendy Britton, Mike Dreps, Holly Ennist, Nancy Kecmer, Joe Mack, Bobby Opolin (who once stayed all summer and part of the fall), Rob Patterson, and Brian Wadman.

And to all the other distractions—guitars and stereos, jangling phones, Blair Academy Sideliners' Association, Jerry Salvatore's motorcycle—all of which are discernible in the following pages.

About the Author

Charles S. Phillips has over twenty-five years of experience as a journalist and public relations practitioner. His professional positions have included Senior Vice President, Carl Byoir & Associates; Vice President-Group Manager, Burson-Marsteller; Director-Corporate Public Relations & Advertising, Combustion Engineering, Inc.

A public relations generalist, Phillips has implemented corporate, investor relations, marketing, and public affairs strategies for many of America's leading corporations.

Currently, Phillips lives on north Florida's Atlantic coast, where he walks his Labrador and golden retrievers on the beach, serves as Director-Account Services for William Cook Public Relations, Jacksonville, and works on three novels.

A graduate of Rutgers University, Phillips served as a U.S. Army Paratroop officer during the Korean Conflict. He and his wife, Phyllis Irwin Phillips, have four children.

Preface

Secrets are bewitching. They captivate, mesmerize, infuse us with the need to know, the need to be in on the sources of mystery and intrigue.

Secrets are all-abiding. They are big and small, important and unimportant, personal and impersonal.

Secrets are universal. Every person, every company, every industry has them.

The public relations business teems with secrets—secrets about what is disclosed, what should be disclosed, what will never be disclosed. Secrets about the chairman, the chairman's wife, the chairman's Lhasa apso. What makes the public relations business so secretive is that it deals with confidential matters: business strategies, competitive situtations, problems and opportunities that affect people, products, and profits.

THE ALPHABETICAL ASSAULT

There are more secrets than ever before in the public relations business. That's because of the alphabetical assault that was made on America's corporations during the 1960s and 1970s, when OSHA, EEO, SEC, DEP and FTC forced more regulation of consumerism than had been advanced in the previous century. NAACP, SANE, NOW, AARP, CORE, ACLU, AFSCME demanded social change on issues that had smoldered since the birth of the nation. AP, UPI, CBS, NBC, ABC fueled national discontent with detailed reporting of discordants' demands.

THE SOCIAL-POLITICAL-ECONOMIC CORPORATION

As a result of this alphabetical assault, American corporations became social and political, as well as economic, entities. Management, professionally ill-equipped to combat such sweeping change, rushed battalions of public relations people to the front. With only light weaponry—basically publicity and marketing skills—PR practitioners attempted to sanctify the corporate presence in the eyes of a disbelieving public. Their success, at best, was measured. But the public relations arsenal was vastly improved during this skirmish. New weapons such as sophisticated audit and research procedures, issues management and government relations techniques, public issues/public affairs counseling methods, employee motivation, community and investor relations approaches were developed. The arsenal includes satellite communications, computerized word processing, and paperless news dissemination, and the list is still expanding.

THE NEW PUBLIC RELATIONS PERSONALITY

At the same time, the public relations practitioner is taking on a new personality. Public relations people are no longer only writers and editors. They are businesspeople. Writing and creativity are still vital to the function, but public relations people today are just as apt to be financial analysts or lawyers as they are journalists—people trained not only to *react* to news, but to *make* news by implementing programmed strategies.

This is important, because more is expected of individuals in the public relations business than ever before. With American business in a survival-oriented period, public relations practitioners are expected to combine the talents of a forecaster, writer, economist, researcher, media expert, sociologist, legislator, industrial psychologist, and more.

Because of the nation's survival-oriented business stance, some of the most effective business techniques, including public relations methods, have been guarded jealously. This book presents some of the more advanced public relations weapons that have, to some degree, been kept under wraps. It is hoped that they will help all practitioners to be everything they are expected to be.

Introduction

ABOUT VOCATIONAL TIME PINCHES, AND KEEPING PACE WITH PUBLIC RELATIONS TRENDS

It is in the nature of public relations that most practitioners are saddled with many recurring, "must do" responsibilities that leave little time for planning strategies or for learning about the expanding role that their profession is assuming in the affairs of corporate America.

Because of this vocational time pinch, many practitioners dwell on the public relations periphery. Their views of the expanding role of public relations are usually shadowy, and they lack the perspective necessary for decisive implementation of the advanced strategies that are being demanded in the wake of the cyclonic changes that occurred in America's social, political, and economic structures in the 1960s and 1970s.

Despite glazed vision, and because American business is facing new and unprecedented challenges, public relations practitioners are being asked to wear many hats: those of versatile writer, press relations advisor, economic strategist, industrial psychologist, union relations counselor, employee motivator, government relations expert, and many more. It is small wonder that much of this headgear is ill-fitting.

HOW CAN THIS BOOK HELP YOU?

Secrets of Successful Public Relations was written to sharpen practitioners' views of the contemporary public relations function, to be their partner and advisor when it is necessary to don ill-fitting hats. The author was in the eye of the storm when American corporations were transformed from economic entities to social/political/economic entities. He helped develop some of the public relations techniques and strategies (many of them, until this book, proprietary) that business is implementing to help guide it through the present turbulent times.

This book can sharpen an individual practitioner's performance in several ways:

- By encouraging clear-eyed examination of new public relations horizons. By allowing practitioners to look beyond their normally-assigned responsibilities; to grasp the significance of the contemporary public relations approaches that are being employed in areas as diverse as audits/research, multinational relations, business-to-business and consumer marketing, and employee motivation.

- By applying explicit guidelines to permit practitioners to execute programs even in unfamiliar areas.

- By significantly broadening an individual's knowledge about today's business trends, and of their effects on corporate America.

- By sharpening practitioners' counseling abilities, by providing knowledge of advanced public relations techniques.

- By helping practitioners to better articulate the necessity to implement advanced public relations strategies.

WHAT PRACTICAL AIDS DOES THIS BOOK CONTAIN?

What specific, practical aids does this innovative book contain that might dramatically increase your perceptiveness and creativity as a public relations practitioner?

- *Proprietary Knowledge*
  Insights developed, tested, and perfected by international leaders in the public relations business, innovators who are setting the pace and helping public relations evolve from a trade press placement function to a full-fledged management service.

- *The Action Areas*
  Secrets zeros in on those public relations areas where the action is, the hot target areas where whirlwind change is occurring, the centers of action that are capturing management's attention, and that offer the maximum challenge and reward for today's public relations practitioners.

- *Graphics*
  One-hundred-eighteen exhibits, including charts, checklists, schedules, questions and answers, lists of associations, speaking platforms, data bases, and other practical information that can be used here and now.

Secrets of Successful Public Relations can help you to focus on the urgency and importance of the public relations function. This text can help you—as a member of management or a practitioner, as an advanced student or an instructor—to focus on up-to-the-minute public relations practices.

Contents

Chapter   7:   EMPLOYEE RELATIONS

New Tactics for an "I-Oriented" Environment   192

Chapter   8:   EMPLOYEE MOTIVATION

**A Master Plan for Getting Top Efforts Out
of a Troubled Work Place   210**

Chapter   9:   INDUSTRIAL INTRIGUE

**How Business-to-Business Public Relations
Is Changing Along with the American Work Place   227**

Chapter 10:   INTERNATIONAL CONNECTIONS

**The Latest Trends and Techniques in International
Public Relations   251**

Chapter 14:   AGENCY-CLIENT RELATIONSHIPS

Secrets of Successful Courtship   **295**

SECRETS OF
SUCCESSFUL
PUBLIC RELATIONS

The Communications Audit

Uncovering the Secrets of the Corporate Universe

The communications audit can provide penetrating insight into the effectiveness of a company's communications strategies and practices. And it can uncover secrets of a more delicate nature, such as the existence of employee frustrations, corporate strengths and weaknesses, and managerial deficiencies.

The audit was originally employed by public relations and advertising agencies to acquire start-up knowledge of a new client's communications activities. Marketplace communications were traditionally stressed. But when special-interest activist organizations and government regulatory agencies targeted corporations for social and legislative reform in the 1960s, the audit was employed as an investigative strategem. The tool was used to gain first-hand knowledge of how important sections of the public—such as employees, customers, the press and financial communities—judged sensitive topics including management effectiveness, product durability and design, and compliance with environmental regulations. Today, the audit is employed in any area that management thinks important enough to warrant obtaining timely, accurate information.

Communications audits are not to be confused with research. They are first cousins. Sometimes, such as with audits of local communities, audits are combined with research. But demographics and statistical evaluations are usually not important to an audit's conclusions; competitive factors are not always involved, either. And, most important, the interviewers are familiar enough with their audiences to know, without the benefit of qualitative or quantitative research, that they are receiving objective responses to questions. Audits permit public relations people to see things the way specific audiences see them. This permits the development of targeted communications strategies.

A communications audit also differs from research in the way interviews are conducted. Marketing research interviews are usually accomplished quickly, frequently on the telephone, and a knowledge of the research topic is not always presumed. The audit, however, is directed at respondents with moderate to exhaustive knowledge about a specific topic. The interviews are almost always face-to-face, and comprehensive questioning is desirable. Also, public relations personnel are able to conduct audits without time-consuming reliance on outside research firms.

ESTABLISHING OBJECTIVES FOR INTERNAL/EXTERNAL AUDITS

There are two types of audits: internal and external. Internal audits are evaluations of "inside" audiences such as salaried and hourly employees, management, and plant communities. Internal audits are gaining in importance as mergers and acquisitions increase, because they assist management in assessing the corporate assimilation process, and they spotlight problems early. External audits provide evaluations of the way outside audiences perceive a company. Audits frequently combine both internal and external audiences.

Common objectives of internal audits are:

- To gather information necessary to update communications programs.
- To gain insight into what division and plant management believe the communications function can realistically accomplish.
- To diagnose the problems and opportunities facing a corporation.
- To determine management and blue-collar appraisal of communications efforts with important publics: employees, customers, prospects, the press, financial and government communities.
- To recognize the company's strengths and weaknesses.
- To evaluate the Marketing and Public Relations and Advertising Departments' effectiveness and potential.
- To understand the proper image to project and develop communications programs that project this image effectively.

External audits are more diverse and more challenging than internal audits. Within "the family," even within a company that is experiencing labor difficulties, auditors usually encounter a willingness to talk. But it can be difficult to diagnose and measure the emotions of a diverse and unregimented public toward a company or other organization. Members of the press, the financial community, shareholders, pressure groups, plant communities, social activists, environmentalists, customers, consumers, government and religious organizations all have different demands, and different ways of measuring a company's responsiveness.

Also, an external audit can have extremely diverse or extremely narrow objectives. For example:

Objective #1: Determine the degree of acceptability of a company's minority hiring, environmental, and community-improvement policies among environmentalists, social activist organizations, and the religious and press communities in cities where the company operates manufacturing facilities.

Objective #2: Determine the degree of receptiveness in Lyndhurst, New Jersey, to the construction of a light manufacturing facility which will employ 170 workers.

External audits frequently require the assistance of professional researchers. Contrary to internal audits, where company personnel are readily available for interviews, external respondents are elusive and sometimes difficult to pin down for interviews. Researchers are especially valuable at keeping external audits moving along on schedule, because of audience diversity: everything from militant women's and black rights advocates to Boy Scout leaders and representatives of longshoremen's unions.

Some of the objectives of external audits are:

- To understand the effectiveness of communications efforts.
- To gain insight into the degree of public understanding of a company's financial and technological commitment to alleviate air and water pollution.
- To determine corporate recognition in the college community.
- To determine effectiveness of corporate advertising on key publics.
- To determine a company's visibility among customers, the corporate/business press, and members of the financial community.
- To survey the impact of a plant closing.
- To determine the reputation of the company's products among customer audiences for: (a) durability, (b) design, (c) technology, (d) warranty, (e) service.
- To determine the effectiveness of international marketing communications.

CONDUCTING THE INTERNAL AUDIT

In terms of the number of plants or offices involved, internal audits run the gamut from a single facility to dozens of operations. All audits, though, have one important element: a need to know. There is always a need to acquire information that, when interpreted objectively, can lead to the implementation of procedures that will make a single plant or an entire corporation operate more effectively.

Multi-Location Plant Selection: Introducing the Parts to the Whole

In wide-ranging corporate audits, several plants, representing a cross section of a company's operations, are usually selected for auditing. For example, if a paper company is auditing hourly employees, a mill location, a converting operation, a manufacturing plant, plus small to large facilities would be included. Frequently, the mind-set of workers is different depending on plant location, type of operation, union representation, and pay scale. Also, especially with medium-to-large companies, the employees in one plant may not necessarily possess knowledge of other operations. Many *Fortune 500* companies have grown rapidly through acquisition, and it is common to find that the "parts" have not been introduced to the whole.

A Sample Notification Letter

A notification letter like the one that follows should be sent to the managers of all facilities selected to participate in the audit. The letter should include: a brief explanation of the audit's objectives; an explanation about why the manager's plant was selected for participation; a positive statement concerning the benefits anticipated as a result of the audit.

The letter, signed by the chairman, president, or other key operating officer, should attempt to allay suspicions that "problem" plants were selected for auditing. The following letter accomplishes this. Additionally, because the letter is signed by a key officer, it assures cooperation by presenting a mandate for the audit.

Dear Fred:

To assist in the development of our company's new and considerably more aggressive corporate communications program, your plant has been selected to participate in a "communications audit." Employees in corporate headquarters, plus those in the Philadelphia, Mobile and Jacksonville production facilities, will also participate. The manufacturing facilities selected represent a cross section of our product line and union affiliations, as well as large, medium, and small work forces.

Objectives of the audit are:

- To determine the level of common understanding that Excel Company employees have of the company's goals and of its expanding product lines and markets.
- To learn how effectively management has been communicating to employees, and vice-versa.
- To determine how effective our traditional employee communication techniques—including the house organ, supervisors' meetings, and hot lines—have been, and to institute changes if necessary.

Our corporate public relations agency, Carl Byoir & Associates, will conduct the audit. They will be supported by our own Public Relations Department, under Henry Reidel. Hank will be contacting you shortly to arrange for a September date for the Carl Byoir people to visit your facility. Employee interviews will require one day or less.

When the audit is completed early next year, we will share the results with you. We will also implement any changes in our communications practices that will help to make us a more proficient company.

Sincerely,

Henry T. Wolcott
President

When Troublemakers Come in Handy

A cross section of employees should be interviewed. The cross section should include "company-oriented" workers, troublemakers, men, women, blacks, whites, Hispanics, foremen, machine operators, sweepers, new hands and old. Employees at hourly, supervisory, and management levels should be interviewed. Sometimes, plant management will present a list of company-oriented workers who will present only the positive side of operations. A perceptive troublemaker often possesses more valuable insight than a company-oriented employee.

The number of hourly respondents selected in each plant will vary. It would seem appropriate, for example, to interview at least 100–150 employees from a work force of 2,000–2,500, while 10–15 respondents could be adequate in a plant with a work force of 125–150.

Although not necessary, it is helpful for hourly employees to have some advance notice of the interview. This permits them to give the subject some thought, and eliminates the necessity for interviewers to explain the purpose of the discussion before each interview.

Face to Face: The Interview

Interviews should be conducted in a well-structured manner. Recording devices should not be used, as they tend to inhibit meaningful conversation. Employees should be informed at the outset that all remarks will be considered confidential. Interviewers should work from question sheets prepared in advance, and all employees should be asked the same questions. Not uncommonly, however, employees will depart from the standard interview format and reveal specific insights their own way. These are sometimes the most productive interviews. In these cases, interviewers should discontinue the structured line of questioning, and home in on the respondent's personal observations.

Telephone interviews are not recommended in public relations audits. They lack the sincerity of face-to-face interviews, and it is difficult for the interviewers to evaluate respondents.

For reference purposes, it is advisable for interviewers to include a few pertinent comments about each respondent at the end of their notes. This helps the person who prepares the final audit report to evaluate each respondent. These notes should be brief, but meaningful, such as: "Respondent evasive. Poor eye contact. Offered vague and incomplete observations. Length of interview: 14 minutes."

Interview lengths vary. Usually, they last from 20 minutes to 1½ hours. Short interviews result when respondents are suspicious and distrustful. Antagonistic interviews should be avoided. Usually, nothing of value is gained, and the respondent could sour other employees by reporting a hostile experience.

Key Traits for Successful Interviewers

It is essential that interviewers be mature and competent. If the confidence of respondents is not won immediately, it is probable that information will be withheld and the entire audit could suffer.

Interviewers should be well-versed not only about the operations and the products of a company, but also about competitive industry factors and issues of historical significance. Usually, to speed the interview process, several interviewers are used. One individual should be appointed project leader and should be responsible for scheduling, coordinating results and, most importantly, for preparing the final document. It is recommended that one person write the final report. This guarantees consistent style and maximum readability.

Copious note-taking by interviewers is recommended. It is almost never acceptable to telephone a respondent for follow-up information. This suggests poor preparation or inadequate knowledge of the company. Notes should also contain substantial quotes. Quotations—which should never be attributed to a respondent by name, but can sometimes refer to a title—lend credibility, and make for lively reading.

For example, here is the same statement, first with quotes and then in straight prose:

> If a label or a theme could be attached to the personality of the company's audit, it would be: "Here Comes Tomorrow." Respondents impart a strong awareness of momentum. An awareness that "Something positive is happening…" that "We've got direction now…" that "We're in a period of transition that will see us become one hell of a firm." "It's slow," one New York executive summed up, "because of the old traditions. But you can feel it starting, because of the new management. We're moving, and it's a great feeling."

> Respondents mentioned that the future of the company seemed bright. They stated that there seemed to be momentum, that something positive was happening. They also mentioned that the company was in a transitional period, because of the new management taking control and instituting changes. Even though positive change was coming slowly, it was agreed that change *was* coming, and this was applauded.

Twenty-three of the Most Frequently Asked Questions in Internal Audits

The following questions are frequently asked of white collar respondents in internal audits.

1. What are some of the adjectives that you think best describe the company? (Offer examples: "stodgy," "aggressive," "leader," "follower," "innovative," "creative," "decisive," "lethargic.")
2. Let's talk about what is right about the company. What are its strengths: Its people? Management? Patents? Manufacturing facilities? Capital position? Shareholder loyalty? Have these strengths been communicated effectively to important audiences?
   - Shareholders
   - Employees
   - Financial community
   - The press
   - Customers and potential customers
3. Now, what about weaknesses? What do you consider to be the company's primary weaknesses? (Interviewer should probe: Do weaknesses hinder corporate operations? Are weaknesses known to important publics?)

4. Let's take several important publics one at a time. Tell me what you think these publics think of the company. (Discuss five publics listed.)

    Do you think some of these publics should receive more attention than others? Which?

    Do you think some of the publics are getting too much or too little attention?

5. In the near term—say, the next five years—where do you see your company going? (Interviewer to question about formalized growth plans. Have plans been explained to those with responsibility for executing growth strategies, etc.?)

6. What about management? Are the managers capable of moving the company forward? Are there enough of them? Do they have the proper backgrounds?

7. Is the corporate marketing function effective? (Interviewer to inquire about competency of all disciplines—advertising, public relations, marketing.)

8. Is management, both divisional and corporate, involved enough in the marketing function? If not, should they be? (Attempt to find out what is meant by "enough.")

9. Does management support the communications function? If you were the person responsible for communications, would you (increase) (decrease) (leave about the same) the function?

10. What do you think is right or wrong with the company's present communications efforts?

11. If you knew *The Wall Street Journal* was going to run a front page story about your company tomorrow, what would you most want to see come across in it?

12. What do you think are the most favorable opportunities in domestic or international markets?

13. What are the major marketing problems?

14. Let's say you are responsible for advertising and public relations strategies. What themes would you use for these campaigns, and why?

15. Does your company assume an aggressive spokesperson role in the industries it serves? If not, should it?

16. Are you aware of an overall marketing plan that coordinates the communications and promotional efforts of all divisions and all departments?

17. Do you think the marketing role is understood throughout the company? (If not, ask how the respondent would increase knowledge of the function.)

18. Are the corporate Public Relations and Advertising Departments' activities coordinated effectively with the divisions? (If not, why not?)

19. Is there an overall marketing plan coordinating the efforts of the divisions? Should there be?

20. Do the divisions have their own advertising and public relations agencies?

21. Do the divisions have their own communications personnel in the field? Is this beneficial or not? Why?

22. Is the public affairs function effectively integrated within the Public Relations Department?

23. Who do you think the corporate spokesperson(s) should be? Why?

Sixteen of the Most Frequently Asked Questions in Employee Relations Audits

When employees are audited, it is recommended that two questionnaires be used—one for hourly employees, who, it can be assumed, lack sophisticated knowledge about the communications function, and one for salaried employees.

The following questions are recommended for interviews of hourly employees:

1. What bugs you the most about your job and about the company? (Interviewer should probe, attempt to touch possible areas of discontent: management, benefits, pay, condition of facilities, job assignment, job security, supervisory personnel, the future, etc.)

2. Could communications help eliminate the problems? (Interviewer to insure that respondent considers all types of communications—print, videotape, section meetings with supervisors, etc.)

3. If you were to rate your company and your plant as a place to work on a scale of 1 to 10—10 is highest—how would you rate it? Why?

4. How do you think communications could help you improve your work habits?
   a. Make you more productive?
   b. Improve craftsmanship?
   c. Help to fill customers' orders faster?

5. In companies, we communicate both from the top down, and from the bottom up. When your plant manager tells his superintendents to inform the work force of something, that is top-down communication. Let's talk about how communications rate in this plant.
   a. Do you talk often and easily with your immediate supervisor?
      (1) How? Regular meetings?
      (2) Why not?
   b. How about your supervisors? Do they communicate frequently with plant management?
      (1) Does this do any good?
      (2) Why not?
   c. How about the company generally; do you think the executives communicate openly enough with employees in all plants?
      (1) What good does this do?
      (2) How can this be improved?

6. What new methods can the company use to communicate with employees?

7. How do you get your company news? (Interviewer to probe, attempt to gain insight into effectiveness of all company communications, such as newsletters, magazines, video, etc.)

8. Do you think you should know something about the people, plants, and products of other divisions?

9. How many employees do you think your company has?

10. Does your company sell products overseas?

11. How much money did your company make last year? What percentage of this do you think is profit?

12. What does the company do with its profits? Give them to management? To shareholders? Put up new plants? Install new and faster equipment? Give them to employees by way of benefits?

13. What makes you proudest of this company?

14. What are the biggest problems facing the company today?
    a. If problems are mentioned, interviewer should ask the respondent how employees could help alleviate them.
    b. If employee says there are no problems, the interviewer should mention some—inflation, energy, pollution control, competition—and ask respondent how employees can help lessen them.

15. If you were the chairman, how would you attempt to instill pride in the work force?

16. Suppose the chairman came to you and asked what you thought the biggest communications problem in the company was? What would you tell him?

"What's the Buzz?"—Rating Communications Within the Company

When interviewing line management and white collar employees, questions pertaining to communications between management and hourly employees should also be included.

1. Do you use the expertise of the Public Relations Department to help you communicate effectively with your employees and with the community? (Interviewer should ascertain whether or not plant management has a valid concept of the services available to them.)

2. On a scale of 1 to 10—10 is tops—how would you rate communications in your company?
   a. How about in your plant?
   b. And other plants that you are familiar with?

3. Let's talk about communications. Do you think you have effective communications with your supervisory personnel and with your hourly workers?

    a. Why is this true?

    b. Why is this not true?

4. How about corporate management? Do they communicate enough with your employees? Or should they leave this function entirely up to you?

5. Do you think it is important for employees to have extensive knowledge about their plant, and about the company?

6. Do you insist that your supervisors hold regular meetings with the hourly work force?

7. Do you know how your hourly workers feel about:
   a. You and your managers?
   b. Their benefits?
   c. Wages?
   d. Condition of the plant?
   e. Individual job assignments?
   f. Job security?
   g. Their supervisors?
   h. The future?

8. How do you think management and workers can improve their relationships?

9. Do you think improved management-worker relationships would result in increased productivity and product quality? (Why or why not?)

10. Do you think there are some kinds of communication you need more of, some you need less of? (Give examples.)

11. Your primary daily responsibility is getting products manufactured and shipped on time. Do you consider communications an important function? Do you think communications can have an effect on employee morale? Product quality? Production?

12. You should be involved in the communications function if your plant is going to benefit. Would you be willing to spend more time on the communications function?
    a. If not, why not?
    b. If yes, what do you think the gains will be?

13. Do you think employee morale, product quality and production level would be affected if all communications in your plant were to stop?

14. Are you familiar with employee motivation programs? (Interviewer should explain the concept and solicit whether there is a need to institute a program.)

15. In your plant, you have "older" and "younger" employees. Do you think your younger employees are more difficult to deal with? (If so, do you think the communications function can help?)

16. What are the greatest problems facing the company today?

17. Can communications help the company lessen problems?

18. What are you most proud of your company for?
    a. Have you communicated this fact to your employees?
    b. If not, why not?

19. How would you use communications to help instill pride in your work force?

20. Would you like to evaluate the results of this audit with a member of the Public Relations Department?

21. Exactly what is the corporate Public Relations and Advertising Department responsible for?

22. How do you presently use the services of this department?

23. What sort of communications do you need more of, and what sort do you need less of?

24. What are the major problems confronting you as a line manager today?

Conducting the Communications Audit:
PR Agencies vs. Management Consulting Firms

Communications audits are conducted both by public relations agencies and by management consulting firms. The results are sometimes quite different, since the corporate relationships shared by agencies and consultancies are dissimilar.

Public relations agencies and departments rely on audits to provide the information necessary to develop effective communications programs. Generally, since public relations people share ongoing relationships with their clients, an abundance of pertinent information, frequently of a privileged nature, is available. This permits the preparation of wide-ranging audits with penetrating observations. The scope of these audits is also increased by the fact that public relations practitioners are often involved with many corporate publics, including employees, customers, the press and financial communities, during the routine discharge of their duties.

Management consultants restrict their audit activities to the employee audience. Services offered by the three largest management consulting firms in the field—Towers, Perrin, Forster & Crosby; Hewitt Associates; and Hay Associates—include:

- Employee communications audits
- Development of employee relations programs
- Economic education programs for employees
- Communications problem-solving
- Employee communications campaigns

Management consultants' employee communications services are contracted for on a project basis, or as "add-ons." That is, these activities are added to more traditional services, such as salary and benefits planning. If, for example, a salary and benefits program is undertaken for a corporation, employee communications activities are often added "to make sure the work force gets the message about our new salary and benefits package."

Cluster Comparisons from One of the "Big Three" Consulting Firms

Management consulting firms rely extensively on charts, graphs, and other statistical documentation to substantiate audit findings. The following cluster comparisons, taken from an audit compiled by one of the "big three" consulting firms, illustrate how these organizations present statistics.

The language of reports compiled by management consulting firms tends to be "statistical." The following paragraphs were taken from the big three audit:

> In the *Management/Supervision* cluster, hourly employees ranked openness of discussion with supervisor at the 39th percentile (62%). Both salaried groups ranked this issue at the 59th percentile (77% and 78% respectively).

> Regarding *Organization* issues, quality of working conditions was ranked significantly low by the hourly group at the 20th percentile (31%). The exempt group ranked this at the 71st percentile (66%), and nonexempts placed it at the 57th percentile (54%).

> Quality of working conditions is *the* organization issue at the hourly level. Repeatedly in group interviews, complaints were voiced about crowded conditions, polluted air and excess noise in shop areas. Quality of working life is negatively affected by these conditions. Conversely, this was not an issue for salaried employees.

> Based on group interviews at all locations, there is a common perception among salaried nonexempt employees, hourly employees and shop supervisors, that advancement opportunities are limited. This may tie in with comments about inadequate training and preparation for bigger jobs.

And On the Other Hand—A PR Agency's Audit

The following extract from a public relations agency's audit of a large commercial bank offers a contrast in styles. It reads easily, delves into the corporate psyche, and, in deliberate fashion, discusses weaknesses in the areas of "internal communications, strategic thinking and planning."

> The lack of effective internal communications and strategic thinking and planning were lambasted, probably more than any other weaknesses.

> Respondents repeatedly mentioned that continuing and meaningful dialogue were missing at all levels: from management to employees, vice versa, and even sideways. As one respondent noted, "Communications are even weak at the individual bank level, even between the heads of each bank."

> One key manager also noted that, "Our internal communications are so poor that our own people don't know our capabilities, internationally and domestically."

> And a foreign executive said, "Precise instructions are not issued to branch managers," with the result that operations "get messed up. We have to know," he

Communications

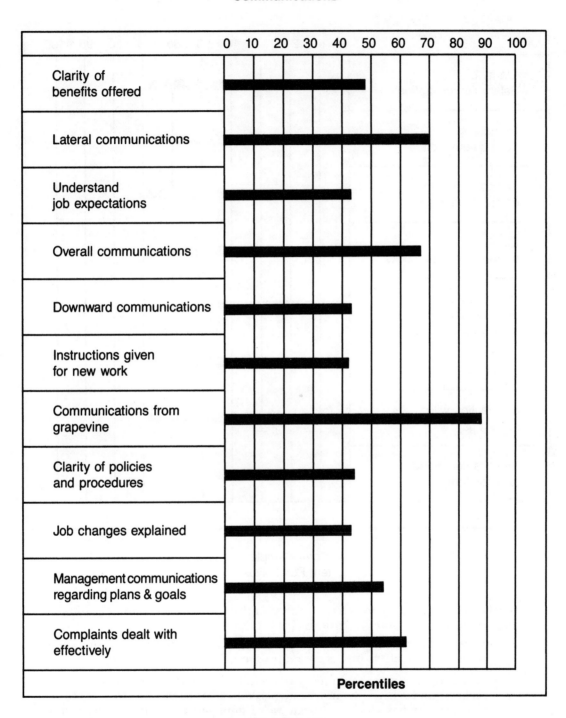

Total Sample
Item Percentiles

Total Remuneration

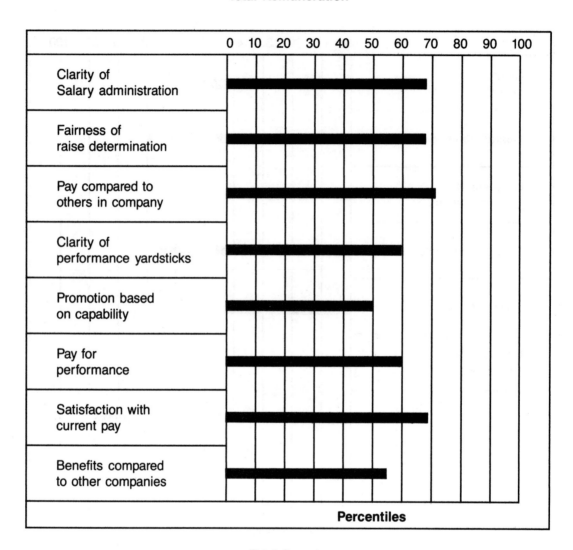

Total Sample
Item Percentiles

concluded, "if we're able to extend for six months or a year, but communications don't even work on issues as basic as that."

A consensus shows that this lack of planning and meaningful dialogue has significant negative effect on corporate progress. Respondents believe:

Number One: It must be decided what kind of bank the company wants to become, and where planning and marketing emphasis are to go. "Top management has to decide what we're going to be, and they have to communicate this internally," one respondent emphasized. "We're fishing in all ponds," another said. And the president remarked: "Growth is

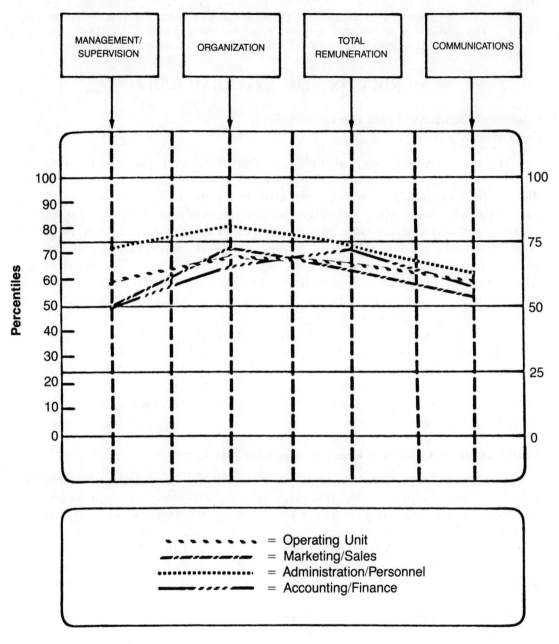

critical in the businesses we're in. Maybe we shouldn't be in some of them, but we are."

Number Two: Corporate objectives must be established, and all departments in the company must organize their plans within this framework. "The Planning Committees of the internal banks don't coordinate activities," one respondent complained. "They all do management by objectives alone. We desperately need direction." Another respondent claimed that "lack of goals and strategies hinder me personally in getting things done."

Number Three: The corporate personality, when it emerges, must be forcefully communicated to outside publics—not only to customers and potential customers, but to Wall Street, shareholders, and to the press.

CONDUCTING THE EXTERNAL AUDIT

Selecting Locations: From the Local Pub to the Rotary Club

When conducting external audits, you must evaluate possible information sources, and select those that will provide objectivity and the greatest return in the shortest time period. This could mean visiting the local Chamber of Commerce, the daily newspaper, a women's bridge club, or the corner bar. One clever staffer of a New York City public relations agency starts external audits in a tavern. He poses as an out-of-town welder looking for employment, and gets an earful when he asks questions such as, "What's it like working for this company?" External audits frequently require working unusual hours. You may attend a Rotary Club meeting at lunch and an investment club meeting after dinner. Or, you may visit the local pub just as the guys from the swing shift show up.

There are several cooperative sources that usually provide reliable information for external audits. These include the mayor's office, the Chamber of Commerce, the local newspaper, and civic clubs such as Rotary and Kiwanis. If you are able to divulge the purpose of your audit activities, the mayor's office and the Chamber of Commerce are good places to start. They can save time by pointing auditors in the right direction.

Notification: Who Should Know About Your Mission?

You will be able to submit a letter of notification containing information about your mission to local organizations such as the Chamber of Commerce, but much of your external auditing will be spontaneous. Stopping citizens on the street for spot opinions is one of the simplest and most productive methods of obtaining information. The external audit presents many opportunities to improvise. It is best likened to newspaper reporting. Just as a newsperson goes after a story, an auditor goes after information, and similar methods are employed by both.

Selecting Respondents: Cutting a Slice of the Public Pie

Here again, it is difficult to apply a methodology to selection procedures. Start with the most obvious respondents, then add others from recommendations and from your own observations. Frequently, it is possible to go right to the source. When soliciting opinions from the general public, you can reach the elderly, minorities, political conservatives and liberals, parents, religious organizations, and many other slivers of society, by approaching organizations such as senior citizens' clubs, NAACP, the local Conservative Party, the Liberal Party, local Republican and Democratic Clubs, parent-teacher associations, Hadassah, and churches.

Face to Face: The Interview

The primary difference between external and internal audits is that the knowledge of your subject will vary profoundly with external respondents. For example, you can gain valid insight into a local company's operations by asking this one question of shoppers on Main Street: "Which local company do you think is most concerned about the future of our town and the people in it?" But, if you were interviewing members of the Chamber of Commerce, you would want to delve into matters such as employment levels, wages, benefits, employee turnover, competitive employment practices, and viability and profitability of operations.

Letting Questionnaires Do the Asking

Questionnaires should be developed specifically for individual audits. There will undoubtedly be similarities in questions, however, since audit objectives and audiences are frequently similar.

When planning audits of the general public, it is important to remember that the legitimacy of samples directly affects results. Frequently, audit interviews alone cannot do the job. Questionnaires must be mass-mailed, or hundreds of street interviews accomplished, to be sure that an adequate percentage of the public is reached. Usually, this requires research, not an audit. But if the audience is small, audits will suffice.

Sixteen of the Most Frequently Asked Questions in Audits of the General Public

It is difficult to compile a list of questions for an audit of the general public, because the reasons for conducting such audits are extremely diverse. They might be done for instance, to learn how a particular company is viewed by minorities; how a community views corporate taxation; how workers and their families react to poor workmanship that resulted in the loss of several contracts; how the local citizenry would accept the doubling of foundry capabilities at a facility on the outskirts of town; how the company's pollution control efforts are viewed compared to other industrial concerns in the area.

If audits of the general public were conducted on behalf of the Tall Timber Paper Company, for example, some typical questions would be:

1. Which local company do you think is most responsible for polluting the air?
   a. Company "A"
   b. Company "B"
   c. Tall Timber Paper Company
   d. Company "D"
   e. Company "E"

2. Why do you think that company is most responsible?

3. Which local company do you think is most responsible for polluting the water in the Gogetcha River?
   a. Tall Timber Paper Company
   b. Company "B"

c. Company "C"

d. Company "D"

e. Company "E"

4. Are you familiar with the government's pollution control regulations?

5. Do you know that all companies are required to install pollution control equipment? One local company has spent more than $14 million on equipment to control air and water pollution. Do you know which company?

6. Do you think the air and water in our town is cleaner than it was ten years ago?

7. Do you know employees who work in all five of the local industrial companies?

8. From the comments of these people, how would you rate the local companies as good places to work?

9. Why did you mention that company as the best one? Why did you rate the other company as the worst one?

10. Which company do you think gives more back to the community than any other? Why?

11. Which company do you think does less for the community than any other? Why?

12. Which company management is most visible? Why?

13. If you were going to work at one of these companies, which would you choose? Why?

14. If you were going to buy stock in one of these companies, which would it be?

15. Do you know that three new species of fish have returned to the Gogetcha River in the past five years?

16. Do you know that companies discharging water into the Gogetcha River must return this water cleaner than when they took it from the river?

Eleven of the Most Frequently Asked Questions in Financial Relations Audits

Financial relations audits are the most frequently conducted external audits. They are usually conducted by persons thoroughly experienced in the financial relations discipline because proficiency in the language and professional practices of the financial community are necessary to conduct interviews of this sophisticated public.

The two most common financial relations audits are conducted to determine the investment community's opinion of a company, including its management and viability, or to determine the professional reaction to an event such as a financial analyst's presentation. Topics normally covered with respondents in "opinion" audits include: the influences which affect coverage of, and interest in, a company; the impact of external influences on a company; assessment of a company's competitive situation, including historical performance, product quality, pricing, and marketing; impressions of corporate management and of operational strategies; projections of a company's viability and solvency; earnings projections and investment recommendations or nonrecommendations; opinions of the effectiveness of a company's communications with the financial community.

Respondents should be mixed to assure veracity. The respondent mix should include long-time company followers, newcomers, representatives of brokerage firms that do and do not have positions in the company, analysts, portfolio managers, industry followers, and generalists.

Questions include:

1. Does the financial community have a (high) (medium) (low) interest in XYZ Company? Why is this?

2. What do you think are the primary outside factors currently affecting the operations of XYZ Company? Will these factors change?

3. There are four primary competitors in XYZ's markets. How do you rate XYZ against them? Why?

4. What are your impressions of XYZ's management? Do you think they have an effective strategy in areas such as: (a) capitalization; (b) diversity; (c) research and development; (d) manufacturing efficiency?

5. Do you think the company is placing the proper emphasis, as far as growth potential is concerned, on its present line of products and services?

6. Where do you see the most limited product growth opportunities? Should XYZ Company divest of these products?

7. How do you see foreign competition affecting XYZ's product lines, now and in the future?

8. Are you presently recommending the purchase of XYZ Company's shares? (Why or why not?)

9. What are your earnings projections, year end, for XYZ Company?

10. How would you rate XYZ's ability to grow and to compete given the capital restraints in today's business environment?

11. What do you think of the quality of, and the frequency of, the communications you receive from the company? How does this material compare to what you receive from its competitors?

Rating Professional Response to Company Events

Questions asked during audits conducted to determine professional response to events such as analyst presentations include:

1. What was your opinion of the quality of information provided in the recent presentation?

2. What changes would you make to improve future meetings?

3. What is your opinion of management's growth/diversification strategies? (Interviewer should probe, attempt to obtain respondent's impressions of this company's strategies compared to those of the competition.)

4. Do you currently have a position in the company? If yes, do you plan to increase, decrease, or keep it at the same level? Why?

5. Did the recent meeting change your ideas about your investment in the company? How?

6. Do you have a position in any companies that are competitive? Which ones? Why did you take these positions originally?

7. What do you think the company should do to encourage investment in its shares?

8. What is your opinion of management?

9. What is your opinion of the company's current communications efforts? Specifically, how do the following corporate communications rate with those of the competition, and what would you do to improve them?
   a. Analyst meetings?
   b. Corporate spokesperson availability?
   c. Annual report?
   d. Interim reports?
   e. Management speech reprints?
   f. Other written communications?
   g. Miscellaneous?
      (Interviewer to probe, attempt to obtain valid criticisms of communications efforts.)

10. Do you hear any comments in the financial community regarding the quality of the company's communications efforts?

Auditing the Press: "I'm Going to Level with You"

The public relations practitioner should decide up front whether or not he or she will divulge corporate identity when auditing members of the fourth estate. Normally, the client's name is not disclosed. This permits candid appraisal and comparison with competitive factors.

However, since public relations people maintain close and ongoing relationships with the press, the practitioner may wish to level, and disclose the company's name. This approach could be called: "I'm going to level with you and tell you the name of the client. Please give me your absolute honest opinions of this company and please keep everything confidential."

Another strategy is to use a combination of the confidential and the "I'm going to level..." approaches. You would save the latter for trusted friends, while maintaining secrecy with strangers and with those members of the press whom you do not know or with whom you would feel uneasy revealing client confidences.

The obvious risk in this approach, however, is that one member of the press could reveal corporate identity to another.

Questions asked of the general readership press and of the trade press would vary somewhat, because it is assumed that the trades have in-depth knowledge of the industry and of the company, its products and management. Staffs of daily newspapers, even business reporters, would not be expected to possess such detailed knowledge.

It is essential that all elements of the press have an accurate picture of a company, its divisions and subsidiaries, its products, and capabilities, if that company is to gain as much recognition as possible.

Fifteen of the Most Frequently Asked Questions in Audits of the Press

The following line of questioning would be appropriate for the trade and business press. Not only would these questions provide the interviewer with an accurate idea of how the press views a company, but a foundation for an ongoing relationship could be established.

1. What do you think is the major business of each of these companies? (List several competitive or partially competitive companies.)

2. How large are the following corporations? (In total sales.) (List competitors.)

3. Could you identify which industry or industries the following companies serve? Or, if they serve several, can you identify which of the following companies could be described as "diversified industrial concerns"? (List competitors.)

4. Can you identify which of the following companies has recently been acquired, and can you name the acquiree? (List competitors.)

5. Which domestic industrial companies do you think do the best job of explaining themselves to the press?

6. How do they do this?

7. How good a job do you think XYZ Company does?

8. Do you recall receiving any press or collateral materials from XYZ Company during the past year? If yes, what did you think of the material? (Well written, good design, well illustrated, message clearly presented, etc.?)

9. How would you describe XYZ Company? (Size by revenues, products manufactured, major divisions, headquarters city, etc.)

10. What are the major operating units of XYZ Company?

11. What material would you like to receive regularly from XYZ Company?
    Annual report
    Interim reports
    Technical literature

Major executive speeches
Reprints of professional proceedings
News releases of a general nature
Contract announcements
Corporate fact sheet
Ad reprints
Other

12. How do you think XYZ Company can best communicate its recent corporate changes to the press?

13. (For headquarters city respondents.) Would you be interested in attending a year-end briefing session by XYZ Company's management, about the company and the industries it serves?

14. Are you familiar with XYZ Company's management?

15. (After explaining some of the recent advances of XYZ Company and outlining the company's product lines.) What interests you the most about this company?

LAYING IT ON THE TABLE: HOW TO PRESENT YOUR FINDINGS

Audits can be difficult, especially when management does not like the conclusions. This is one reason why it is recommended that outsiders such as a reliable public relations agency handle the project. A reputable agency will most likely have staffers with auditing experience. The agency will be able to commit as much time and manpower to the project as necessary to assure completion on time. Agency personnel will be better received by the respondents as specialists and as outsiders. And they will be experienced at preparing palatable final documents, regardless of how critical.

The outside source should have one key contact on the corporate staff available for assistance on a daily basis. Ideally, this would be an individual of stature, perhaps the vice president of communications. The inside audit participant should be capable of impressing senior management with the urgency and importance of the project, and of assuring that internal interviews take place as scheduled.

The inside representative should also be the first to review a draft of the agency's final written report. He must decide how, and how much, of the material to present to top management. A general rule of professionalism for agency personnel charged with preparing audits should be that an accurate, completely candid first draft be provided their company contact. That draft could contain some pretty hard stuff, as these examples from internal audits of industrial companies illustrate.

No area was harder hit than the area of management. And, nowhere else did the respondents exhibit as much knowledge or voice as much pessimism as they did on this subject. "Their management is poor. That's why it is too late to save that company," one respondent noted. "The chairman is arrogant; he alienates people. The whole industry knows this."

"The reputation for poor customer service will last for quite a while," another respondent believes, "because of the closeness of the industry. When you have exhibited a lack of integrity many times in the past, you get fixed with that reputation," he says.

"Specifically," another officer said, "our upper echelon executives…are not good managers….they never managed anything."

Since all audits are different, the form in which the results are prepared for management should be different, too. Whatever format is most readable and most easily understood should be used. The final document should also contain: a list of objectives; a list of interview techniques employed; a list of the questions asked; an in-depth presentation of the audit findings; and a detailed summation of both conclusions and recommendations. If the company audit representative believes that management would react negatively to the audit in the form presented, the written document should be more palatable.

When the document is in the desired format, a decision should be made about how to present it to management. Presentation methods range from providing copies to the chairman and president and reviewing audit results with them privately, to a formal showing using slides and taped comments (actual statements, but not the respondents' voices or names).

The slide presentation is the most dramatic and credible method of presenting audits. This method also permits the opportunity for open discussion about audit conclusions. Slide presentations can be made to large or small audiences. However, a drawback to slide presentations is that audit findings quickly spread from the viewers of the slide presentation to other employees, and management usually desires that this sensitive information remain close to the top.

How One Company Prepared Its Findings: A Sample Audit Script

The following audit script, prepared for presentation to personnel of the Public Relations & Advertising Department of a large forest products company, is a good example of how to present audit findings in a logical and interesting manner.

It is recommended that the agency's audit supervisor present the findings in conjunction with the company's staff coordinator. The audit supervisor has the most intimate knowledge of the project, and is the only individual qualified to field many of the questions that will be asked.

AUDIO/VISUAL	SPEAKER

TAPE

"WE'RE BEHIND THE TIMES."

"THIS COMPANY IS TOO CONSERVATIVE. THE INDUSTRY RESPECTS COMPANIES THAT KNOW WHO THEY ARE."

"WE'RE FOLLOWERS. GOD DAMN, CAN WE FOLLOW!"

These are actual quotes by your company's managers. The voices have been changed, but the words are exactly as they were spoken during the communications audit recently completed.

SLIDE

200 INTERVIEWS
• CORPORATE
• DIVISIONAL
• LOCAL

Almost 200 interviews were conducted with managers at corporate ...divisional...and local levels.

Purpose of the audit was to find out exactly where the company stands at this point in time. With this knowledge, we can develop a meaningful communications program.

BUILD-UP SLIDE

1. MANAGEMENT'S VIEW
2. MAJOR PROBLEMS
3. PRIMARY MESSAGES
4. COMMUNICATIONS EFFECTIVENESS
5. COMMUNICATIONS ROADBLOCKS

Specifically, we wanted to know:
• How managers see the company's strengths...weaknesses...and objectives.
• What major problems and issues we face.
• The primary messages that should be communicated about the company.
• How effectively we have traditionally communicated with employees...shareholders... customers...the press and others.
• What communications roadblocks must be overcome.

What you are going to hear today are audit highlights. Detailed findings will be presented in a written report. To start, let's find out how we view ourselves.

TAPE

"WE COULD BE A LEADER, BUT WE'RE PLODDERS."

"WE'RE SOLID. NOT EXCITING, BUT SOLID. WE HAVE FINANCIAL AND MANUFACTURING MUSCLE."

"WE HAVE GOOD FORESTS, AND EXCELLENT BAG PACKAGING TECHNOLOGY. WE DEVELOPED THE FIRST CONTINUOUS DIGESTER."

AUDIO/VISUAL	SPEAKER

AUDIO/VISUAL

SPEAKER

So, if we listed the adjectives that best describe the company, they would be "conservative"... "solid"... "follower." There are some definite strengths—financial muscle and basic technological know-how. But our managers see the company as not taking advantage of its muscle. Not being innovative...not seeking a leadership position.

BUILD-UP SLIDE
1. DIVERSIFY
2. EXTEND PACKAGING ACTIVITIES
3. INCREASE INTERNATIONAL MARKETING

We are becoming more aggressive under new management, though. The respondents think the company will diversify...extend its packaging activities into new areas...and increase international marketing.

SLIDE
CORPORATE STRATEGY

When it comes to corporate strategy, the respondents give the company a failing grade.

TAPE
"THE ONLY CORPORATE PLAN WAS IN THE CHAIRMAN'S HEAD. AND HE'S IN FLORIDA."

"I'M AN OFFICER OF THIS COMPANY, AND I CANNOT TELL YOU OUR CORPORATE GOALS."

"BELOW THE TOP LEVEL, THERE'S NOT MUCH UNDERSTANDING OF THE PLANNING FUNCTION."

Obviously, we're starting at ground zero. Traditionally—dating back to an era when the company was family-owned—there was little strategizing. But this is also changing.

TAPE
"NEW MANAGEMENT KNOWS WHAT HAS TO BE DONE...HOW MUCH MONEY AND MANPOWER WE NEED."

"WE'RE STARTING TO MOVE, WITH THE NEW GUYS. IT'S SLOW, BUT IT'S A GREAT FEELING."

What makes the respondents think new management is capable of changing things?

Most managers think new management is aggressive...open-minded...decisive, although conservative...and profit-oriented.

AUDIO/VISUAL	SPEAKER
	"They're starting to divest of the marginally profitable operations," one executive said. "They know the directions they want to go in, like packaging," said another. And a third said, "They keep their minds open, and they're acting like they know what they want to go after."
PIX COMPANY RESEARCH FACILITY TAPE "RESEARCH DOESN'T ADDRESS OPERATIONAL PROBLEMS." "THESE ARE IVORY TOWER GUYS." "THEY'RE NOT RESPONSIVE TO OUR PROBLEMS."	Technical research was singled out as an area that needs attention, also.
PIX FOREST TAPE "THE FAMILY REALLY PUT SOMETHING TOGETHER. OVER EIGHT MILLION ACRES OF WOODLANDS." "WHAT A DISTRIBUTION OF WOODLANDS: NORTH, SOUTH, EAST, WEST." "OUR FOREST BASE IS ONE OF THE BEST IN THE WORLD."	But the company's primary natural resource—its forests—are considered a magnificent asset.
TAPE "PROBABLY TOPS IN THE BUSINESS. OUR FORESTERS ARE GOOD." "THIS COMPANY WROTE THE BOOK ON TIMBERLANDS MANAGEMENT."	And, the company has woodlands and management strengths.
TAPE "OUR OFFICERS ARE SPREAD TOO THIN." "WE CAN'T HOLD MANAGERS BECAUSE OF OUR WAGE BASE." "A FEW GREAT BRAINS, SWIMMING IN A SEA OF MEDIOCRITY."	But, management operates under obvious handicaps.

AUDIO/VISUAL	SPEAKER

SLIDE
PROBLEMS AND ISSUES

Leaving internal operations, we discussed the company's position in society. What the problems and issues are...how we are responding to them.

PIX
POLLUTION CONTROL EQUIPMENT

Pollution abatement is considered the major social issue facing the company. Not only where the public is concerned, but where finances are concerned, too.

TAPE
"WE HAVE SO MUCH CAPITAL TIED UP IN POLLUTION CONTROL, IT'S HARD TO ACQUIRE, DIVERSIFY."

PIX
MACHINE FELLING TREE

High on the social list was the trend toward restrictive land use legislation. "We're losing control over land management," one manager emphasized. "Cutting is ridiculously restrictive," another said.

PIX
PACKAGING MATERIALS

Interestingly, packaging legislation was not singled out as a problem. Apparently, this is one area that Congress started to scrutinize, then backed off.

SLIDE
THE CORPORATE IMAGE

We have discussed the respondents' views of their company. Now, what about the corporate image? What image should be projected to important publics such as the financial community...the press... shareholders?

PIX
CORPORATE LOGO

Well, since we still have major problems—and since we have few distinguishing characteristics—there was some waffling. But with a company as large...and as well established...as this one, there has to be something to promote. And, what is most realistic is:

TAPE
"OUR WOODLANDS. A GREAT STRENGTH."

"NEW MANAGEMENT. WE HAVE SOME OF THE GREATEST NAMES IN THE INDUSTRY."

So, at least for the near term, the company's communications program will feature its natural resources, and its management potential.

PIX
WOODLANDS

PIX
MANAGEMENT

We will have to go slow with management for awhile, though. As the chairman told us, "We must be honest. We haven't done much yet. But in a year or so you can start talking about some accomplishments."

AUDIO/VISUAL

SLIDE
CORPORATE COMMUNICATIONS

TAPE
"WE DON'T COMMUNICATE. NOT WITH EACH OTHER, OR ANYBODY ELSE."

BUILD-UP SLIDE
1. HOURLY WORKERS
2. FIRST-LINE SUPERVISORS
3. MIDDLE MANAGERS

SLIDE
MAP WITH COMPANY LOCATIONS

TAPE
"WE NEVER TRIED TO TALK TO WALL STREET."

"OUR GOVERNMENT RELATIONS ARE OKAY AT THE STATE LEVEL. BUT, WE HAVEN'T BOTHERED WITH WASHINGTON."

"WE IGNORE THE PRESS."

SPEAKER
The interviewers spent most of the time talking about communications. Not surprising, since this is a communications audit. What they discovered was not surprising, either. This is a conservative company, operating within a conservative industry.

The absence of an organized employee communications effort was considered especially serious. "We have EEO problems," one plant manager said. "And we have productivity problems. We have to talk to the workers...get them to pull the oar with us."

The primary audiences where communications emphasis should be placed—the respondents said—are: hourly workers...first-line supervisors...and middle management. The lower levels require information about their individual importance to the company. The middle managers have to be informed about corporate goals, long-range planning.

A dangerous phenomenon has occurred in the company during the years without organized communications. It simply does not know itself.

A worker in Maine has no idea what his brothers in the state of Washington are doing. A mill hand in Savannah has no identity with a plastic converter in Toledo.

And, if we are to forge ahead...assume a leadership role in the forest products industry...we must know who we are, where we are going.

How about other communications areas?

AUDIO/VISUAL

Those comments pretty well sum it up. A quiet company—we have said—in a quiet industry.

Because of this, the Public Relations and Advertising Department was not singled out for praise. It wasn't condemned, either. Just kind of overlooked.

TAPE

"I KNOW THERE ARE SOME PEOPLE IN NEW YORK, BUT I DON'T KNOW WHAT THEY DO."

"THEY'RE UNDERMANNED."

"THEY'RE NOT INNOVATIVE. THEY'RE MEDIOCRE."

The company's managers displayed little knowledge of the specific services offered by the PR&A Department. When interviewers asked about corporate public relations services such as local press relations…employee communications programs…crisis communications…they responded with the old, "Why, I didn't know that!"

BUILD-UP SLIDE
1. MANAGEMENT'S VIEW
2. STRENGTHS & WEAKNESSES
3. MAJOR PROBLEMS
4. COMMUNICATIONS EFFECTIVENESS

That summarizes the bottom line…presents the results of the communications audit. What these results tell us is: "You've got a long way to go, baby." Remember, these results were not dreamed up. This is what 200 company managers think. When we started, we wanted to find out what we thought about ourselves. Our corporate direction…our corporate strengths and weaknesses…the major problems facing us…and how effective our communications were.

What we discovered was:

• The company is solid, with good natural resources. But it is also plodding… unimaginative…conservative.

29

AUDIO/VISUAL

<u>BUILD-UP SLIDE</u>

1. SOLID, PLODDING
2. GOOD RESOURCES AND
   MANAGEMENT
3. NO CORPORATE STRATEGY
4. POLLUTION, LAND-USE NEED
   ATTENTION
5. COMMUNICATIONS IGNORED

<u>PIX</u>

COMMUNICATIONS PROGRAM
(BOOKLET)

<u>TAPE</u>

"I DON'T KNOW WHETHER I'D LAUGH
OR CRY."

<u>SPEAKER</u>

- New management is a strength. But, too new to boast about.
- Corporate strategy is nil.
- Pollution abatement and land-use restrictions need attention.
- And communications have been almost totally ignored.

We are now developing a corporate communications program for presentation to management. It will be the first formal program in the company's sixty-year history.

What we have here is a professional communicator's dream. A major forest products company—a major *worldwide* forest products company—which, to this point, has not communicated. Not to the outside world, or to itself. What a great opportunity to make a mark! Or, as one senior manager put it:

Research
Illuminating a Dark Door of Public Relations

While the audit, the first cousin of research, is employed routinely in the public relations business today, research is still not used as much as it should be. One reason is that the audit can be implemented readily by public relations practitioners, while research generally requires the expertise of outside research firms, plus supplemental budget. Also, public relations research has suffered somewhat from "back-of-the-mind" treatment. Public relations practitioners are not conditioned to think of research as an integral part of their business, the way advertising people do.

The argument is also advanced that, in the area of measuring public relations/publicity results, research is not a professionally suitable tool. There is more than a grain of truth to the contention that measurement research is difficult to apply to public relations. Media staffers will judge a story's merits differently—some will feature it, some will not use it. Any effort to research the effectiveness of a public relations/publicity campaign, the argument goes, will necessarily be weakened in a way that advertising research—with its "bought" space and air time—does not have to contend with.

If this argument contains grains of truth, there are boulders of truth to the premise that measurement research has been deferred because many public relations practitioners are fearful of the answers to questions such as, "Does public relations really work?" and, "To what degree did public relations help us to achieve our marketing objectives?"

Despite these obstacles, the dark door of public relations research is being illuminated by the electronic storage of numbers and information that increases tremendously every day, and by managements and numbers-oriented marketers who are scrutinizing expenditures more closely than ever before. These forces are accelerating the evolution of the research function in public relations to an extent never before realized. Research is being used for program development, market intelligence, surveillance of the financial and business communities, development of new business presentations, community relations, issues analysis, employee attitude surveys, and many other purposes.

Research is divided into two categories: primary and secondary. Primary research is fresh exploration, and it is undertaken for a specific purpose or purposes. For example, primary research could be conducted to ascertain the awareness of Americans residing west of the Mississippi River that Rutgers is the State University of New Jersey.

Secondary research is knowledge, frequently in abundance and usually in print, available from any source. This information has been compiled for reasons other than the research project being undertaken, but could contain information of significance to the present research project.

PRIMARY RESEARCH: BREAKING NEW GROUND

Primary research is much more complex, and, therefore more expensive, than secondary research. Primary research is "untainted." Each project is fresh, and is usually undertaken for fairly demanding reasons: an industrial facility is experiencing turnover and production problems; the investment community is not sponsoring a company's shares; a new product is to be launched in the near term; customers are reacting negatively to a proposal to close a domestic plant in favor of one in Japan. Primary research is fresh, plowing new ground each time it is attempted. There would be no way to acquire the information—and to analyze and interpret that information—from secondary research sources.

Primary research is divided into two parts. One pertains to qualities, the other to quantities. The results of qualitative research provide the foundation for quantitative research.

QUALITATIVE RESEARCH: PUTTING OUT YOUR FEELERS

The objectives of qualitative research pertain almost exclusively to the development of the next step in primary research—the quantitative study. The primary objective of qualitative work is to gain sufficient information about the survey topic to be able to develop objectives, structure a questionnaire, and conduct a successful quantitative study.

Some research purists might disagree, but I think it is also possible for experienced public relations practitioners—those with extensive knowledge of the markets and the customers involved in a research project—to work against other objectives during the preliminary phases of primary research. These additional objectives, which apply only to experienced practitioners, would include:

- The auditing of a specific public or publics regarding the research topic.
- The compilation of corporate, product, industry, or marketing information for use in new business presentations.

- The partial or complete development of a marketing program.
- The partial or complete development of a strategy to combat a problem confronting a corporation.
- The preparation of preliminary management reports concerning the situation being researched.

Qualitative research can be dangerous. It involves small numbers of respondents, it is frequently unstructured (in large part, qualitative work is meant to provide substance and format for a research project), and it can be rife with subjectivity and supposition. Focus groups and individual interviews generally comprise qualitative work.

What to Expect from Focus Groups

Focus groups usually involve fewer than a dozen respondents—if participants are knowledgeable about the subject being addressed, four to six would suffice— and are conducted by an interviewer skilled at "carrying" a group discussion and in eliciting pertinent, worthwhile information. An experienced moderator is essential for conducting a successful encounter group, because a knowledge of people and of their interaction with others is essential if the session is to move smoothly.

For example, it is normal for focus group members to divulge only shallow information. Participants react guardedly in groups, and with as many as a dozen people discussing a given topic, time becomes a factor.

The moderator should strive to involve all participants, because it is important to explore as many areas, and to develop as many ideas, opinions, facts, and approaches as possible. Because of the natural reticence to speak candidly about sensitive matters, the moderator should also be skilled at evaluating "halves"—half comments, half truths. And, the moderator should be adept at massaging participants' egos. The opportunity for a respondent to appear knowledgeable in front of his or her peers frequently loosens tongues.

Focus sessions should be recorded. Participants sometimes talk at such a fast pace that note-taking is impossible. Also, tapes provide the opportunity to evaluate the meeting.

Focus group discussions are sometimes undertaken to expedite the fact-finding process or to save research dollars. These sessions should only be conducted for legitimate reasons or they could be harmful. The following letter from a Research Director of a major New York City advertising agency to the Director-Public Relations of a *Fortune 150* corporation explains why. The public relations man was considering organizing a focus group to evaluate the effectiveness of a new employee communications program.

Dear Larry:

I am negative regarding your proposal to have a focus group to evaluate the effectiveness of your new employee television series.

Based on my extensive experience with focus group research, I'd like to point out some pitfalls of this research technique.

1. *A focus group cannot assure respondent anonymity.* It is extremely difficult to get employees to talk freely about their company in a company-sponsored, face-to-face encounter. Even if management is removed from the scene, tape recorders must be used. This frequently arouses suspicion. Participants know that management is behind the project, selected them, and would have no trouble identifying who said what. They might even be suspicious of the other employees in the group. No one feels so secure in his job that he would risk his future by being completely candid.

2. *A focus group is not representative.* We never advise conducting one focus group—or several—for the purpose of aiding management decision-making. These sessions are preliminary, exploratory, inconclusive research techniques. The groups normally consist of eight to ten people, a few of whom seem to do most of the talking. These two or three individuals may be quite atypical of the majority, their views hardly representative of thousands of other employees. The net effect, thus, can be quite misleading.

3. *A focus group provides qualitative, not quantitative, evidence.* Focus group discussions, by design, are excellent for eliciting a wide range of ideas and reactions on a given subject, but are not suitable for evaluating the success of a product or service among a large group of people. While a focus group may elicit a range of positive and negative reactions, you cannot determine in what proportion the negative weighs against the positive. Further, the subject matter in this instance is not of such depth that an hour's taped discussion is required. Ideas as well as reaction levels could be more efficiently elicited using other research methods.

I therefore propose that we use a semi-structured (both open- and closed-ended questions), self-administered questionnaire for this research. The questionnaire would be mailed to 400 employees at each of the company's nine plants. We could anticipate a return of 25 percent. This approach will provide us with quantitative measurements important to decision-making. Anonymity will be assured. There will be no reason for respondents to put their names on the forms. Candid responses are anticipated. We should be able to learn much more about the effectiveness of your new communications technique than if we attempted a focus session.

Sincerely,

QUANTITATIVE RESEARCH: THE NUMBERS GAME

Questionnaires, respondent selection and interview techniques are carefully structured through quantitative research. The empirical approach—the probing, the reasoning, the calculating—of the initial qualitative phase is over. Now, the quantitative research effort is tightly structured, as the information gained earlier is applied to substantiate preliminary findings and to obtain accurate information as it pertains to numbers and statistics.

There are two types of quantitative research studies: specialized and shared-cost. Specialized studies are designed for a specific corporation or other type of organization. Shared-cost studies are designed by research companies for several participants. The cost of this generalized approach is usually significantly less than it is for specialized studies, but the degree of "personalization" found in the latter is missing.

The primary companies offering shared-cost surveys include:

Company	Sample	Frequency
Opinion Research Corp. North Harrison Street Princeton, N.J. 08540 (609) 924-5900	The public, business persons	Quarterly
The Gallup Organization 53 Bank Street Princeton, NJ 08540	The public	Monthly
Trendex, Inc. 15 Riverside Avenue Westport, CN 16880 (203) 227-0851	The public	Daily
R. H. Bruskin Associates 303 George Street New Brunswick, NJ 08903	The public	Weekly
Cambridge Research Institute 44 Brattle Street Cambridge, MA 02138 (617) 492-3800	The public	Quarterly

Quantitative research electives include specialized store audits, purchase panels, and in-place panels. These techniques measure product performance and purchase behavior. Several major research organizations routinely conduct these studies.

A Primary Research Project, Step By Step

The following step-by-step procedure shows how the need for a primary research project develops, and how it is implemented.

First, a problem is identified. It could concern product performance in the marketplace, apprehension about the assimilation of an acquired company, or a number of other matters.

Second, research objectives are developed to evaluate the problem.

Third, a list of respondents is developed.

Fourth, qualitative and quantitative research is undertaken. Focus groups may be instituted, and several in-depth employee interviews conducted to permit cross-checking focus group findings.

Fifth, a questionnaire is drafted.

Sixth, a self-administered questionnaire is distributed to samples of respondents.

Seventh, the survey is analyzed and interpreted, and a written report is prepared.

Generally, public relations research is broken down into the following categories:

- Employee attitude
- Measurement
- Employee readership
- Trade marketing
- Consumer marketing
- Investor relations
- Community attitude
- Issues determination

A SAMPLE EMPLOYEE ATTITUDE SURVEY

The management of Rosie the Riveter Enterprises is concerned about the assimilation of an acquired company. To evaluate the situation, Rosie management retained employee communications specialists to research the situation, and to recommend improvements if necessary.

The questionnaire for the Rosie the Riveter research follows.

1. Does Rosie the Riveter Enterprises provide you with adequate information about their plans for your plant, for the corporation as a whole, and about company policies?

   <u>Mark only one</u>

   Yes, I get enough information   _____
   Sometimes I get enough,
      sometimes not enough   _____
   I never get enough information   _____
   I don't have an opinion   _____

2. If you think you do not receive enough information, explain what type of information you want more of:

   _____

   _____

   _____

3. Since your company's acquisition by Rosie the Riveter Enterprises, have communications on company policies and procedures:

   Improved   _____
   Improved slightly   _____
   Stayed the same   _____
   Gotten worse   _____

4. Did you receive an orientation from the Personnel Department when you joined the company?

   Yes   _____
   No   _____

5. If you did not receive a formal orientation program when you joined the company, do you think you should have?

Yes _____
No _____
No opinion _____

6. What do you think an orientation program should include?

_____

_____

7. How do you receive information about Rosie the Riveter Enterprises?

Number in order of importance. Number as many as you wish.

The Rosie house organ ( )
The grapevine ( )
My supervisor ( )
The town newspaper ( )
Radio and television ( )
Notices on the bulletin board ( )
Letters from the plant manager ( )
Employee meetings ( )
Other _____ ( )
I don't receive any information ( )

8. Which are the best ways—in your opinion—to receive information about Rosie the Riveter Enterprises?

Number in order of preference. Number as many as you wish.

The Rosie house organ ( )
The grapevine ( )
Your supervisor ( )
Your town newspaper ( )
Radio and television ( )
Notices on the bulletin board ( )
Letters from your plant manager ( )
Employee meetings ( )
Other _____ ( )
I don't want any information ( )

9. Did you receive an employee handbook?

Yes _____
No _____

10. Do you think the handbook contains useful information?

Yes _____
No _____
Somewhat useful _____

11. Do you believe what Rosie the Riveter management tells employees?

I always believe management _____
Sometimes, I believe management _____
I never believe management _____
No opinion _____

12. Did you believe what your previous management told you?

Always _____
Sometimes _____
Never _____
No opinion _____

13. How would you rate communications since your company was acquired by Rosie the Riveter Enterprises?

Better than before _____
About the same _____
Worse _____
No opinion _____

14. Why did you rate communications the way you did in question #13?

_____

_____

_____

15. How do you rate Rosie the Riveter as a place to work?

Mark only one

The best possible ( )
Better than average ( )
Average ( )
Below average ( )
Bad ( )

16. How do you rate your individual plant?

Mark only one

The best possible ( )
Better than average ( )
Average ( )
Below average ( )
Bad ( )

17. Since Rosie the Riveter took your company over, what has happened to working conditions in your plant?

Mark only one

Conditions have improved a lot ( )
Conditions are a little bit better ( )

Conditions are about the same   ( )
Conditions are a little worse   ( )
Conditions are much worse   ( )

18. Why did you answer question #17 the way you did?

_____

_____

_____

19. Do you like your job? Are you happy with your work?

Mark only one

My job is great   ( )
My job is okay   ( )
I dislike my job   ( )

20. Are you proud of the products your plant turns out?

Mark only one

Very proud   ( )
Our products are so-so   ( )
Not proud   ( )
No opinion   ( )

21. What do you think about your company, compared to others that you know about, in the following areas?

Mark one in every category

	Excellent	Good	Average	Below average	Poor
Wages	( )	( )	( )	( )	( )
Promotions	( )	( )	( )	( )	( )
Managers concern for workers	( )	( )	( )	( )	( )
Handling of complaints	( )	( )	( )	( )	( )
Communications	( )	( )	( )	( )	( )
Benefits	( )	( )	( )	( )	( )
Abilities of supervisors	( )	( )	( )	( )	( )
Opportunities	( )	( )	( )	( )	( )
Job training	( )	( )	( )	( )	( )
Quality control	( )	( )	( )	( )	( )
Production capability	( )	( )	( )	( )	( )
Growth prospects	( )	( )	( )	( )	( )
Work scheduling	( )	( )	( )	( )	( )

	Excellent	Good	Average	Below average	Poor
Cooperation between departments	( )	( )	( )	( )	( )
Layoffs	( )	( )	( )	( )	( )
Safety	( )	( )	( )	( )	( )
Cost reduction	( )	( )	( )	( )	( )
Overtime	( )	( )	( )	( )	( )
Scheduling of overtime	( )	( )	( )	( )	( )
Working with community officials	( )	( )	( )	( )	( )

22. What items are most important about your job?

Rank in order of importance, 1 through 10

Wages	( )
Safety	( )
Advancement	( )
Steady work	( )
Benefits	( )
Being treated right	( )
Good supervision	( )
Working conditions	( )
Participating in planning	( )
Staggered work hours	( )

23. How do you rate Rosie the Riveter's benefits?

Mark each category

	Excellent	Very good	Average	Poor
Vacations	( )	( )	( )	( )
Retirement plan	( )	( )	( )	( )
Life insurance	( )	( )	( )	( )
Health insurance	( )	( )	( )	( )
Cafeteria	( )	( )	( )	( )
Lockers	( )	( )	( )	( )
Other _____	( )	( )	( )	( )

24. What do you think of the job conditions in your plant?

Mark each category

	Excellent	Very good	Average	Poor
Noise	( )	( )	( )	( )
Safety	( )	( )	( )	( )
Ventilation	( )	( )	( )	( )

	Excellent	Very good	Average	Poor
Lighting	( )	( )	( )	( )
Cleanliness	( )	( )	( )	( )
Orderliness	( )	( )	( )	( )
Temperature	( )	( )	( )	( )
Lockers	( )	( )	( )	( )
Tools and equipment	( )	( )	( )	( )

25. How do you rate your managers since Rosie the Riveter Enterprises acquired your company?

Mark each category

	Excellent	Very good	Average	Poor
Availability	( )	( )	( )	( )
Communicating with workers	( )	( )	( )	( )
Letting workers know where they stand	( )	( )	( )	( )
Listening to complaints	( )	( )	( )	( )
Fairness	( )	( )	( )	( )
Knowledge of how to manage	( )	( )	( )	( )
Decision-making	( )	( )	( )	( )
Friendliness	( )	( )	( )	( )
Discipline	( )	( )	( )	( )
Giving credit when it's due	( )	( )	( )	( )
Policy-making	( )	( )	( )	( )
Setting objectives	( )	( )	( )	( )

26. Read the following statements, and mark whether you agree or disagree with each one.

	I Agree	I Do Not Agree	No Opinion
Our production is poor because the workers don't care.	( )	( )	( )
Our quality is poor. Nobody cares about it.	( )	( )	( )
We make a damned good product.	( )	( )	( )
Our plant is very well organized.	( )	( )	( )
Our sales staff is good at moving our products.	( )	( )	( )
The competition does better in the marketplace than we do.	( )	( )	( )
Our monthly plant meetings are good.	( )	( )	( )
Our communications need to be improved.	( )	( )	( )

	I Agree	I Do Not Agree	No Opinion
The old management had better communications with employees than the new management does.	( )	( )	( )
Employees should be able to work staggered shifts.	( )	( )	( )
Employees should be able to rotate their jobs.	( )	( )	( )
I am prouder to work for this company than I was before it was acquired.	( )	( )	( )
Workers are afraid to say what's on their mind since the acquisition.	( )	( )	( )

27. Answers to these questions are used only to guide the research team. Remember, this is a confidential survey! Please do not sign your name. These forms will not be seen by anyone but the researchers!

How old are you? _____

Are you Male _____ Female _____?

Are you a Manager? _____ Supervisor? _____ Foreman? _____ Hourly? _____

How long did you work for the company before the acquisition by Rosie the Riveter Enterprises? _____ years.

28. Please mention anything else—either positive or negative—about the company that is important to you.

_____

_____

_____

_____

_____

_____

Up-to-the-Minute Methods of Measuring Public Relations Effectiveness

The most interesting research trend is that of attempting to measure public relations effectiveness. For decades, this was done by adding numbers of clippings and circulation totals. Or, if the public relations effort was directed at the electronic media, it was measured by adding numbers of appearances by a spokesperson, minutes of air time, references to message points, or numbers of viewers. What was missing was the element that *must* be measured to determine public relations success or failure: impact on target audiences.

There are new methodologies, however, that—while not profound—do make honest attempts to evaluate changes in awareness levels of target audiences; these are reasonably dependable measurements of the effectiveness of public relations.

Burson-Marsteller, the large international public relations agency, uses two measurement methods: change design and size design. Ketchum Public Relations, another international firm, employs what it calls the Ketchum Publicity Tracking Model, a computerized method of evaluating numbers of placements, numbers of sales points in placements, and the numbers of targeted consumers (not total circulation) reached by all the media. Hill & Knowlton uses a computerized system to measure effectiveness, as does PR Data of Wilton, Connecticut, AT&T, Bacon's PR and Media Information Systems, and the News Analysis Institute of Pittsburgh.

The promise and the pitfalls of measurement research are evident in the Burson-Marsteller approach. Measurements are taken before and after promotional activity, to provide an indication of changes in target audiences. This approach is called change design.

The Pros and Cons of Change Design

Change design is referred to as "pre" and "post," because of the before and after measurements. If publicity is to appear during a certain time period, a random sampling of newspaper readers and television viewers is conducted to evaluate pre-campaign awareness levels. Normally, 200 telephone interviews are conducted before the campaign (or before an article that is to be evaluated appears in print), and 200 interviews are conducted following the campaign or after the article appears.

This type of research—also called tracking research—is problematic. It must be accomplished quickly or external factors could contaminate findings. A solution to this problem is to take repeated measurements during a publicity campaign, and also to attempt to evaluate circumstances that might alter findings. But this runs expenses up.

Sometimes, tracking research should not be attempted, or should only be conducted locally or regionally. The cost of meaningful tracking research on a national scale—the United States has an adult population of approximately 230 million—is prohibitive. Also, the chances for inconclusive studies are high, since it is impossible to achieve consistent and similar publicity placements in several cities at the same time.

In an individual market, however, change design can be effective once publicity has been generated. It is important, however, that researchers measure audiences only in areas where publicity has actually appeared.

Another type of change design survey is referred to as test-and-control. Researchers interview respondents in control markets—areas where a product has not been introduced—and in a number of test markets, or areas where promotional campaigns are being implemented. Several measurements are taken in both groups, and the pre-post difference that is obtained in the control markets is subtracted from the pre-post difference obtained in the test markets. The final figure is called an incremental effect, and is attributed to promotional efforts.

There are problems with test-and-control, too. It is frequently difficult to find comparable markets to survey, and it cannot be guaranteed that control markets will remain free of public relations or advertising that would influence respondents.

Many times, research is asked to separate the results achieved from advertising and from public relations campaigns. Hopefully, there are separate but similar markets. Then a workable approach would be to introduce advertising and publicity jointly in one set of markets, and advertising only in the other set.

Sometimes, a publicity program is implemented in support of an ongoing advertising campaign. A measurement of the change resulting before publicity was launched can be obtained by using one market or several market pre-publicity program measurements. If multiple surveys are achieved before publicity is introduced, the effectiveness of advertising and publicity can be measured separately.

When to Use Size Designs

Size designs primarily measure audience recall and recognition of a public relations message. They are employed for post-measurement only. Size designs, which are usually conducted by telephone, can indicate the size of the audience reached through public relations/publicity efforts, and they can provide an indication of message point recall.

Customarily, measurement requires monitoring a single story—usually one of high visibility—that appeared in a daily newspaper or in a trade publication, or which has been aired on television or radio.

Public Relations Measurement Objectives
• Determine the effect of public relations or publicity activities on target audience's awareness of and knowledge about a product or service.

The Sample
• "Pre" (Control Group) and "Post" (Test Group). Number of respondents in each group is 150–200.
• Sample is probability, and may require pre-survey telephone screening, or review of newspaper or magazine subscribers.

Interview Method
• Telephone. Surveyors must determine before interviews that Pre and Post respondents are available in sufficient numbers to execute measurement activity when publicity is imminent.

Analysis
• Comparing Pre to Post, and attributing the difference to public relations/publicity activity.

A SAMPLE QUESTIONNAIRE FOR MEASURING CONSUMER PRODUCT USE

The following hypothetical measurement of a consumer product involves a small, regionally marketed product, Chilton paint, and those of large, well-known competitive factors—Sherwin Williams, Benjamin Moore, and Cook & Dunn. A story concerning the economies of house painting—including how to evaluate the condition of existing paints on frame homes, how to ventilate a house to prolong the life of paint most effectively, and how to select the most economical paint—is to appear in the March 7 issue of the New York *Daily News.* The article will quote a Chilton Paint Company executive, and will mention a new brand of paint the company is marketing that is less expensive than the nationally advertised brands of the larger companies.

1. What newspaper did you read today?

   New York Daily News   ( )
   New York Times   ( )
   New York Post   ( )

   (IF *DAILY NEWS* NOT READ, TERMINATE INTERVIEW)

2. Which sections and features in the *Daily News* do you usually read?

   Sports   ( )
   Local news   ( )
   Gossip   ( )
   Home/Living Section   ( )
   Sylvia Porter   ( )
   Business Section   ( )

3. Which of these sections did you read today?

   Sports   ( )
   Local news   ( )
   Gossip   ( )
   Home/Living Section   ( )
   Sylvia Porter   ( )
   Business Section   ( )

   (IF SYLVIA PORTER NOT READ, TERMINATE INTERVIEW)

4. I'd like to ask you a few questions about Sylvia Porter's column.

   First, what was the subject of the column today?

   _____

   _____

   Second, what was the message of the column? PROBE.

   _____

   _____

   Third, do you recall the name of any company in the column? PROBE.

   _____

   _____

5. When it comes to painting your house, what paint companies do you expect to be offering "how to" advice?

_____

_____

_____

6. Of the companies I am going to mention, which ones do you think offer the public advice on how to paint a house?

Sherwin Williams	( )
Chilton Paint	( )
Benjamin Moore	( )
Cook & Dunn	( )

7. Do you think a homeowner can save hundreds of dollars in one painting of his house?

Yes	( )
No	( )
Don't know	( )

8. How do you think this is possible? _____

_____

_____

_____

9. Finally, do you think a fresh paint job can increase the value of your home, and by how much? _____

_____

10. Now, may I ask a few questions about yourself so we can categorize our rspondents?

a. Which age group are you in?
(READ IF RESPONDENT HESITATES)

18 - 21	( )
22 - 27	( )
28 - 35	( )
36 - 45	( )
46 - 58	( )
59 - 65	( )
Over 65	( )

b. Are you employed full time?

Yes	( )
No	( )

c. What is your occupation? _____

    d. How large is your house? _____

    e. How often do you paint your house? _____

    f. Have you ever used Chilton Paint?
        Yes   ( )
        No   ( )
        Don't know ( )

    g. (INTERVIEWER NOTE WHETHER RESPONDENT IS MALE/
       FEMALE)

Thank you for your help.

Employee Readership Survey: A "Tuning Key" for the House Organ

One of the most common public relations surveys involves employees. Employees are also one of a company's most important audiences. They are essential to productivity, to product quality, and, ultimately, to the success of a corporation. The employee audience is also important because it is undergoing dramatic, and sometimes unpredictable changes.

Communications surveys are one of the most frequently employed analytical tools. A lack of communiation, a the wrong type of communication, can cause major problems on the plant floor. Even where more obvious problems are involved, such as the changing emotional and professional demands of the American workers, communications can frequently help resolve serious and persistent problems. In just about all cases they can help management understand what is happening on the plant floor.

The most basic communications survey, and the one implemented most often by public relations practitioners, is the one that attempts to learn the effectiveness of the company house organ or other communications vehicle. Sometimes, the house organ is under management fire as a needless expense. Other times, because the house organ does not seem to be "doing the job it did in the old days," surveys are undertaken to ascertain whether the publication's design, format, or editorial content should be changed, or if the money budgeted for its production should be expended for a more up-to-date communications format such as closed circuit television.

Readership Survey Objectives
- To determine effectiveness of a publication in delivering corporate news.
- To evaluate a publication's credibility among its readership.
- To evaluate the effectiveness of its publishing frequency.
- To rate story types for reader appeal.

The Sample
- Employees (although others, such as customers and family members, may be added if they are substantial readership segments).
- A minimum sample depends on readership size. Small readership, about 500, should have at least a 20 percent sample. Large readership, say 50,000, should have a minimum sendout of 5,000 questionnaires.

- The sample should be demographically balanced, and representative of a company: factory and office personnel, salaried/hourly employees, etc.
- Preliminary focus groups frequently help to zero in on potential problems.
- Post-survey telephone calls can be helpful in determining if nonresponding employees react similarly to respondents.

Interview Method

- Mail, plus telephone if post-survey check is deemed necessary. Return is unpredictable. Hope for 25 percent. Enclose copy of publication with questionnaire.

Analysis

- Evaluation of respondents (hourly, salaried, divisions).
- Individual evaluations of publication's value.

A SAMPLE LETTER OF INTRODUCTION

Dear Employee:

Our research organization, Let's Discover, Inc., has been retained by your company to find out what you think about the corporate newspaper, THE BUGLE. Your answers are vital to our survey, because if employees don't like THE BUGLE, changes will be made. If you do like it, it will remain pretty much the same.

Your responses are confidential. We do not want to know who you are or why you are answering the questions the way you are. But it is important that you answer the questionnaire, because that is the only way we have to find out what has to be done to make THE BUGLE the kind of publication the employees think it should be.

Please use the enclosed, stamped envelope to mail your questionnaire. And please remember that complete honesty is important to this survey, as well as to our planning for the right type of publication for you in the future.

Thank you for your help!

Sincerely,

John T. Aires
Research Assistant

A SAMPLE EMPLOYEE READERSHIP QUESTIONNAIRE

SURVEY OF THE BUGLE

1. Do you read THE BUGLE?   Yes ( )   No ( )

2. If "No," why not? _____

_____

3. Is THE BUGLE mailed to your home?   Yes ( )   No ( )

      a. If "No," should we put your name on the mailing list?
      Yes ( )   No ( )

4. Who else in your house reads the publication?

         Nobody   ( )
         My spouse   ( )
         The kids   ( )
         Others (state who)   ( )

5. Do you like receiving THE BUGLE in the mail, or would you rather pick it up at work?

         Home   ( )
         At work   ( )

6. Does THE BUGLE help you to know what is going on at the company?

         Yes, a lot   ( )
         A little, but not much   ( )
         Are you kidding?   ( )

7. Do you think you know what's going on at the company? If so, how do you get the word?

     _____

     _____

     If not, why not?

     _____

     _____

8. Does your plant have a local newspaper also, in addition to THE BUGLE?
     Yes ( )   No ( )

9. If so, do you like your plant newspaper better than THE BUGLE?
     Yes ( )   No ( )

10. If yes, why?

         a. Coverage is more honest. ( )
         b. I know the people in it. ( )
         c. I get my name in it. ( )
         d. My family likes it. ( )
         e. I don't care about the rest of the company. ( )
         f. I get tired of seeing things about management in THE BUGLE. ( )

         g. Other _____

         _____

11. Do you think the company should publish THE BUGLE?

         a. Yes, I think it's very important. ( )
         b. I don't know, maybe. ( )
         c. Heck, no! ( )

12. How frequently do you think THE BUGLE should be published?

        a. Every other week ( )
        b. Once a month ( )
        c. Once every three months ( )
        d. Never ( )

13. If you never saw another copy of THE BUGLE, how would you feel?

        a. Very upset ( )
        b. A little bothered ( )
        c. Happy ( )

14. Read the statements below, and then mark—very carefully—the statement that best matches your feelings.

	I agree	I disagree	I don't know
THE BUGLE gives me more information about the company than any other source.	( )	( )	( )
I am usually interested in the articles in THE BUGLE.	( )	( )	( )
I like the headlines in THE BUGLE.	( )	( )	( )
I like the pictures in THE BUGLE.	( )	( )	( )
The subjects in THE BUGLE don't interest me.	( )	( )	( )
I think management plans the subject matter.	( )	( )	( )
The subject matter is just right for employees.	( )	( )	( )

15. Who likes THE BUGLE the most? (Mark 1-2-3-4, with "1" the highest.)

        a. Management ( )
        b. Salaried employees ( )
        c. Hourly employees ( )
        d. People in the plant ( )

16. Which type of stories do you like the most? (Put a check mark next to the categories you like the best.)

        Management ( )
        Company finance ( )
        Sports ( )
        Families ( )
        Safety ( )
        Company plans for future ( )
        Plant towns ( )
        New products ( )

Industry stories ( )
Individuals like me ( )
Union news ( )

17. How *interesting* and how *believable,* overall, do you find THE BUGLE? Circle a "10" for high score, a "0" for the lowest score.

INTERESTING
   10 9 8 7 6 5 4 3 2 1 0

BELIEVABLE
   10 9 8 7 6   5 4 3 2 1 0

18. If your company decided to stop printing THE BUGLE in favor of another form of communication, what do you think it should be?

     a. A magazine with color pictures ( )
     b. Something on TV in the training room ( )
     c. Something completely different (explain)

     _____

     _____

     _____

19. Do not sign this form, but please answer the following questions.

     a. How long have you worked for the company? _____
     b. How old are you?   17-25 _____
                         26-35 _____
                         36-45 _____
                         46-50 _____
                         51-55 _____
                         56-65 _____
     c. Did you finish grade school?   Yes ( )   No ( )
        Did you finish high school?   Yes ( )   No ( )
        Did you go to college?   Yes ( )   No ( )
        If you went to college, how long?   (1) (2) (3) (4)

20. Are you male ( ) female ( )?

21. How many in your family are living at home? _____

Trade Marketing Survey: Quick and Revealing

Trade marketing surveys are easier to implement than consumer surveys, because manufacturers and distributors of industrial products are knowledgeable about the industry or industries they serve, and they know who and where their customers and potential customers are. These revealing surveys can be executed quickly, and they can frequently influence sales and marketing efforts in the short term.

Trade Marketing Survey Objectives

- Determine marketplace awareness of, and regard for, a product or service.
- Evaluate the effectiveness of sales, advertising, and other promotional efforts.
- Obtain information about competitive products and services.
- Determine how purchasing decisions are made in specific companies, and which individuals influence purchasing decisions.

The Sample

- Probability sample of customers drawn from knowledge of marketplace. Size of sample varies, depending upon size of market. In the survey which follows, involving an industrial pump market, a minimum of 150 respondents would be queried.
- Noncustomers are important to trade marketing surveys. Names can be gathered from sales force, industry associations, trade magazines.

Interview Method

- A combination of personal and telephone interviewing is recommended. Some research firms also use mail, but this could violate the survey's confidentiality.
- Since these interviews involve well-placed executives, and since they sometimes require considerable time, it is best to advise potential respondents of the survey by letter about one week before contact is made.

Analysis

- By user/nonuser categories, by size and type of company, and by respondent's professional qualifications, including job title, knowledge of and years in the business.

A SAMPLE LETTER OF INTRODUCTION

The following letter is of the type recommended to alert respondents to the forthcoming telephone contact. To assure confidentiality, the letter should not reveal the survey sponsor or provide any information from which industry sources could determine the sponsor. The letter should stimulate the recipient's interest and willingness to participate in the survey.

Dear Mr. Smith:

Industry sources have recommended that we contact you regarding participation in an upcoming survey, because of your extensive knowledge about the application of pumps in the food processing and other industries.

Our research firm is presently conducting a survey regarding contemporary heavy-duty pump applications, and we would appreciate it if you would share some of your knowledge about this topic with us. We will telephone you in about one week and see if we could discuss the topic for ten minutes or so.

You may be interested to know that this is one of the most exhaustive studies ever attempted on this subject. Approximately 150 professionals in responsible positions like yours are cooperating in the study.
Thank you in advance for your assistance.

Sincerely,

Mark T. Janckovitch
Vice President-Survey Coordinator

A SAMPLE TRADE MARKETING QUESTIONNAIRE

Questionnaires for individual studies might vary somewhat if several different corporate disciplines—such as purchasing, manufacturing, engineering, finance—were to be interviewed. Usually, though, only one audience is involved. The following questionnaire would be characteristic of those used for engineering/manufacturing audiences. The objectives of this hypothetical study, if conducted by a manufacturer such as Ingersoll-Rand, for example, would be to determine purchasing influences within customer companies, to measure the acceptability of I-R pumps compared to those of the competition, and to judge the effectiveness of sales and marketing efforts.

1. When you think of pumps used on manufacturing and processing lines, what names first come to mind? (DO NOT READ LIST. THIS IS A CROWDED INDUSTRY. PROBE.)

   Gardner Denver ( )
   Chicago Pneumatic ( )
   Ingersoll-Rand ( )
   Gould ( )
   Duriron ( )
   Gorman Rupp ( )

   _____ ( )

   _____ ( )

   _____ ( )

2. Which company/companies do you think of as the leader(s)? (PROBE.)

   _____

   _____

   _____

   _____

3. What improvements do you expect over the long term—say, five to ten years—in heavy-duty pumps for manufacturing and processing applications? _____

   _____

   _____

4. Are manufacturers working on these improvements at the present time? (PROBE. WHICH MANUFACTURERS?) _____

   _____

   _____

5. Do you think pump manufacturers have been keeping people like yourself informed about developments in this field? Have they been:

       Doing a good job? ( )
       Doing a fair job? ( )
       Doing a poor job? ( )
       Don't know.   ( )

6. What techniques do they use to keep you up-to-date?_____

   _____

   _____

7. What pump manufacturers have been doing the best job of keeping you informed? PROBE. _____

   _____

   _____

8. Which people in your company—by job title—are involved in the selection of new pumps?

     Title

     President   ( )
     Executive vice president ( )
     Purchasing officer   ( )
     Production manager   ( )
     Manufacturing manager ( )
     Design engineer   ( )
     Other _____   ( )

9. Which individual(s) has the most influence on the purchase of this equipment?
   _____

   _____

10. Why does this person(s) have the most influence on the purchasing decision?

   _____

   _____

11. How much influence does a manufacturer's salesperson have on your company's purchasing decision?

     A lot of influence ( )
     A fair amount ( )
     Not much influence ( )
     We don't listen to them ( )

12. Why is this so? _____

_____

_____

13. Some companies' sales staffs have reputations for being very good technically. Do any companies come to mind? (PROBE. DO NOT NAME COMPANIES.)

_____

_____

_____

_____

14. Also, some companies have reputations as technological leaders in the area of pump development. What companies come to mind? (PROBE. DO NOT NAME COMPANIES.)

_____

_____

_____

_____

15. How about meeting manufacturing and shipping deadlines? Are some manufacturers better than others? (PROBE. DO NOT NAME COMPANIES.)

_____

_____

_____

_____

16. What is most important in selecting a pump manufacturer? The sales staff? Technological leadership? Meeting manufacturing and shipping deadlines?

_____

_____

17. Which manufacturers' pumps do you presently have on line, and why were they selected? _____

_____

_____

18. How many, and what type, of pumps do you have on line?

_____

_____

19. How important is parts supply and service to your buying decision?

_____

_____

20. Does any company(ies) have the edge in this area?

_____

_____

_____

21. What factors count the most to you when selecting a pump?

_____

_____

22. What do you think of Chicago Pneumatic equipment?

_____

_____

23. How about Ingersoll-Rand? _____

_____

_____

24. And Gardner Denver? _____

_____

25. How do you rate these three manufacturers in the following important areas?

	Ingersoll-Rand				Gardner Denver				Chicago Pneumatic			
	Good	Fair	Poor	Don't Know	Good	Fair	Poor	Don't Know	Good	Fair	Poor	Don't Know
Professionalism of salespeople	( )	( )	( )	( )	( )	( )	( )	( )	( )	( )	( )	( )
New products frequency	( )	( )	( )	( )	( )	( )	( )	( )	( )	( )	( )	( )
Quality of products	( )	( )	( )	( )	( )	( )	( )	( )	( )	( )	( )	( )
Technical reputation and advice	( )	( )	( )	( )	( )	( )	( )	( )	( )	( )	( )	( )
Parts and service	( )	( )	( )	( )	( )	( )	( )	( )	( )	( )	( )	( )
On-time shipments	( )	( )	( )	( )	( )	( )	( )	( )	( )	( )	( )	( )

26. What do you think is the best method of keeping up with what's happening in your industry?

        Trade magazines ( )
        Trade shows ( )
        Manufacturers' and distributors' salespeople ( )
        Other _____ ( )

27. Which trade magazines do you read regularly?

        _____

        _____

        _____

        _____

        _____

28. Respondent's name _____

        Title _____

        Company, plus address _____

        _____

        _____

Consumer Marketing Survey: Capitalizing on Computerized Data

Consumer marketing surveys have benefited substantially from an abundance of computerized data that includes everything from the flow of grocery and household goods, to consumer reactions to specific products, to product inventory levels, and much more. There is very little that cannot be learned about a product or service, and about competitive factors in the marketplace.

Consumer Marketing Survey Objectives

- Determine advertising and brand awareness, plus consumer response to products or services.
- Determine effectiveness of various media in presenting messages about products or services.
- Determine receptiveness among different markets for products or services.

The Sample

- Either a general market, or specific target markets.
- Minimum sample would be about 300.

Interview Method

- Both personal interview and telephone.

Analysis

- Respondent education, sex, age, income, and lifestyle, plus consumer use patterns (such as loyalty to brand, volume, etc.).

A SAMPLE CONSUMER MARKETING QUESTIONNAIRE

If New York City's Citibank were interested in conducting a marketing program with the objective of attracting college seniors, graduate students, and recent graduates to use the bank's services, starting with checking accounts, the effort would logically include research. A questionnaire similar to the following would help researchers ascertain how visible the bank is to the college audience, if the importance of establishing credit was understood, and how visible a (fictitious) service of the bank's, "Student Service," was.

1. Have you ever opened a checking or a savings account?

   Yes ( )
   No ( )

2. If yes, at what bank? Why did you choose that bank?

   _____

   _____

3. Do you think it is important to establish credit?

   Yes ( )
   No ( )

4. If yes, why? _____

_____

5. If no, why? _____

_____

6. What do you think is the best method of establishing credit?

Opening a checking or a savings account ( )
Getting a credit card ( )
Repaying a loan ( )
Getting a job ( )
Paying bills ( )
Using a service such as "Student Service" ( )

7. Have you ever heard of that service— "Student Service" —or anything like it? (IF NO, EXPLAIN SERVICE.) (IF YES, ASK WHERE.)_____

8. Which of the following banks provides "Student Service"?

Chemical ( )
Bankers Trust ( )
Manufacturers Hanover ( )
Chase ( )
Citibank ( )

9. Do you think "Student Service" has advantages that other ways of establishing credit do not have?

Yes   ( )
No   ( )
Don't know ( )

10. If "yes," or "no," ask why. _____

_____

11. What banks in the New York area have you heard of? (PROBE. DO NOT READ LIST.)

Citibank ( )
Chemical ( )
Chase ( )
Bankers Trust ( )
Morgan Guaranty ( )
Irving Trust ( )
Manufacturers Hanover ( )

12. Have you ever used the services of a bank? Which ones?

_____

13. Do you have any credit cards? (PROBE. DO NOT READ LIST.)

       Department store ( )
       Gas ( )
       MasterCard ( )
       VISA ( )
       American Express ( )
       Carte Blanche ( )
       Other _____

14. Do any of these cards—to your knowledge—have minimal eligibility requirements so that students can take advantage of the service, and establish credit?

       Yes   ( )
       No   ( )
       Don't know ( )

15. Do you think a bank's service would be a better way to establish credit than, say, with an American Express card, or with VISA?

       Yes   ( )
       No   ( )
       Don't know ( )

16. If "yes," why? _____

_____

17. FOR RESPONDENTS WHO ARE AWARE OF CITIBANK'S "STUDENT SERVICE," ASK: How did you hear about Citibank's "Student Service?"

       Ad in campus newspaper ( )
       Direct mail piece ( )
       A classmate ( )
       A radio ad ( )
       Application in a Citibank branch ( )

18. Do you think many of your classmates know about "Student Service?"

       Yes   ( )
       No   ( )
       Don't know ( )

19. Do you think "Student Service" is the easiest way for a student to earn a credit rating?

       Yes   ( )
       No   ( )
       Don't know ( )

20. Do you think you are eligible for "Student Service"?

       Yes   ( )
       No   ( )
       Don't know ( )

21. Are you eligible for other types of credit, such as American Express, or MasterCard?

Yes   ( )
No   ( )
Don't know ( )

22. If you had a "Student Service" card, how would you use it? _____

_____

23. To help us with our statistics, would you please answer the following questions?

       What college do you attend? _____
       Do you live (on campus) (off campus) (at home)?
       Do you work (part-time) (seasonally) (full-time)?
       Approximately how much do you earn annually? $_____

24. Record respondent's sex (male) (female).

Investor Relations Survey: Weathering the Whims of Wall Street

The financial/investor relations survey is one of the most frequently employed measurements in the public relations business. Because of the caprice of Wall Street, this survey is also often used on a recurring basis.

Financial/Investor Relations Survey Objectives

- To analyze the financial community's opinions of a company and its industry. (This type of survey is normally initiated immediately following financial analysts' meetings, annual meetings, or tours by selected members of the financial community.)
- To determine shareholder assessments of a company, of its industry, and of competitive factors.
- To determine the attractiveness of a company's—or an industry's—shares, usually following events that generate substantial recognition.
- To reveal the attitudes of active/inactive investors regarding business issues of national or international importance.

The Sample

- National investor panel of 14,000 persons maintained by Market Facts, Inc. Sample includes 2,500 active investors. Fewer than 1,000 panel members usually interviewed per individual study.
- Shareholder assessment studies depend upon number of stockholders in an individual company. Approximately 300 to 3,000 per study.
- Financial analyst studies following important corporate events normally include from 6 to 25 analysts who participated.

Interview Method
- Varies, depending upon study.
  1. Investor panel: telephone or mail.
  2. Shareholder assessment: usually mail, sometimes combination, mail/telephone.
  3. Financial analyst studies: telephone, occasionally in-person interviews.

Analysis
- Varies, depending upon study.
  1. By panel member investment characteristics, plus demographics.
  2. Shareholder composite.
  3. Sponsoring, interested, and uninterested analysts.

Financial Community Survey: Determining the Aftereffects of Major Corporate Events

Probably the most common type of financial relations survey is the one conducted immediately following a major corporate event, such as a financial analysts' meeting. Only a few respondents are necessary for these surveys, since those contacted follow the company on a regular basis and will have attended the meeting.

The following survey can be considered typical of this type of research. A public relations agency prepared this report following a financial analysts' meeting at an important time in the corporate history of a major independent oil company, we'll call XYZ Oil. High prices for foreign oil have weakened the company's profitability and competitive position, and new management had recently been installed.

The agency interviewed 11 of the 120 members of the New York financial community who attended the year-end, review-of-operations meeting. The audience was comprised of security analysts, retail-brokers, institutional salespeople, portfolio managers, and investment advisors, as well as the oil company's investment bankers.

The following few pages from the survey are presented to illustrate the type of report that is prepared after a major corporate event.

EXCERPTS FROM A SURVEY OF THE FINANCIAL COMMUNITY

The company's presentation played to mixed reviews because levels of interest in the company varied so widely.

The audience composition resulted in mixed feelings about both the quality and quantity of information in XYZ Oil's presentation. Security analysts who knew the company very well thought the meeting lacked substance. Financial content was "light" in the eyes of many seasoned observers. Analysts were disappointed that the presentation seemed to be nothing more than "a speech read from a podium." More than one observer noted that XYZ did not make enough use of comparative numbers in order to accentuate the financial positives of the company.

One analyst, a relative newcomer to XYZ, was disappointed because the presentation "concentrated too much on the past, and not enough on the future, in terms of specific numbers." He thought management "talked in generalities," ignoring specifics such as gasoline prices, crude oil costs, and six-month projections. Other analysts as well wanted "some forward looking" on supply and demand for petroleum products. One individual who has followed XYZ for about fifteen years made the following observation:

> The company, out of perhaps an excess of conservatism or caution, didn't tell a story that they are in a better period for their earnings—which they are. They could have been more aggressive and said, "Hey gang, we're on the move. Industry conditions have improved, our cash flow is up, our earnings are up, we are headed for better days."

Improved cash flow at XYZ Oil raised an important question for some attendees—a question which remains unanswered, according to one analyst. He explains:

> It comes down to what happens next year when they have an enormous cash flow and don't have to spend it on the refining sector. They claim they are going to pump money back into their other businesses, but there's a limit to how much money can be absorbed by those segments. They will still have excess cash.

Another investment professional noted that the short shrift given to XYZ's positive cash flow and the lack of comparative financials did not do justice to the dramatic turnaround being experienced by the company. He observed:

> ...they never really showed you just how big cash flow was or how big it could be. They should have segmented out the first half of the year versus the second half of the year and showed the contrast....They really ought to show the momentum changing from despair to optimism. Instead, they basically lumped everything together. Analysts who didn't follow the company closely wouldn't have known that there was a dramatic turn-around in the past six months.

Brokerage firm representatives thought the meeting gave plenty of information; they were also pleased with the opportunity to socialize with management.

Several investment professionals voiced little concern about the actual quality and content of management's presentation. They were more concerned with the chance to mingle one-on-one with members of the management team in order to get their "real questions" answered. One analyst admitted that he had visited XYZ recently, so he knew the numbers were going to look good. "The meeting was sort of a social event," he commented, adding, "All the oil analysts go to see what the refiners are doing."

Another long-time XYZ follower noted that for a detail-oriented analyst such as himself, management's presentation was simply "a place to start." This analyst was pleased because he was able "to nail" a management team member after the formal meeting and get "all the details about the economics of the RCC and all the crude cost questions." He explained:

> For a generalist who follows biscuit companies one day and XYZ Oil the next, the content was all right. But I got the details I wanted by having management present and being able to nail them later. I think that's what detail analysts tend to do, anyway.

Another, a long-time follower of the company, was far more blunt about his attendance. He came "purely to show face" and didn't expect to gain any information from the presentation, since he does all his research on a one-on-one basis with management.

Survey participants made several constructive criticisms which management should consider for improving their communications efforts.

Given the diverse interests of the audience, XYZ should not expect to have satisfied each individual attendee's informational needs. For the most part, the meeting did offer a comprehensive picture of the company for brokers and portfolio managers. Management was viewed as both credible and able, as well as responsible for the improved condition of the company's financial position.

Detail-oriented analysts would have been more satisfied by a greater emphasis on comparative financial data and future cost projections; greater focus on the refining and marketing area, XYZ's lead business; and a long-term scenario for next year when cash flow will become substantial. Greater elaboration on diversification results to date and future plans would satisfy both broker and institutional analysts.

The meeting format did not show management to its best advantage. The CEO, for example, received some criticism for "reading from the podium," and was seen as awkward in handling the question and answer period.

A SAMPLE QUESTIONNAIRE FOR INVESTORS

If a company (for example, a high-flyer in a high-technology field) desired to find out how investors arrive at stock purchase decisions, and if there were general interest on the part of individual investors in the industry the company served, the following questionnaire would be appropriate.

1. How many times a year do you purchase stock? _____
2. What usually influences your decision to buy stock?
    My own personal knowledge of the business
    world ( )

    Discussions with my broker ( )

    Discussions with other professionals (list)

    _____   ( )

    Newspaper articles (list where)

    _____   ( )

    Magazine articles (list where)

    _____   ( )

    Radio or television (list shows)

    _____   ( )

    Trade magazines (list)

    _____   ( )

3. After you decide you like a stock, what do you do?
   Buy it ( )
   Investigate the situation further ( )

4. If you investigate further, how do you do this?
   Call my broker ( )
   Contact the company ( )
   Obtain an annual report ( )
   Talk it over with friends ( )
   Call people I know in the industry ( )
   Read press clippings ( )

5. When did you last buy stock? _____

_____

6. What industry was the company in? _____

_____

7. Why did you buy that stock? _____

_____

8. How did you first hear about the company? _____

_____

9. What is your opinion about (name of sponsoring company's industry)? _____

_____

10. Have you been following it? (Yes) (No)

11. Do you know of (name of sponsoring company)? (Yes) (No)

12. IF YES: How? _____

_____

_____

13. What do you think of investing in its shares?

_____

_____

14. What are those qualities that you normally look for in a company to invest in?
   Strong capital position ( )
   Good management ( )
   Growth industry ( )
   Yield ( )
   Strong performance historically ( )
   Unusual products ( )

Opportunity for quick profit ( )

Other _____( )

15. Does size of company influence your decision to buy stock?
(Yes) (No)

16. What size company are you most interested in?
Under $300 million sales ( )
Under $800 million sales ( )
Up to $1.5 billion sales ( )
Over $1.5 billion sales ( )
The bigger the better ( )

17. Do you usually invest in:
NYSE companies ( )
ASE companies ( )
OTC companies ( )
Other (specify) _____

18. What is your occupation? _____

19. How old are you? _____

20. How much education do you have? _____

Thank you for your assistance.

Community Attitude Survey: PR's "Preventive Medicine"

Community attitude surveys became important public relations weapons when the American corporation became a social entity. Management suddenly needed to know what the community thought of a company's environmental practices, its Equal Opportunity and OSHA compliance, and—especially in multi-company communities with competitive hiring situations—about the public's opinions of the company as a place to work.

These surveys can pinpoint trouble areas before they become serious, thereby permitting corrective public relations procedures to be implemented before damage is done. Or, if problems have reached damaging proportions, community attitude surveys can reveal the extent of the damage and help determine the type of corrective action that should be taken to reinstate the community's good faith in the company.

The following hypothetical survey could be undertaken to find out the community's attitude toward one company compared to other employers in town.

Community Attitude Survey Objectives

- To reveal potential social problems that could involve a company, a community, or both.
- To permit an evaluation of the standings of all firms in a multi-company community.
- To determine the importance of different community activities and of a company's involvement in these activities.

- To determine community reaction to specific events, such as the purchase of a local facility by an outside source.

The Sample

- Probability sample of residents.
- Probability sample of employees.
- Numbers of respondents would vary according to size of community or payroll. Generally, at least 100 employees and 250 residents are required. (In extremely small communities, surveys are not generally required because the people's mind set is usually known.)

Interview Method

- Always by telephone. Respondents should not be made aware of the survey sponsor's identity.

Analysis

- Two groups, residents and employees (length of time with company is important when analyzing employees). All demographics should be considered, including age, sex, media habits, and years in the community.

A SAMPLE COMMUNITY ATTITUDE QUESTIONNAIRE

Local residents and employees are interviewed from the same questionnaire.

Name: _____ Date: _____

Address: _____

Telephone: _____ Interviewed by: _____

Hello. I'm from Smith Associates, a marketing research firm. We're surveying several hundred people in this area to find out what they think of local companies. May I have a few minutes of your time?

    A. First, we're talking to people of voting age. Are you 18 or older?

    B. Is anybody home who is over 18? (ASK TO SPEAK TO THEM.)

    C. Sex: Male ( ) Female ( )

1. How many years have you lived in Middletown? _____ years

2. Let me ask you about the companies that have plants in your area. What companies come to mind? (PROBE.)

_____

_____

_____

_____

_____

3. I will name some major employers in your area. Please tell me—on a scale of 1 to 10—how you would rate them when it comes to being good citizens, or doing good for the community. If you don't know some of the companies, say so.

   Tru-Steel _____

   Vertical Hoist _____

   Bimmy Cosmetics _____

   Rollaway Trucking _____

   Fast Fizz Soda Pop _____

4. Let's talk about one of the oldest companies in the area—Tru-Steel. What has it done for the community? (PROBE.)

   _____

   _____

   _____

5. What are Tru-Steel's strengths? (PROBE.)

   _____

   _____

   _____

6. What about weaknesses? Can you think of any weaknesses that Tru-Steel has? In any area? (PROBE.)

   _____

   _____

   _____

7. In your opinion, what does it take for a company to be a good corporate citizen?

   _____

   _____

   _____

8. What are the major problems facing Middletown at this time? These problems can be in any area: social, political, economic, or environmental.

_____

_____

_____

9. Let's talk about Vertical Hoist. What are the company's strengths?

_____

_____

_____

10. Has Vertical Hoist tried to help the community through the years?

_____

_____

_____

11. Do you think companies should help solve local problems?

_____

_____

_____

12. What are Vertical Hoist's weak points as a corporate citizen?

_____

_____

_____

13. Okay, let's switch to Bimmy Cosmetics. What are their best points when it comes to being a citizen of Middletown? (PROBE.)

_____

_____

_____

14. Can you name some contributions that Bimmy Cosmetics has made to the community? (PROBE.)

_____

_____

_____

15. What about weak points? Does Bimmy Cosmetics have any weak points when it comes to being a citizen of Middletown? (PROBE.)

_____

_____

_____

16. Now, let me ask you to evaluate several statements I will make about all three companies. Tell me if you *agree* with the statement...if you *disagree*...or, if you don't have an opinion. (REPEAT ALL STATEMENTS.)

	Tru-Steel			Vertical Hoist			Bimmy Cosmetics		
	Agree	Disagree	Don't Know	Agree	Disagree	Don't Know	Agree	Disagree	Don't Know
A good place to work.	( )	( )	( )	( )	( )	( )	( )	( )	( )
Pays well.	( )	( )	( )	( )	( )	( )	( )	( )	( )
Has strict rules.	( )	( )	( )	( )	( )	( )	( )	( )	( )
Levels with workers at all times.	( )	( )	( )	( )	( )	( )	( )	( )	( )
Helps to improve the community.	( )	( )	( )	( )	( )	( )	( )	( )	( )
Concerned about pollution.	( )	( )	( )	( )	( )	( )	( )	( )	( )
Has good benefits.	( )	( )	( )	( )	( )	( )	( )	( )	( )
Really cares about safety.	( )	( )	( )	( )	( )	( )	( )	( )	( )
Donates money to Middletown.	( )	( )	( )	( )	( )	( )	( )	( )	( )
Has good career opportunities.	( )	( )	( )	( )	( )	( )	( )	( )	( )
Hires women and blacks.	( )	( )	( )	( )	( )	( )	( )	( )	( )

	Tru-Steel			Vertical Hoist			Bimmy Cosmetics		
	Agree	Disagree	Don't Know	Agree	Disagree	Don't Know	Agree	Disagree	Don't Know
Management cares about employees and the town.	( )	( )	( )	( )	( )	( )	( )	( )	( )

17. What community activity—and this could include work with charities—do you think Tru-Steel has been involved in? (PROBE.)

_____

_____

_____

18. What community activity—including charities again—do you associate with Vertical Hoist? (PROBE.)

_____

_____

_____

19. What activities of the same sort do you attribute to Bimmy Cosmetics? (PROBE.)

_____

_____

_____

20. Now, I'd like to ask a few questions about how you get your local news. For example:

a. How long do you listen to the radio each day?
   (1) 15 minutes _____
   (2) 30 minutes _____
   (3) One hour _____
   (4) More than one hour _____

b. How about television?
   (1) 15 minutes _____
   (2) 30 minutes _____
   (3) One hour _____
   (4) More than one hour _____

c. What radio station(s) do you usually listen to?

_____

_____

_____

d. What television station(s) do you watch?

_____

_____

_____

e. What part of the day do you usually watch television or listen to the radio?

Early morning _____

Midmorning _____

Late morning _____

Afternoon _____

Evening _____

21. What newspaper(s) do you read?

_____

_____

22. Do you work for any of the companies we have been discussing?
   Yes ( )
   No ( )
   Company _____

23. Do any of your family members work for any of these companies?
   Yes ( )
   No ( )
   Company or companies _____

24. We are trying to get a balance of the community to respond to our survey. Could you please describe yourself, including information such as years of school completed, type of job, and race?

_____

_____

Thank you.

Issues Determination: How to Read the Public's Mind

Issues surveys are important management tools. They help management read the public's mind at a time when society is exerting pressure on companies to operate in "socially acceptable" ways. Issues surveys have been simplified by computerization, with its tremendous information storage capability and its ability to identify target audiences easily. These surveys are usually conducted to gain insight into problems, or potential problems, facing corporations, but they are also undertaken to provide substantiation for public relations/publicity activities.

Issues Surveys Objectives
- Determine public attitudes concerning current issues that are affecting, or that could affect, a company or an industry.

The Sample
- Numbers of interviews would vary widely, depending upon size of target audience. If audience is vast and the subject is highly controversial, several thousands of respondents could be interviewed. Normally, however, 500 to 1,000 are sufficient.
- If survey is undertaken solely for management guidance, a few hundred respondents, carefully selected, will suffice.

Analysis
- Demographic characteristics—age, income, job, sex—of respondents.
- Whatever factors of issue are relevant, such as money and political parties.

A SAMPLE ISSUES QUESTIONNAIRE

The questionnaire for issues surveys should be as brief as possible. It should also be direct, aiming straight at the issues. The demographic characteristics of respondents should be carefully recorded, as they usually have a direct bearing on results.

Let's assume that a pharmaceutical association desires to embark on a public relations/publicity campaign aimed at prodding the U.S. Food & Drug Administration to accelerate procedures for new drug approvals. Part of this effort could involve surveying the general public in major cities regarding its feelings on this subject, and conducting regional publicity campaigns highlighting the results.

Hello. I'm Ted Jones, from the International Consumer Research Company. We are conducting a survey about how people in this region feel about an important health issue. Would you help us by answering a few questions that will help us get to the bottom of this problem? Thank you.

1. First, have you heard the term "drug lag"? It means that prescription drugs to combat illness are being approved in other countries much faster—sometimes years faster—than in the United States.
   Yes ( )
   No ( )

2. Do you take any prescription medicine, or do you know much about this problem?

     Yes ( )
     No ( )

3. From your knowledge, or from what you have read, do you believe that the FDA should:

     Regulate new drug approvals even more strictly than they are now doing? ( )
     Keep regulating approvals the way they are now? ( )
     Liberalize approvals, so new drugs are made available to the public sooner? ( )

4. One argument has it that thousands of American patients have died during the past ten years because important drug therapies have not been available to them. The counterargument claims that American lives have been saved because of strict drug approval procedures. Which argument do you believe?

     That many American patients have died. ( )
     That American lives have been saved. ( )

5. Beta blockers—advanced drugs for heart conditions such as angina pectoris, and for high blood pressure—are primary treatment for these conditions in Europe. Over 30 beta blockers are available in Europe. But, in the United States, only a handful are available. How do you size up this situation? _____

_____

_____

6. Do you recall the problems with the drug thalidomide in the early 1960s? Do you think these problems had anything to do with the protracted drug approval procedure in this country today?

     Yes ( )
     No ( )
     Don't know ( )

7. Do you think there are drug breakthroughs on the horizon that would make drug lag especially damaging in America?

     Yes ( )
     No ( )
     Don't know ( )

8. IF ANSWER TO #7 WAS "YES," ASK: In what areas do you expect drug breakthroughs? _____

_____

9. Has your doctor made any comments about drug lag?

     Yes ( )
     No ( )

10. IF ANSWER TO #9 WAS "YES," ASK: What did your doctor say?

_____

_____

11. Are you presently on any medication?
    Yes ( )
    No ( )

12. IF ANSWER TO #11 WAS "YES," ASK: What is the medication and illness?
    And, do you know if more advanced drug therapy is available in other nations
    for that illness? _____

_____

13. Have you ever obtained advanced drugs for your condition when in other
    nations? Canada? Mexico? European nations?
    Yes ( )
    No ( )

14. Do you know of anybody—a family member, or a friend—who would be helped
    by medications that are available elsewhere?
    Yes ( )
    No ( )

15. Have you ever considered this?
    Yes ( )
    No ( )

16. Have you heard anything about the FDA loosening up on drug approval
    procedures?
    Yes ( )
    No ( )

17. IF ANSWER TO #16 WAS "YES," ASK: What exactly have you heard?

_____

_____

18. Whose responsibility do you think it is to lean on the FDA to liberalize drug
    approval procedures?
    The President's ( )
    Congress ( )
    Industry groups, such as pharmaceutical associations ( )
    Drug companies ( )
    The public ( )

19. It's important that we classify the people the people we speak to. Would you
    please tell me how old you are? (IF RESPONDENT HESITATES, IMME-
    DIATELY START READING CATEGORIES.)

```
18 - 20      ( )
21 - 25      ( )
26 - 30      ( )
31 - 35      ( )
36 - 40      ( )
41 - 48      ( )
49 - 60      ( )
61 - 70      ( )
Over 70      ( )
```

20. How far did you go in school?

    Grammar school   ( )
    Junior high school   ( )
    High school   ( )
    Junior college   ( )
    Four-year college graduate ( )
    Graduate study   ( )

21. How would you describe your everyday outlook on social and political events?

    Conservative   ( )
    Moderate   ( )
    Liberal   ( )
    Not sure   ( )

22. What was your approximate income last year?

    Under $10,000   ( )
    Under $15,000   ( )
    Under $20,000   ( )
    Under $25,000   ( )
    Under $35,000   ( )
    Under $50,000   ( )
    Over $50,000   ( )

23. Do you—or, does anybody in your immediate family—work for a drug company, own or work in a drug store, or have any other affiliation with the drug or medical industries?

    Yes ( )
    No ( )

Thank you for your assistance.

SECONDARY RESEARCH:
AN ABUNDANCE OF INVALUABLE INFORMATION

Secondary research consists of readily available information that is not prepared specifically for a situation being addressed, but which is relevant nevertheless. Secondary research material is abundant and is applied plentifully in the public relations business. Secondary research provides valuable input for:

- Preparations of important corporate documents such as articles, annual and interim reports, speeches, financial analysts' presentations, position papers, and proposals.

- Development of new business presentations by public relations agencies.

- Substantiation of recommended procedures for correction of corporate or marketing problems.

- Providing input for the preparation of product marketing plans.

- Situation analysis for the development of issues and strategies.

- Substantiation of facts and positions for the development of government relations strategies.

- Understanding and anticipating social change.

- Understanding consumer motivation.

- Development of financial relations strategies.

- Evaluation of corporate performance compared to that of the competition.

- Development and refinement of direct mail programs.

- Evaluations of trade shows, conventions, and seminars.

- Evaluations of specific markets and of marketing strategies.

- Targeting of specific consumer markets.

- Validation of product acceptance in the marketplace.

- Discerning public viewing, listening, and reading preferences.

- Research for a wide variety of public relations and publicity programs.

Secondary research material abounds. It is in books and catalogues, on film and tape, in libraries, trade associations, universities and government agencies, in magazines and newspapers. And secondary research material is available from data banks and computerized services, which are proliferating like mushrooms in damp caves. Public relations practitioners are utilizing computer-generated information at a torrid and accelerating rate. This trend will continue. Computers are fast, their information storage capabilities are both practical and immense, they provide up-to-date information, and they have become so specialized that valuable documentation concerning almost any business topic is available literally at the push of a button. Computerized information services that are appropriate for the public relations business are included in the following section.

A Listing of Computerized Information Services Around the Country

Allstate Research and Planning Center   (415) 324-2721
Allstate Census Use System
321 Middlefield Road
Menlo Park, CA 94025

Specialty of census-based information system is comparison/evaluation of small market segments and the larger portions of which they are a part. Especially suitable for direct mail marketing, environmental analysis, minority marketing activities.

N. W. Ayer ABH International   (212) 974-6411
Ayer Information Center
1345 Avenue of the Americas
New York, NY 10019

Demand information service specializing in advertising, marketing, general business. Utilizes information services such as The Information Bank, Lockheed/DIALOG, System Development Corporation, plus own materials.

Bill Communications   (215) 563-0680
Successful Meetings Databank
1422 Chestnut Street
Philadelphia, PA 19102

Information regarding conventions, trade shows, seminars, association meetings. Output can be requested as reports, statistical studies, mailing labels, specialized directories.

Business International Corporation   (212) 750-6300
Associate Client Program
One Dag Hammarskjold Plaza
New York, NY 10017

International business data retrieval through computerized master key index. Issues weekly reports on international business trends, and analyses of international markets.

Capitol Services, Inc.   (202) 546-5600
511 Second Street, N.E.
Washington, DC 20002

Monitors federal legislative, administrative functions through Federal Register and the Congressional Record; prepares daily reports.

Chase Manhattan Bank, N.A.   (212) 667-7350
Information Services Department
Chase Econometrics Associates, Inc
555 City Line Avenue
Bala Cynwyd, PA 19004

Extensive economic consulting services covering broad spectrum of American, some international, economies. Included are industrial production and shipments, foreign exchange rates, materials prices.

Claritas Corporation   (703) 841-9200
PRIZM
1911 North Fort Myer Drive
Rosslyn, VA 22209

Processes government information, including census data. Helpful service for public relations people is PRIZM—Potential Rating Index by ZIP Markets—which is used for shareholder profiles, programming and implementing consumer marketing activities. PRIZM analyzes the more than 35,000 ZIP code neighborhoods in the United States, forms 40 regional clusters after evaluating approximately 1,000 characteristics such as age, education, and income. The system surmises that humans are attracted to those of similar status, and that homogeneous neighborhoods develop from socioeconomic factors.

Similar ZIP code clusters are given descriptive names: Blue Blood Estates; Money & Brains; Levittown, U.S.A.; Bunker's Neighbors; Sun-Belt Singles; Old Brick Factories; Shotguns & Pickups; Urban Renewal; Back-Country Folks. But the important thing to public relations people attempting to plan business activities with as much accuracy as possible is that the 40 homogeneous clusters have similar motivational and lifestyle characteristics. PRIZM's information is used to:

- Develop characteristics that can be applied to purchase practices, readership preferences, information about how people in the individual clusters live, eat, read, entertain.

- Determine exact locations of different market segments, thereby permitting implementation of targeted retail marketing programs.

- Develop public relations activities that complement socioeconomic characteristics of target audiences.

Corporation for Public Broadcasting   (202) 261-1893
Management Information Systems
1111 16th Street, N.W.
Washington, DC 20036

Surveys public radio and television, provides state-of-the-art information.

Data Courier, Inc.   (502) 582-4111
ABI/Inform
620 South Fifth Street
Louisville, KY 40202

On-line searching with data base aimed at management, economics, marketing, law, finance.

Donnelley Marketing Information Services   (203) 965-5454
(A Dun & Bradstreet company)
1351 Washington Boulevard
Stamford, CT 06905

Perhaps the nation's largest residential data base. Superior aid for direct marketing efforts. Describes services as: "A complete line of demographic data for consumer marketers—1980 Census Data, demographic updates and 5-year projections for areas defined geographically, geometrically, by ZIP Code or 'Clusters.' Catalogues, by name and address, about 90 percent of American households. Neighborhood Director Ensemble breaks out specific local markets, provides names, addresses of consumers." Following are graphic profiles of demographic data.

Dow Jones & Company, Inc.   (212) 285-5225
News/Retrieval
22 Cortlandt Street
New York, NY 10007

On-line access to content of Dow Jones News Service, *The Wall Street Journal*, *Barron's* for a 90-day period. Short time, but up-to-date corporate/financial information of superior quality.

Dun & Bradstreet, Inc   (212) 285-7000
Marketing Services Division
99 Church Street
New York, NY 10007

Diverse services include: Management Information Products, marketing service that assists with identification of markets and potential customers; Customer

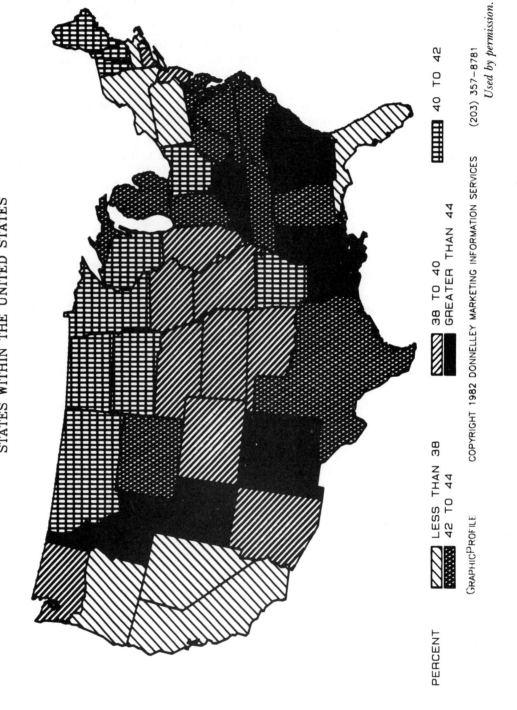

HOUSEHOLDS WITH CHILDREN (1980)
STATES WITHIN THE UNITED STATES

PERCENT

LESS THAN 38
42 TO 44

38 TO 40
GREATER THAN 44

40 TO 42

GRAPHICPROFILE   COPYRIGHT 1982 DONNELLEY MARKETING INFORMATION SERVICES   (203) 357-8781

Used by permission.

PERSONS AGE 0 TO 5
NEW YORK COUNTIES (1980)

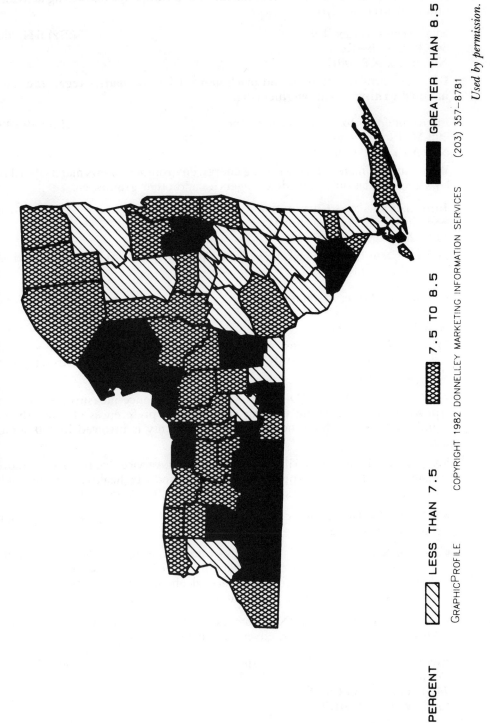

PERCENT

LESS THAN 7.5   7.5 TO 8.5   GREATER THAN 8.5

GRAPHICPROFILE   COPYRIGHT 1982 DONNELLEY MARKETING INFORMATION SERVICES   (203) 357-8781

Used by permission.

Analysis Service, which permits evaluation of a company's marketing activities; other research, analytical services.

Engineering Index, Inc.   (212) 644-7600
345 East 47th Street
New York, NY 10017

Data base provides printed and machine-readable summaries regarding international writings about engineering.

Environment Information Center, Inc.   (212) 949-9494
292 Madison Avenue
New York, NY 10017

Wide range of materials concerning energy, environment: news materials, films, laws and regulations, individuals, agencies and other groups, etc.

Information Access Corporation   (415) 941-1100
885 North San Antonio Road
Los Altos, CA 94022

Software, consulting marketing firm. Monitors 370 American magazines; updated monthly.

Interactive Market Systems, Inc.   (212) 869-8810
19 West 44th Street
New York, NY 10036

Provides some of the most interesting marketing services, from a public relations standpoint, presently available. Data bases, available through time-sharing include:

• ARBITRON TV/RADIO—Television/radio audience-measurement service provides data regarding viewing and listening preferences of more than 2 million American households. Every U.S. county is involved in 160 survey areas.

• SAMI—Designed primarily for manufacturers, service documents the movement to retail outlets of specific warehoused products (health and beauty aids, frozen food, dry groceries, etc.) in more than 40 U.S. markets.

• SIMMONS—Documents consumption of specific brand products for more than 500 categories.

• NIELSEN STATION/TV INDICES—Continuous retail sales audit reports consumer reactions to pricing, packaging, advertising, other incentives. Includes data about mass merchandisers, alcoholic beverages, food and drug outlets. Also reports on retail inventories, prices, profits.

• NIELSEN RETAIL INDEX—Provides retail sales, inventory audits by brand. Also reports prices, profits, advertising expenditures.

Investors Management Sciences, Inc.   (303) 771-6510
Compustat
7400 South Alton Court
Englewood, CO 80110

Source of financial information about several thousand corporations; used for merger and acquisition searches, company and industry comparisons, portfolio evaluations, etc. Machine-readable.

K&M Publications, Inc.   (502) 897-6736
Foods Adlibra
2000 Frankfort Avenue
Louisville, KY 40206

Documents events in international food industry, including marketing developments, new product introductions.

Lockheed Information Systems   (415) 493-4411
DIALOG
3251 Hanover Street
Palo Alto, CA 94304

Provides access to more than 70 data bases internationally. Public relations people like Dialog's diversity—it can provide information on many areas of human involvement, from sports to science to business.

Mead Corportion   (212)883-8560
NEXIS
200 Park Avenue
New York, NY 10017

Probably the most used data bank in the public relations field. Includes the old *New York Times* Information Bank, which Mead purchased and merged with its existing capability. On-line index holds editorial content of all major domestic publications, including *Fortune, Time, Newsweek, Los Angeles Times, Chicago Tribune, Business Week, U.S. News & World Report, Financial Times, Barron's, Dun's Review,* Associated Press, United Press International. Excellent source for information about business, current events, people.

User-friendly information storage and retrieval system. On-line access.

```
          LEVEL 1 - 15 of 30 STORIES

      Copyright (c) 1982 The New York Times Company;
                The New York Times

    September 13, 1982, Monday, Late City Final Edition


SECTION:  Section D; Page 1, Column 3; Financial Desk

LENGTH:  1442 words

HEADLINE:  SELLING ARTIFICIAL INTELLIGENCE

BYLINE:  By ANDREW POLLACK


BODY:
    Artificial intelligence, the science of making computers
    "think," has long been the preserve of theoreticians who
    were little concerned with practical applications.

    "When they said 'real things,' they ...

    ...going to talk to Wall Street, let alone own a suit."
```

National Bureau of Economic Research   (212) 682-3190
Time Series Data Bank
261 Madison Avenue
New York, NY 10016

Accessible through time-sharing computer systems, service is devoted to providing information for analysis of business conditions, and to assist researchers in developing economic forecasts.

National Planning Data Corporation   (607) 273-8208
20 Terrace Hill
Ithaca, NY 14850

Provides complete 1970 census counts.

Newsbank, Inc.   (203) 357-8894
P.O. Box #10047
741 Main Street
Stamford, CT 06904

Newsbank library, which subscribers may purchase complete or in one or more of 13 packages, consists of locally prepared news articles from approximately 210 American newspapers. Almost 137,000 articles from 205 newspapers in 130 cities and towns—every state, plus District of Columbia—are catalogued annually.

A.C. Nielsen Company   (312) 498-6300
Nielsen Plaza
Northbrook, IL 60062

Fifty-seven services to assist product marketers. Public relations people use Media Research Services, which measure television audiences; Retail Index Services, which measure sales rates of individual products in the United States and over twenty foreign nations; Neodata Services, which handle magazine subscription list maintenance and fulfillment; and Custom Research Services, which evaluate marketing strategies and problems. On-line access to extensive range of surveys.

On-Line Systems, Inc.   (412) 931-7600
115 Evergreen Heights Drive
Pittsburgh, PA, 15229

Services include On-Line's Accessible Securities System (OASES), interactive computer service with data bank of approximately 30,000 securities in the United States and Canada; National Bureau of Economic Research data bank, from 1945; demographic data base with 107 socioeconomic factors for all counties in the United States, plus other composites.

Predicasts, Inc.   (216) 795-3000
200 University Circle Research Center
11001 Cedar Avenue
Cleveland, OH 44106

Extensive research capabilities include reports on wide range of industries worldwide, specialized research, consultation and forecasting, business seminars, etc.

Selling Areas-Marketing, Inc.   (312) 329-6800
SAMI
541 North Fairbanks Court
Chicago, IL 60611

Documents the movement of grocery and household products in over forty major markets across the United States. Reports are prepared from once each year to once each month, depending upon speed with which specific products sell.

SRI International   (415) 326-6200
333 Ravenswood Avenue
Menlo Park, CA 94025

VALS—for Values and Lifestyle Program—while subjective, has added an important new dimension to public relations and advertising marketing efforts. VALS analyzes changing values and lifestyles using more than 1,000 variables, including consumption patterns and demographics. The marketplace, then, becomes one of segmented groups of people instead of an undifferentiated mass.

VALS helps public relations and advertising practitioners to better understand the needs and motivations of consumers, and to project how their values will affect their spending habits. It also permits an improved comprehension of the nation's changing ethics and lifestyles. "We are what we believe, what we value," says an SRI executive. "For the most part, we try to mold our lives to make our beliefs and dreams come true."

VALS distinguishes between nine different types of consumers, or market segments: Survivors, Sustainers, Belongers, Emulators, Achievers, I-Am-Me's, Experientials, Societally Conscious, and Integrated.

Survivors, for example, are the most underprivileged Americans. They are poverty stricken, poorly educated, old, and uninformed. They bake bread and pastries, watch television, but score low in almost all the major consumption areas.

Achievers, on the other hand, are well-educated leaders. About one out of four Americans falls into this category. They are independent, materialistic, success-driven, industrious. They believe strongly in capitalistic America, own homes and cars, are sports minded, attend cultural events, and use credit cards.

United States Travel Data Center   (202) 293-1040
1100 Connecticut Avenue, N.W.
Washington, DC 20036

Nonprofit concern maintains data center with wide range of travel/tourism facts and statistics. Sponsors annual travel seminar.

Ward's Communications, Inc.   (313) 962-4433
Ward's Autoinfobank
28 West Adams
Detroit, MI 48226

Maintains data bank of marketing/production information concerning automotive industry.

Wharton Econometric Forecasting Associates, Inc.   (215) 243-6451
4025 Chestnut Street
Philadelphia, PA 19104

Forecasting service provides information about national industrial and economic developments. Several econometric models provide short- and long-term forecasting, analysis. Subscribers access Wharton's data bases through RFA's time-sharing system.

World Trade Center   (212) 466-3063
World Trade Information Center
One World Trade Center, Lobby
New York, NY 10048

Serves worldwide business with research capabilities in areas of international trade and global business.

There are countless secondary research sources, many of which are comprehensive and up-to-date, and which are also inexpensive, or available at no cost. Additional popular secondary research sources include the government, academe, trade magazines and associations, market research services, and reports dealing with socioeconomic issues.

Names and Addresses of Important Government Statistical Sources

Non-profit statistical sources of a highly credible nature include the United States Census Population Reports, which contain demographic characteristics; the Department of Commerce Census of Business, which provides information concerning products and markets, numbers of employees, etc.; and many other reports from government departments and agencies. The following compilation contains the names and addresses of frequently used federal government information sources, all of which have computer-based information capabilities.

U. S. Bureau of the Census   (301) 763-2400
Data User Services Division
Washington, DC 20233

Supplies materials explaining how to use its services, including computer programs, statistical reports, surveys, maps. Twelve regional offices.

U.S. Department of Agriculture   (202) 447-5455
Statistical Reporting Service
Washington, DC 20250

Information on crops, livestock, estimates regarding supply, demand, pricing. Over forty regional offices.

U.S. Department of Commerce   (202) 523-0777
Bureau of Economic Analysis
Washington, DC 20230

Data pertaining to regional and national business conditions and economics, balance of payments, budgets, projected economic growth, many other topics.

U.S. Department of Defense   (202) 274-6881
Building Number 5
Cameron Station
Alexandria, VA 22314

Information concerning defense research and other activities (unclassified).

U.S. Department of Energy   (202) 566-9085
Energy Information Administration
Washington, DC 20461

Materials relating to the supply and utilization of the nation's energy resources. Also operates Technical Information Center, P.O. Box #62, Oak Ridge, TN, 37830.

U.S. Department of Justice   (202) 376-2607
Room #4016
Chester Arthur Building
Washington, DC 20530

Computerized system for researching legal items.

U.S. Department of Labor   (202) 523-1154
Bureau of Labor Statistics Data Bank
441 G Street, N.W.
Washington, DC 20212

Statistics pertaining to number of employed, types of employment, salaries, industry and consumer price indexes, imports-exports, employment turnover, unemployment, etc.

U.S. Federal Energy Regulatory Commission   (202) 275-4006
Office of Regulatory Information Systems
Washington, DC 20426

Information pertaining to regulation of interstate natural gas, electric power industries.

U.S. Geological Survey   (703) 860-6696
Office of Energy Resources
Petroleum Data System
Reston, VA 22092

Information regarding oil and gas fields, plus most effective and efficient utilization of these natural resources.

U.S. National Aeronautics & Space Administration   (202) 755-3219
Office of Technology Utilization
NASA Headquarters
600 Independence Avenue
Washington, DC 20546

Conducts programs pertaining to space. Nine regional centers. Also, Scientific & Technical Information Office, 300 Seventh Street, S.W., Washington, DC, 20546.

U.S. National Technical Information Service   (703) 557-4650
5285 Port Royal Road
Springfield, VA 22161

Consolidates technical, engineering information for U.S. Department of Commerce, and 350 other federal government units. Government-sponsored research included.

U.S. Patent & Trademark Office   (703) 557-3050
Technology Assessment & Forecast Reports Data Base
Washington, DC 20231

Maintains data pertaining to U.S. patents. Also provides information about global technological development.

Major Academic Information Sources

Most major universities have at least moderately impressive research and information storage capabilities, although some are locally or regionally oriented. Some academic institutions, however, have developed excellent computerized services pertaining to specialized courses of instruction.

Examples of university research and information storage capabilities that are available to assist public relations practitioners are:

- The University of Michigan Survey Research Center's Survey of Consumer Expectations, which provides data regarding national and personal expectations.

- The Illinois Institute of Technology's data regarding advanced techniques in the fields of information retrieval and library sciences.

- The Aerospace Research Applications Center of Indiana University/Purdue University at Indianapolis, which provides technical information and other assistance.

- Ohio State University's Center for Human Resource Research, which, through its National Longitudinal Surveys, provides information about the U.S. labor market.

- The University of Connecticut's New England Research Application Center, with an extensive information base featuring literature and information-searching capabilities that include an unusually broad number of subjects.

- The University of New Mexico's Technology Application Center, which operates an Industrial Information Program, Energy Information Program, and Remote Sensing-Natural Resources Program.

- The University of Pittsburgh's Knowledge Availability Systems Center, which stores more than 10 million pieces of information about NASA research.

- The University of Southern California's Western Research Application Center, which maintains extensive literature services, plus awareness and data base development services.

What You Can Learn from Trade Magazines and Trade Associations

Popular, and cooperative, sources of secondary research information are trade magazines and trade associations. These sources provide valuable data about products, economics of and trends within industries, purchasing characteristics, and other information. An important feature is that these sources also frequently sell mailing and subscriber lists.

Taking Advantage of Market Research Services and Socioeconomic Reports

Commonly employed sources for secondary research include the materials of market research services, such as those developed by organizations such as:

Yankelovich, Skelly, & White; The Roper Organization; Louis Harris & Associates, Inc., and Opinion Research Corporation. These companies routinely compile studies about important social, economic, and business issues.

Other socioeconomic reports abound. They are prepared by government, banks, universities, research organizations, and many other public and private institutions. They are valuable because they are usually current, and because they provide both narrow and wide views of American society and of the nation's economy.

When to Combine Primary and Secondary Research

Frequently, research projects combine primary and secondary research. The latter, for instance, might be utilized for educational purposes by those conducting a primary research project. Or, computerized information from a data bank might substantiate or invalidate information learned in individual interviews. And a focus group or several in-depth interviews might be conducted to elaborate on, or to authenticate, secondary research findings.

BLUEPRINT FOR A SUCCESSFUL SURVEY

Surveys are inquiries, scrutinies, ways of obtaining information about specific topics. Surveys can be basic—such as obtaining intelligence through observation—or they can involve elaborate questionnaires and/or interviews.

There are four steps to a survey: development of a realistic sample; interviewing; processing and tabulation; evaluation and presentation of findings.

The Sample

Samples are pieces of a whole. A sample can be a model of an industry, a market, the nation; a sample breaks an entity down into segments that can be readily observed and evaluated. Samples can be of many different things: people, households, corporations, newspapers and magazines, cars and trucks, or any other piece of a whole. It is important that individuals familiar with the research function develop samples at the start of a survey, or the entire project could be based on false assumptions.

Interviewing, Processing, Tabulation

Interviews can be conducted in three ways: by mail, telephone, or in person. Surveys can be conducted using one of these methods, or a combination. There are advantages and disadvantages to each. The method or combination should be determined by evaluating the type of survey, the type of information being solicited, the amount of time available, and budget limitations.

Generally, mail interviews provide a poor return rate, but they can be conducted at the least expense. Telephone surveys can also be accomplished speedily and at a low budget, but they tend to be shallow. Face-to-face interviews permit the greatest depth because interviewers have the opportunity to probe and to evaluate a respondent's answers. But this method is expensive and requires the most time.

The following chart, used by many researchers, provides information regarding the various types of interviewing methods.

INTERVIEWING METHOD

	Most Preferred			Least Preferred
Most Representative Sample	T	IHP	M	IPC
Shortest Time Completing Survey	T	IPC	IHP	M
Most Number Of Questions Which Can Be Asked	IHP	T	M	IPC
Widest Range, Most Complex Questions Which Can Be Asked	IHP	IPC	M	T
Lowest Cost Per Completed Interview	T	M	IPC	IHP

T   = Telephone
IHP = In-Home Personal
M   = Mail
IPC = In-Person Central Location

Following interviews, information is categorized, interpreted, and results are tabulated.

There are several types of questionnaires employed for surveys. The most basic is an outline of topics to be covered during qualitative research sessions, which could be focus group meetings or individual interviews. This type of questionnaire is generally in outline form, and serves primarily to keep sessions on target.

Quantitative surveys, on the other hand, require structured questioning in a logical manner, and can employ three types of questions: closed-ended, open-ended, or scalar.

Closed-ended questions provide easy-to-check categories. They are appropriate when numerical estimates are important to findings, and in situations where respondents are available for only short periods of time. For example:

"Do you think Product B is sweeter tasting than Product A?"

Yes . . . . ( )

No . . . . ( )

About the same . . . . ( )

With *open-ended* questions, interviewers write down respondents' comments, as close to verbatim as possible. This line of questioning is used for audits, and for face-to-face interviews, but can also be employed in other situations. For example:

"Do you think Company A's advertising is as interesting as Company B's?"

PROBE: If yes, why? Use of women in bathing suits? Catchy tunes? Contest?

If no, why? Do women in bathing suits seem contrived? Too many elements, including music and a contest?

Using *scalar* questions is a closed-ended approach that provides rankings for answers. For example:

"Which company is doing the best job at controlling air and water pollution in the metropolitan area?" (Put a "1" next to the leader, "2" next to second best, etc.)

Clifford Serrell Co. . . . . ——

Chip Cracker Co. . . . . ——

Gina Apparel . . . . ——

Lindsey Kip Enterprises . . . . ——

The value of research to the public relations function will continue to gain importance during the 1980s. Research will continue to grow as an aid in the areas of program development, financial, community and employee relations, and as a marketing tool. It will also be used increasingly to measure the effectiveness of public relations and publicity, whether for an individual story placement, a media tour, or for entire programs.

3

The Press Conference
Learning to Live Again After the Death of a Friend

It's no secret that the traditional press conference is dead. It expired in the late 1960s, in full view of an agonized public relations community. Although public relations people lament the demise, they were guilty of mistreating the press conference when it was robust and flourishing. Quite simply, the press conference was worked to death by practitioners who used the ploy to create press attention and clippings even when there was no reason for the recognition. But editors—who enjoyed the lunches, the booze and the junkets—were influenced by the skepticism and censorious introspection that was blowing across America during the 1960s and 1970s, so attendance at press conferences waned. Finally, the public relations corps consumed the last of the canapes, drained the vodka and the champagne, and closed the door on the press conference as it had been known.

Occasionally, there is hard news that deserves a press conference. And, when this happens, the press attends. But there is precious little news that would qualify.

To a large extent, the press conference void has been filled by meetings between the corporate world and the press that are educational in nature. These meetings are not billed as press conferences and they seldom involve fast-breaking news or trips to exotic locations. Such get-togethers are referred to as press meetings, editorial board meetings, or editorial round tables. The affairs provide the press with the opportunity to gain insight into a significant industry or into an important company or business trend. The educational legitimacy of these meetings is of such caliber as to win the endorsement of the Fourth Estate.

EDITORIAL BOARD MEETINGS:
HOW TO PUT YOUR COMPANY IN THE SPOTLIGHT

Meetings with the editorial boards of prestigious publications such as *The New York Times, The Los Angeles Times, The Chicago Tribune, The Washington Post, The Wall Street*

Journal, Fortune, and *Business Week,* are recommended for companies that wish to draw attention to their management, corporate strategies and progress, or issues confronting their industries. Editorial boards determine the editorial policy and direction of a publication, and consist of the publisher and key executives and journalists. Many publications do not have formal editorial boards. Some, such as *Newsweek* and *Time,* have the reputation in public relations circles of using editorial board meetings to sell advertising. Other boards, such as the one at *Forbes,* are believed to be totally influenced by strong-willed publishers.

Editorial board meetings are off-the-record, informational sessions, and are not expected to result in immediate ink. The value of these sessions lies in the increased editorial awareness afforded a company and its management. Publications tend to follow companies more closely if management has an identity with staff members.

Another benefit of these meetings is that corporate managers have the opportunity to position themselves as industry leaders before the most influential media in the nation, and to gain insight into publishing operations.

Either company public relations personnel or representatives from a company's public relations agency can approach a publication regarding the possibility of an editorial board meeting. The proposal should be in letter form, and should be addressed to a senior representative of the newspaper or magazine. This could, but does not have to be, the publisher. If a key executive is known to a public relations staffer, it would expedite matters to work through this channel. A response frequently requires one or two months, depending upon travel schedules and availability of executives at the publication. A refusal is usually tendered with alacrity, however.

How to Propose an Editorial Board Meeting:
A Sample Attention Grabber

The letter proposing an editorial board meeting (or any of the other press events described in this chapter) must be a real grabber. No puff. No vague references or false drama. Simply interesting facts presented in provocative fashion. The following letter, from the chairman of a large American pharmaceutical firm to the publisher of a major business magazine, is right on target.

Dear Mr. —————————:

For many years, subtle changes in the pharmaceutical industry have been gaining momentum. These changes have now achieved such stature that they are making the present decade the most exciting and challenging in the pharmaceutical industry's history.

Perhaps you will agree that the business press should be apprised of these events. If so, I would appreciate the opportunity to meet with your editorial board to explain the forces that are changing the industry and this company. These forces include:

> The fiercest competition ever encountered, not only from domestic firms, but also from European and Japanese companies interested in tapping the world's largest market for therapeutic compounds.

Astounding growth in the generic drug area. These compounds presently account for 25 percent of all drug sales. State and federal regulations permit generic substitution, thereby increasing their market share, and threatening to stifle pharmaceutical manufacturers' research and development incentive.

Crowded drug categories which will continue to expand because of accelerating FDA approval procedures, and because Research and Development efforts—which are alarmingly costly—are targeted at high-incidence maladies that promise greatest financial reward.

Consistent market growth, about 4 percent each year, which will see the industry reach $33 billion in sales during 1988.

New understanding of fundamental biological processes—such as breakthroughs in cellular biology—that are helping to speed laboratory exploration.

These are a few of the challenging factors that are making the pharmaceutical industry one of the most challenging and interesting businesses in America.

Shall we explore today's pharmaceutical industry in depth?

Sincerely,

What to Expect at the Editorial Board Meeting and How to Prepare for It

The format for an editorial board meeting is unstructured. There is small talk, some comment about the general state of business and the economy, perhaps even some observations about the status of the Mets or Cubs or Dodgers.

A visiting executive can request that one additional company officer also attend the meeting; this is frequently the vice president for finance. The publication is usually represented by the publisher and/or editor-in-chief, and other publishing executives. Usually, a reporter or editor whose assignments include the industries in which the visitor's company operates is included.

The corporate spokesperson should have in mind the topics that he or she wants to discuss. The topics that will receive the most interest should involve the company, business and society, or all three. The tree famine issue, for instance, would be a good topic for a paper company. Steel company representatives might discuss efforts by domestic manufacturers to combat foreign competition, touching on diversification and "regionalized" steel production. Prepared remarks should never be used in these sessions. Visiting executives should feel free to bring up any topic, and ask any questions they have a mind to, even if the topic involves previous reporting that the executive considered poor or inadequate.

Approximately one week before the meeting, the company, or its agency, should be provided with the names and titles of the publishing executives who will attend. If a public relations agency is involved, it should provide its client with biographical information about the journalists.

COMPANY-SPONSORED PRESS MEETINGS:
ASKING MOHAMMED TO COME TO THE MOUNTAIN

Press meetings are company-hosted affairs that are usually held in New York, because it is the nation's communications capital. But they are also held in key regional communications centers such as Atlanta, Chicago, Houston, Dallas, Los Angeles, and San Francisco. These meetings are recommended for visible companies that are operating in industries undergoing change (such as technological advances, foreign competition, or deregulation), or companies that have unusually positive stories to tell.

Press meetings, which can be held on-the-record or off-the-record, permit the press to gain insight into the business developments and management strategies of leading corporations, as well as the opportunity to meet leading business executives.

Press meetings provide management with unusual opportunities, too: the opportunity to present the corporate story informally, without the pressure of structured interview situations; to describe their corporate profile in a detailed and well-planned manner; and to cultivate positive, long-term relationships with the nation's most important business editors.

All companies cannot participate in press meetings, because the press is simply not interested in all companies. To attract the press, a company must be a leader, a factor in an emerging industry, or undergoing changes significant enough to arouse the intrigue of investors and the financial community.

Successful press meetings are presented in a straightforward manner, and allow the editors to question management at length. Informality and candor should be stressed. The information that the press is primarily interested in includes:

- Growth and marketing strategies
- Cash flow and liquidity
- Sales and earnings projections
- Growth strategies
- Problems and opportunities facing the corporation
- Evaluation of management

Press meetings are both for-the-record and off-the-record. However, since it is not uncommon to host twenty-five journalists at a New York City press event, it is difficult to guarantee the sanctity of a promise of silence. It is recommended that these meetings always be on-the-record, and that management's presentations be open and honest, with problems being discussed as candidly as possible. The Fourth Estate understands that problems are a fact of business life. They become suspicious when problems are omitted from corporate discussions.

Where to Hold the Press Meeting and How to Run It

Convenient, midtown meeting/dining facilities are most appropriate for press meetings. Popular locations in New York City, for example, include the Waldorf-Astoria, The University Club, Park Lane, Helmsley Palace, Yale Club, Princeton Club, Harvard Club, the Board Room, the Intercontinental Hotel, and the Sky Club. Meetings should start late enough to accommodate journalists on daily morning newspapers who are working against deadlines in the late afternoon and early evening. An appropriate schedule would be:

6:15 P.M.	Cocktails
6:45 P.M.	Dinner
7:15 P.M.	Management presentation
7:40 P.M. (Approximate)	Question/Answer
8:15 P.M. (Approximate)	Adjournment

A company's chief executive officer usually starts the management presentation with a ten to fifteen minute talk. His comments should include a company profile, a description of how the enterprise is prepared to meet the challenges of the future, and industry trends.

Comments by officers directing operations of a company's major divisions usually follow. Each would talk for five to eight minutes, and touch on the technologies and objectives of their operations. The company's president also frequently participates in press meetings by leading the question/answer session. The chief financial officer should also attend to field financial questions.

Visuals are important. They help to maintain a fast pace, and to heighten interest.

The question and answer period is also important. It permits journalists to obtain information that they might have been pondering for months. Such sessions usually last twenty to sixty minutes, and should continue until all questions have been asked.

Whom to Invite to Your Press Meeting

Invitation lists should include the leading business/financial press and selected trade publications. The following publications would be invited to attend a New York City meeting:

The New York Times

The Wall Street Journal

Newsweek (Business Section)

Time (Business Section)

U.S. News & World Report

Fortune

Forbes

Business Week

Barron's

Dow Jones

Reuters

Associated Press

United Press International

The Economist

The Financial Times

Dun's

Wall Street Transcript

Journal of Commerce

Financial World

Institutional Investor

The industrial/business press should also be invited, if an industrial company is involved. The list might include:

Iron Age

Industry Week

American Metal Market

Television and radio are almost never invited to press meetings. They seldom attend because they have little to gain. Their story coverage is of a far different nature than printed media, and a strong knowledge of the business community is not required.

"Bouncing" press meetings to cities other than New York is sometimes recommended, particularly if a company has major facilities in the region. These are scaled-down affairs, with fewer attendees and fewer corporate officers involved. A regional meeting could be conducted by officers other than the top three, such as the manager of a local facility, or the officer in charge of divisional operations of which the local plant is a part.

Press meetings should be held about every eighteen months if a company is interested in establishing and maintaining a position in the minds of the press. A minimum of eight to ten weeks should be allowed for preparation and execution of a press meeting. This is considered sufficient to reserve meeting facilities, develop management presentations, produce slides and other graphics, and invite the press. The press should be polled at the very start to assure that there is sufficient interest to hold a press meeting.

THE PORTABLE PRESS BRIEFING

There is another acceptable press approach which came to life after the traditional press conference died; it could be called the "Portable Press Briefing."

This approach is especially appropriate for the trade press, but, depending upon the message, it can be effective with daily newspapers, too.

The Portable Press Briefing puts a corporate expert on a particular product or service at an editor's desk to review the subject and help the editor develop story lines.

These sessions are sometimes hyped by clever mailings, such as a bottle of wine and a wedge of cheese, delivered by messenger to the editor with a note requesting that he or she stay at the desk during lunch one day to meet a representative from a company that produces an unsual product.

If pitched properly, the Portable Press Briefing can:

- Allow for discussion in a one-on-one situation that assures the editor's complete attention.

- Provide the editor with an unusual opportunity to pursue exclusive story lines with a recognized expert.

- Allow the publication to educate its entire staff on the topic being presented.

- Dramatically improve story pick-up potential by personalizing the editorial approach.

Press briefings are frequently moved from city to city, especially if appropriate trade publications are located in several different cities.

When Is Your Story Worth a Briefing?

You must have a relatively strong story in order to conduct a successful Portable Press Briefing. And, if the story is genuine enough to interest daily press editors—in automotive, transportation, business, or home and garden sections—they should be included. Reporters on the staffs of morning dailies are prime targets for Portable Press Briefings. They generally arrive at the newspaper late in the morning, and lunchtime is a slack period.

What sort of story would qualify for approaches to both trade magazines and daily newspapers for a Portable Press Briefing? A company which has an advanced jackhammer technology for instance, might have such a story. Suppose the company is marketing a tool that is vibrationless and makes significantly less noise than traditional equipment. There would be both trade and general readership interest in this technology. But, since the new jackhammer represents a technological advancement, not a revolutionary breakthrough, a full-scale press conference would not be appropriate.

If a company is represented by a public relations agency, the Portable Press Briefing can be a mutual effort. The agency can utilize its knowledge of editors and publications to arrange briefings, and the company can provide the spokesperson. A company and agency representative should make the tour together. Also, a comprehensive press kit, including fairly elaborate technical material, should be left with editors.

HOW CORPORATE "KNIGHTS" CAN USE EDITORIAL ROUND TABLES

Editorial round tables are specialized meetings conducted by companies willing to share proprietary or unusual information about significant industrial developments, such as trends in emerging industries like robotics, digital office equipment, and separations technology. Such meetings are another method of attracting attention to corporate achievements.

Even if a technology is dated and does not qualify for new product attention, the press might be interested in receiving an educational overview if, for societal, economic or technological reasons, there is sufficient interest in the industry involved.

Editorial round tables are usually conducted for the enlightenment of trade book editors and the business financial press, but they are also suitable for customers and potential customers. The press and customer audiences can be mixed, or they can participate separately. It is important that technical experts from the company participate. Penetrating questions are usually asked by attendees who are knowledgeable about the products and technologies involved. Also, these affairs are usually programmed for at least a half-day, providing ample opportunity for give-and-take.

Usually, round tables consist of technical sessions that address five elements:

- State of the art of the technology
- Development of the technology
- Description of traditional approaches to the problems addressed by the technology
- Anticipated benefits of the technology
- Future applications and economic significance of the technology

If it is appropriate to include a government speaker or a representative of an industry association who could lend perspective and credibility to the session, this should be attempted.

The site for an editorial round table should be carefully selected. One of the company's facilities is recommended, especially if it is located near a major airport and if a plant or laboratory tour would enhance the educational value of the session. If not, a large hotel in a major city is acceptable.

UNDERSTANDING THE MEDIA: WHAT PR PEOPLE DON'T KNOW WILL HURT THEM

It is a disquieting fact that, during the present period of expansion—both in numbers of public relations practitioners and in the variety of assignments they handle—those who practice this oft-denigrated art of persuasion are becoming alarmingly insensitive to the needs of the general readership press. Since public relations people deal most frequently with the wire services and daily newspapers, the deficiency is most obvious in these areas.

At the hub of the problem is the fact that, until the late 1960s, most public relations people were recruited either from the trade or general readership press; they knew how to approach the Fourth Estate, and how to write for it. Today, as the public relations business becomes more specialized, it is recruiting experts from backgrounds as diverse as the legal, government, medical, and engineering professions. The creative prowess and knowledge of press operations that these people possess is frequently minimal or nonexistent. Many of this new breed view newspapers as unnavigable seas of gray type. They do not understand the basics: what type of corporate stories the wire services and dailies want, how they want them prepared, and how to work with the press.

What Kind of Bait the Media Bites

Fundamentally, there are five types of stories in which the daily press is interested.

1. *Earnings stories.* The financial/business press helps American companies meet Securities Exchange Commission regulations for prompt disclosure of meaningful corporate news by printing, at the minimum, box copy of interim and annual sales and earnings. Meaningful quotes from key executives and explanations of a company's performance enhance the possibility of receiving a story in addition to box copy.

2. *Product marketing stories* are popular. New product coverage is most common.

3. *Corporate news and feature stories* are found in large newspapers every day. This coverage usually involves business strategies, turnarounds, interesting operational procedures, and acquisitions. Local companies are favored.

4. *Management profiles,* most frequently of the chairman, president, or chief financial officer, abound. The better the corporate performance, the better the chance for a story.

5. *Issues stories* are also in demand, but are frequently negative. Nuclear power, dioxins, phosphates, acid rain, and environmental controls are examples of issues that have received press attention.

The unenlightenment of many public relations people to the ways of the press is demonstrated in dramatic fashion in the press placement primer of one of America's largest public relations agencies.

"Beyond headline news," proclaims the training booklet, "there are few things that appear in the media that do not have public relations origins. To secure space, placement people must compete with hundreds of their counterparts with similar enthusiasm and determination."

It is simply just not true that "there are few things that appear in the media that do not have public relations origins." It would be far more accurate to state, "In any edition of any large city daily newspaper, there are few stories that have public relations origins, and there are hundreds of public relations people—many of whom have little or no knowledge of how to work with the press—competing for this limited space."

Ten Keys for Turning the Press On

Those practitioners who do know how to work with the press have the greatest opportunity for success in today's competitive placement environment. It is not difficult to understand the media. But success involves working with corporate management in addition to the press. Following are ten of the most important general considerations to which public relations people should adhere.

1. Do not consider pitch letters as final documentation. Pitch letters should be short and catchy, and should convey an interesting message—just as neon signs and billboards do. Editors and reporters receive piles of public relations submissions daily. It is the public relations practitioner's duty to present his or her message in such a way that it arouses the recipient's interest. If background material is necessary to explain a story idea in detail, it should be included as addenda.

2. Expect few courtesies from press "contacts" (editors/reporters who are considered friendly to public relations staffers). Editorial friendships usually result only in reviews of pitch material, but seldom—very seldom with wires and with major publications—do they result in actual stories.

3. Consider the term "exclusive" elusive. Exclusive means story material is provided to one specific publication and not to its competition. However, once the favored publication prints the story, it may be pitched to all other media, competitive or not. And sometimes a story appearing in a major business/financial publication does not preclude its publication in competitive journals. For example, a story in the business section of *The New York Times* would probably kill it for *Business Week, Fortune,* or *Forbes,* unless the story was of such significance that exclusivity became meaningless. However, a story in the business section of *The Christian Science Monitor,* or of a newspaper such as *The Chicago Tribune* would probably not kill it for the three major business publications. Make absolutely certain that you and the editor/reporter you are dealing with have the same understanding of the term "exclusive."

4. Remember to slant all your submittals to the business/financial press to the investor audience. The business/financial press generally presents news of public companies to investors who read the business section daily. Stories about privately owned companies, therefore, receive scant attention unless a company is locally owned or has an impact on the local economy.

5. Provide management with a list of questions that would most likely be asked during an interview. While the interview would almost certainly concern the story suggested in the pitch letter, management should be cautioned that other questions (relating to business generally or to their industry specifically) might also be asked. Also provide management with a biography on the reporter doing the story, and include copies of recent stories by the individual.

6. Brief corporate spokespeople thoroughly before interviews. Make certain that they are familiar with the material contained in the pitch letter, and that they concur with it. Stories can be lost if statements made in pitch letters are not substantiated during interviews.

7. Postpone an interview rather than substitute an executive who is not empowered to represent the company and its management.

8. Explain to management how the wire services work after a story has been filed. Associated Press and United Press International feed evergreen stories into computers, and even reporters do not know when they will be released. Although it is usually within two to four weeks, sometimes several months might elapse. And, occasionally, a story never sees the light of day.

9. Assume a low profile as a public relations staffer, especially if you sense any hostility on the part of an editor/reporter. Chances are you do not have the authority to serve as a management surrogate, and the press probably looks upon you as a management buffer or as an outright obstructionist.

10. Explain to management how it is possible for the press to conduct interviews and sometimes to even write stories that never get printed.

   • Enough hard facts could not be gathered to make the story credible.
   • Another publication printed a similar story first.
   • A senior editor killed the story in favor of another.
   • Business circumstances changed, thereby invalidating or dating the story.

   If a reporter expresses interest in a story but it never appears, drop the matter. The press is not obligated to explain why stories do not appear. Unless a public relations person knows a reporter at least reasonable well, questions pertaining to a story's disposition can alienate the press.

Members of the business/financial press occasionally meet with the staffs of public relations agencies, and with public relations departments of larger companies, to review specific editorial needs and methods of operating.

Do's and Don'ts for Preparing Business News

Two prominent business writers, one from *The Wall Street Journal* and one from the business section of *The New York Times,* are among those members of the Fourth Estate who have addressed public relations audiences regarding what contemporary journalists wish all P.R. people understood about the task of preparing business news for a major publication.

The New York Times writer explains that effective relationships require public relations people to be aware of the way a newspaper operates, and of the requirements of its editorial staffers. He presents a list of ten "Do's" and ten "Don'ts" for public relations practitioners when dealing with the business section of a daily morning newspaper.

Do's

1. Learn deadlines for copy and photographs.
2. Write releases with the press, not your client, in mind.
3. Be a newsman's friend by making company executives available and by helping with liaison work.
4. Suggest industry roundups, and cooperate if you are contacted for roundup information. This is one area where we need help. If you help us here, you score a lot of points.
5. Pass on tips, leads, ideas that might interest the press. We get our ideas by talking to people.
6. Include your night telephone number on all releases. Remember, we go to work late and stay late.

7. Answer all questions fully and honestly. If you can't, explain why. But don't stonewall.

8. Respect prompt disclosure rules.

9. Respect the reporter's exclusive.

10. Know the subject of your release thoroughly.

Don'ts

1. Don't send multiple copies of releases. Call and find out who should receive a release.

2. Don't call an A.M. paper after 4:00 P.M. unless it's urgent. A Ford merger with General Motors would qualify.

3. Don't call to ask if we have received a release.

4. Don't sit in on an interview unless the reporter asks you to. This destroys the give-and-take.

5. Don't try to hide bad news with clever writing or a late Friday release time. We might highlight the story.

6. Don't telephone with feature ideas. Do a one- or two-page outline, and follow that up a few days later with a call.

7. Don't call a press conference unless there is absolutely no other way to do it. You must have something worthwhile for a press conference.

8. Don't ask your secretary to make calls and don't pull a "Hold for Mr. Jones" routine.

9. Don't send a copy of something long, like a speech, without a summary.

10. Don't lie to the press; you might not get a second chance.

What Today's Journalists Wish PR People Knew

The Wall Street Journal editor says, "When I address the topic of what journalists in the 1980s wish public relations people knew, I think of three things, beyond the basic tenants of being straightforward and acceptable:

1. "Be fully informed about what your company is doing and know when to get the reporter in touch with somebody who is up-to-date on things that you are not.

2. "Know the tactical requirements of the major news organization that you are dealing with: deadline, whom to call, what they like and don't in terms of contacts.

3. "Avoid ways of dealing with the press that, in the long run, can backfire and be counterproductive, and put your company or your client in a bad light."

This editor says he respects the public relations person who "says he doesn't know something, and gets somebody else, right away, who can explain things. This is important for people who are working against deadlines. And I like the public relations guy who puts us in touch with his company's chief operating people. This gets the company's point of view across very clearly, and makes the company look like the industry leader rather than just coming out with a 'no comment.'"

In the procedural area, *The Wall Street Journal* representative said public relations practitioners must respect a publication's deadlines. "The absolute deadline for our first edition, and this is the one that goes to half our readers, a million people, is 5:30 P.M. Eastern Standard Time." Also, he stresses the importance of "dealing with the bureau that covers your company. If you are with a Los Angeles-based firm, you must deal with our Los Angeles bureau." In the area of feature story suggestions, *The Wall Street Journal* staffer says public relations people should "write a note to the reporter and the bureau chief in your area, and follow it up with a telephone call."

The biggest complaint received by the *Journal* regarding news coverage, he claims, is lack of copy about earnings. "There are certain companies that are simply so big and have such an effect on the economy that we write an earnings story every quarter. Say, AT&T, GM, IBM, etc." The best chance for small or medium-sized companies to get space, he says, is to include "substantive discussion as to why the numbers were up or down, and to present a forecast." Also, when it comes to executive promotion releases, the *Journal* editor says *Fortune 500* company titles starting with vice president qualify for coverage.

Op-Ed Placements: Ground Rules for Claiming Some of the Finest Print Space Available Today

One of the most important placements that public relations people can make is opposite the editorial page of daily newspapers—or, "op-ed." Thousands of submissions are prepared for this prestigious space every year, because of op-ed's erudite readership and excellent positioning.

But, relatively few of these submissions see ink, because most public relations practitioners do not understand the basic editorial requirements for op-ed pieces. Submissions are frequently not prepared with the distilled intensity that most op-ed editors want, and basic editorial ground rules—number of words required, topics of interest, frequency of column—are ignored.

Op-ed submissions are rejected for the following reasons, presented in order:

- Poorly or improperly written
- Inappropriate length
- Unsuitable topic
- Untimely topic

A Chart of Op-Ed Names, Addresses, and Requirements for the Top Fifty Television Markets in the Country

Most op-ed sections are found in large newspapers. Small dailies seldom provide op-ed space. The following chart documents the op-ed requirements for newspapers in the nation's top fifty television markets. These markets have powerful purchasing, political, and social influence. There are approximately 55 million television homes in these markets, with 57 million adult women, 52 million adult men, 15 million teenagers, and 21 million children.

Newspaper	Name/Frequency of Op-Ed Section	Editorial Page Editor	Subject Matter	Number of Words
Albany KNICKERBOCKER NEWS Box 15-627 Albany, NY 12212	"Public Column" 5 days/week	Howard Healy	Local, state, social, human, and general interest.	3 double-spaced type-written pgs. Include biog. sketch, pix.
Albany TIMES-UNION Box 15-627 Albany, NY 12212	Op-Ed Daily	Daniel Davidson	Local, state, national, inter-national, political, social, general interest.	500-800
Asheville CITIZEN Box 2090 Asheville, NC 28802 (Sunday edition is Asheville CITIZEN-TIMES)	"Other Views" Sunday	Will Curtis	Local, state, national, inter-national, political, business, social, human and general interest. *Usually syndicated journalists.*	500-1,000
Asheville TIMES Box 2090 Asheville, NC 28802	"Other Views" Sunday	Will Curtis	Local, state, national, inter-national, political, business, social, human and general interest. *Usually syndicated journalists.*	500-1,000
Atlanta CONSTITUTION Box 4689 Atlanta, GA 30302	Op-Ed 1-2 pieces/week	Joseph Dolman	General interest.	500-700
Atlanta JOURNAL Box 4689 Atlanta, GA 30302	Untitled *Daily and Sunday Sunday's paper is Journal and Constitution.*	Handled by editorial department.	"Anything, *but we do not accept unsolicited material."*	500-900

Newspaper	Name/Frequency of Op-Ed Section	Editorial Page Editor	Subject Matter	Number of Words
Baltimore NEWS AMERICAN Box 1795 Baltimore, MD 21203	"Letters/Opinions" Daily	William Stump	*"All unsolicited copy is given consideration."* Local, state, and other high-interest material.	850-1,200
Baltimore SUN Box 1377 Baltimore, MD 21203	Op-Ed 2 pieces each day	Stephen Broe	General interest.	750-1,000
Battle Creek ENQUIRER 155 E. VanBuren Battle Creek, MI 49016	"Opinion & Commentary" Daily	Duane Freese	Local, state, national, inter-national, political, business, social, human and general interest.	500-900
Birmingham NEWS Box 2553 Birmingham, AL 35202	"Other Voices" Daily and Sunday	James R. McAdory, Jr.	General interest. *Only occa-sional submitted articles used.* Mostly syndicated columnists.	750-1,000
Birmingham POST HERALD Box 2553 Birmingham, AL 35202	Op-Ed 5 days/week	Karl Seitz	Local, state, national, inter-national, political, human interest.	Max. 1,000
Boston GLOBE 135 Morrissey Blvd. Boston, MA 02107	Op-Ed 1-2 pieces each day	Thomas Gagen	Emphasizes political, eco-nomic, public affairs material.	Max. 650
Boston HERALD 300 Harrison Ave. Boston, MA 02106	Op-Ed Daily and Sunday	Shelly Cohen	Local, state, national, inter-national, political, human interest.	Max. 800

Newspaper	Name/Frequency of Op-Ed Section	Editorial Page Editor	Subject Matter	Number of Words
Buffalo NEWS Box 100 Buffalo, NY 14240	"Viewpoints Page" Daily and Sunday	Lee Smith	Local, state, national, international, political, business, social.	600-700
Charleston DAILY MAIL 1001 Virginia St., E. Charleston, WV 25301	"Commentary" 2 times/week	David Greenfield	Political. "We accept unsolicited material, but don't often use it."	500
Charleston GAZETTE 1001 Virginia St., E. Charleston, WV 25301	"Opinion Page" 2 times/week	Donald Marsh	General interest.	Max. 1,500, short pieces favored.
Charlotte NEWS Box 30308 Charlotte, NC 28230	"Insight" 5 days/week	Thomas Bradbury	General interest.	500
Charlotte OBSERVER Box 30308 Charlotte, NC 28230	"Viewpoint Page" Daily	Frye Gaillard	"Open to anything, but we're inundated." Also use syndicated columnists and local writers.	400-1,200 Optimum 750
Chicago SUN TIMES 401 N. Wabash Ave. Chicago, IL 60611	Op-Ed Occasionally/month	Lois Wille	Local, general interest.	750, with pix.
Chicago TRIBUNE 435 N. Michigan Ave. Chicago, IL 60611	"Perspective" Daily	Kathy Oakley	Social, political, general interest.	Max. 850

Newspaper	Name/Frequency of Op-Ed Section	Editorial Page Editor	Subject Matter	Number of Words
Cincinnati ENQUIRER 617 Vine St. Cincinnati, OH 45201	Untitled Daily and Sunday	Thomas Gephardt	*"We rarely print guest columns from outside our circulation area."*	700-1,000
Cincinnati POST 800 Broadway Cincinnati, OH 45202	"Opinion" Daily	Claudia Winkler	Local, state, national, international, political, business, social, human interest.	700
Cleveland PLAIN DEALER 1801 Superior Ave., NE Cleveland, OH 44114	"Forum" Daily	William Woestendier	Local, state, national, international, political, business, human interest, social, sports.	800
Columbus CITIZEN-JOURNAL Box 1350 Columbus, OH 43216	None	n/a	*"We do not have a typical Op-Ed page. Half of the space is devoted to local and syndicated columnists. The other half is used for local news."*	n/a
Columbus DISPATCH 34 S. Third St. Columbus, OH 43216	"Forum Page" Daily and Sunday	Howard Huntzinger	Local, state, and national news, *either staff written, or by syndicated columnists, or by the Washington bureau.* Submissions used for "background only."	n/a
Dallas MORNING NEWS Box 22537 Dallas, TX 75265	"Viewpoints" Daily	Rena Pederson	Local, state, national, international, political, human and general interest.	Avg. 750

Newspaper	Name/Frequency of Op-Ed Section	Editorial Page Editor	Subject Matter	Number of Words
Dallas TIMES HERALD Box 5445 Dallas, TX 75202	Op-Ed Daily	John Senderline Ronald Ryan	Emphasis on political, social, economic topics.	24-30 standard paragraphs.
Dayton DAILY NEWS Fourth & Ludlow Sts. Dayton, OH 45401	Op-Ed Daily	Hap Cawood	Local, state, national, international, political, business, social, human and general interest.	500-2,000
Dayton The JOURNAL HERALD Box 1061 Dayton, OH 45401	Op-Ed Daily	William Wild	Local, state, national, international, political, business, social, human and general interest.	500-2,000
Daytona Beach EVENING NEWS Box 431 Daytona Beach, FL 32015	"Ideas" Daily and Sunday	Natalie Dix	"Anything." Usually use syndicated material.	1,500 tops
Daytona Beach MORNING JOURNAL Box 431 Daytona Beach, FL 32015	None	n/a	Presently considering initiating an Op-Ed section.	n/a
Denver POST Box 1709 Denver, CO 80201	"Open Forum" Occasional	Frederick Brown	Ten percent of Op-Ed material consists of "guest editorials," primarily local. Rest of page contains letters and syndicated columns. Guest editorials are of general interest.	600-750

Newspaper	Name/Frequency of Op-Ed Section	Editorial Page Editor	Subject Matter	Number of Words
Denver ROCKY MOUNTAIN NEWS Box 719 Denver, CO 80204	"Speak Out" Frequent	Address: Editorial Office	Local, national affairs, general interest.	Max. 750
Detroit FREE PRESS 321 W. Lafayette Detroit, MI 48231	Op-Ed 3 pieces/month	Pat Foley	Local, general interest.	Varies, call first.
Detroit NEWS 615 Lafayette Blvd. Detroit, MI 48231	Op-Ed	Edwin A. Roberts, Jr.	"We don't use unsolicited material on our Op-Ed page."	n/a
Durham MORNING HERALD Box 2092 Durham, NC 27702	"Furthermore" 6 times/week, no Saturday	Jack Adams	State and local. "We're inundated with unsolicited material that we seldom use."	Max. 800
Durham SUN Box 2092 Durham, NC 27702	None	n/a	n/a	n/a
Grand Rapids PRESS Press Plaza Grand Rapids, MI 49503	Op-Ed Daily	Raymond Kwapil	State, national, international, political, general interest.	Max. 1,000
Greenville The DAILY REFLECTOR Box 1967 Greenville, NC 27834	Untitled Sundays only	Alvin Taylor	"Anything is considered." (Also has section called "Public Forum." Maximum 300 words.)	Max. 750

Newspaper	Name/Frequency of Op-Ed Section	Editorial Page Editor	Subject Matter	Number of Words
Hartford COURANT 285 Broad St. Hartford, CT 06115	Op-Ed Daily	Frederick Mann	Local, state, national, international, political, social.	600-800
Houston CHRONICLE Box 4260 Houston, TX 77002	"Outlook" Daily	Hugh Powers	"Open" . . . any topic.	No standard length.
Houston POST 4747 S.W. Freeway Houston, TX 77001	Op-Ed Daily and Sunday	Kuyk Logan, Managing Editor	Local, state, national, international, political, general interest. "We use little free-lance material."	500-800
Huntington HERALD-DISPATCH Box 2017 Huntington, WV 25301	Untitled Daily	James E. Casto	General interest.	No standard length.
Indianapolis NEWS Box 366 Indianapolis, IN 46206	Op-Ed Daily	Harvey C. Jacobs	Local, state, national, international, political, business, human interest.	Max. 650
Indianapolis STAR Box 145 Indianapolis, IN 46206	Op-Ed Seldom	John Lyst	General interest *with an Indiana slant.*	Max. 800
Kalamazoo GAZETTE Box 2007 Kalamazoo, MI 49003	"Viewpoint" Daily and Sunday	Robert L. Stephenson	Will consider all general interest material, but *"the concentration is local."*	750, but "flexible within reason."

Newspaper	Name/Frequency of Op-Ed Section	Editorial Page Editor	Subject Matter	Number of Words
Kansas City STAR 1729 Grand Ave. Kansas City, MO 64108	Op-Ed Infrequent	Virginia Hall	General interest.	No standard length.
Kansas City TIMES Box 191 Kansas City, MO 64108	Opinions/Columns Daily	Virginia Hall	National, international, political, economic.	500-1,500
Los Angeles HERALD-EXAMINER 1111 S. Broadway Los Angeles, CA 90015	Op-Ed Daily and Sunday	Michael Gordon	Local, state, national, international, political, business, social, human interest.	800, sometimes longer, depending upon topic.
Los Angeles TIMES Times Mirror Square Los Angeles, CA 90053	Op-Ed Daily and Sunday	Robert Berger Maureen Murphy Marc Kessler	"General timely issues." Exclusivity required.	Max. 800
Memphis COMMERCIAL APPEAL Box 364 Memphis, TN 38101	Untitled Daily	Richard McFalls	Local, state, national, international, political, business, social, human and general interest.	600-700
Miami HERALD One Herald Plaza Miami, FL 33101	Op-Ed Daily	Joanna Wragg	General interest, usually with local involvement.	Max. 750
Miami NEWS Box 615 Miami, FL 33152	"Columns Page" 5 times/week	Louis Salome	Local, state, national, international, political, business, social, human and general interest.	1,000

Newspaper	Name/Frequency of Op-Ed Section	Editorial Page Editor	Subject Matter	Number of Words
Milwaukee JOURNAL Box 66 Milwaukee, WI 53201	Op-Ed Daily and Sunday	Address: Op-Ed Editor	General interest.	500-600, biog. sketch, pix.
Milwaukee SENTINEL Box 371 Milwaukee, WI 53201	Op-Ed	Robert A. Witas	"Occasions when we use unsolicited manuscripts are extremely rare."	Max. 800
Minneapolis STAR & TRIBUNE 425 Portland Ave. Minneapolis, MN 55488	Op-Ed Daily and Sunday	James Boyd Robert J. White	General interest, usually with local angle.	No standard length.
Nashville BANNER 1100 Broadway Nashville, TN 37202	"Forum" 4 times/week	Mary Hance	Local, state, national, international, political, general interest.	750-1,250
Nashville TENNESSEAN 1100 Broadway Nashville, TN 37202	Untitled, except for Sunday edition which is called "Perspective." Daily and Sunday	Linda Harrell	"It's rare for us to run unsolicited material." Mostly syndicated writers. However, access column called National Eye accepts political, human interest, and humorous pieces of 500 words.	650
Newark STAR-LEDGER STAR-LEDGER Plaza Newark, NJ 07101	"Forum" Sunday	Address: Forum Editor	Consists mostly of staff-written and syndicated material, with occasional piece by nationally renowned person.	Max. 1,800

Newspaper	Name/Frequency of Op-Ed Section	Editorial Page Editor	Subject Matter	Number of Words
New Orleans TIMES-PICAYUNE/STATES-ITEM 3800 Howard Ave. New Orleans, LA 70140	Op-Ed	Malcolm Forsyth	*Restricted to local citizenry.*	250
Newport News DAILY PRESS Box 746 Newport News, VA 23607	"Commentary" Daily	Roberta Nicholls	Local, state, national, international, political.	600
Newport News TIMES-HERALD Box 746 Newport News, VA 23607	"Insight" 3 times/week	Richard Wagner	National, international, political, business, general interest.	"Short articles."
New York DAILY NEWS 220 E. 42 St. New York, NY 10017	Op-Ed Daily and Sunday	Earl King	Local/regional orientation.	700, but call first. Prefers up-front relationship.
New York POST 210 South St. New York, NY 10002	Op-Ed Daily and Sunday	Stephen Cuozzo	*Almost always staff-written and syndicated material.* Occasionally politico by-lines article on local topic.	650-800
New York TIMES 229 W. 43 St. New York, NY 10036	Op-Ed Daily and Sunday	Robert B. Semple, Jr.	Local, state, national, international, political, business, social, human and general interest. Current events pieces frequently appear.	Max. 750
Norfolk The LEDGER-STAR 150 W. Brambleton Ave. Norfolk, VA 23501	Op-Ed 1 time (or less)/week	George Herbert	General interest.	Max. 750

Newspaper	Name/Frequency of Op-Ed Section	Editorial Page Editor	Subject Matter	Number of Words
Norfolk VIRGINIAN PILOT Box 449 Norfolk, VA 23501	Untitled Daily and Sunday	James C. Raper, Jr.	International, political, national. *Syndicated columnists and guest journalists only.*	600-900
Oklahoma City OKLAHOMAN Box 25125 Oklahoma City, OK 73125	None	n/a	n/a	n/a
Oklahoma City TIMES Box 25125 Oklahoma City, OK 73125	None	n/a	n/a	n/a
Orlando SENTINEL Box 2833 Orlando, FL 32801	Op-Ed Daily and Sunday	Harry Wessel	Local, state, national, international, political, business, human interest, social, sports, media, general interest.	450-750
Philadelphia DAILY NEWS 400 N. Broad St. Philadelphia, PA 19101	Op-Ed Daily and Sunday	Richard Aregood	*"We have committed virtually all our opposite-editorial space to staff columnists and contracted writers."*	n/a
Philadelphia INQUIRER 400 N. Broad St. Philadelphia, PA 19101	Op-Ed Daily and Sunday	Philip Joyce	General interest, "not personalized."	Max. 750
Phoenix The ARIZONA REPUBLIC Box 1950 Phoenix, AZ 85001	Op-Ed	Pat Murphy	General interest, with local slant. *However, submitted manuscripts seldom printed.*	500

Newspaper	Name/Frequency of Op-Ed Section	Editorial Page Editor	Subject Matter	Number of Words
Pittsburgh POST-GAZETTE Box 957 Pittsburgh, PA 15230	"Perspectives" Daily	Michael McGough	Local, state, national, inter-national, political, business, social, human and general interest.	Max. 800
Pittsburgh PRESS Box 566 Pittsburgh, PA 15230	None	n/a	n/a	n/a
Portland OREGONIAN 1320 S.W. Broadway Portland, OR 97201	Op-Ed Daily and Sunday	Philip Cogswell	State issues.	Varies, call first.
Providence EVENING BULLETIN 75 Fountain St. Providence, RI 02902	Op-Ed 5 times/week	Robert Ramaker	Local, state, national, inter-national, political.	700-800
Providence JOURNAL 75 Fountain St. Providence, RI 02902	"Commentary" Daily and Sunday	Robert Ramaker	Local, state, national, inter-national, political, business, social, human and general interest.	750
Raleigh NEWS & OBSERVER 215 S. McDowell St. Raleigh, NC 27602	"Other Opinion" Daily and Sunday	Ferrel Guillory	Local, state, national, inter-national, political, general interest. "We usually don't print pieces from out-of-state corporate or political figures, unless topic is especially compelling."	500-750

Newspaper	Name/Frequency of Op-Ed Section	Editorial Page Editor	Subject Matter	Number of Words
Raleigh TIMES 215 S. McDowell St. Raleigh, NC 27602	Op-Ed Daily and Sunday	Robert Brooks, Managing Editor	*Almost always syndicated writers.*	500-800
Sacramento BEE Box 15779 Sacramento, CA 95813	No name, but appears daily. Commentary section called "Forum" appears Sunday.	Bill Moore	"Any topic is acceptable."	Daily, 800-1,000. Sunday, 1,200.
Sacramento UNION Box 27 Sacramento, CA 95812	Op-Ed Daily and Sunday	Fred Reinsch	Local, state, national, international, political, general interest.	600-800
St. Louis GLOBE DEMOCRAT 710 N. Tucker Blvd. St. Louis, MO 63101	None	n/a	n/a	n/a
St. Louis POST-DISPATCH 900 N. Tucker Blvd. St. Louis, MO 63101	"Mirror of Public Opinion" 4 times/week	Edward Higgins	General interest.	600-800
St. Petersburg TIMES Box 1121 St. Petersburg, FL 33731	"Other Opinions" Daily and Sunday	Robert Pittman	*National, international, economic, general interest. By syndicated writers, and guest journalists with other publications.*	500-1,200
Salt Lake City DESERET NEWS Box 1257 Salt Lake City, UT 84110	Op-Ed Daily and Sunday	Richard Laney	Local, state, national, international, political, social.	Varies, call first.

Newspaper	Name/Frequency of Op-Ed Section	Editorial Page Editor	Subject Matter	Number of Words
Salt Lake City TRIBUNE Box 867 Salt Lake City, UT 84110	Untitled Daily	Robert Blair	National, international, political, general and human interest. "Only rarely use submitted material."	No limit
San Antonio EXPRESS-NEWS Box 2171 San Antonio, TX 78297	Two Pages "Commentary I" "Commentary II"	Sterlin Holmesly	Mostly local and state affairs. "We do accept pieces from outsiders."	Max. 800
San Antonio LIGHT Box 161 San Antonio, TX 78291	"Viewpoint" 6 times/week. None Sat.	Joe Carroll Rust	Local, state, national, international, political, human and general interest.	500-600
San Diego EVENING TRIBUNE Box 191 San Diego, CA 92112	Op-Ed 5 times/week	R.B. Bennett	Local, state, national, international, political, general interest.	700
San Diego UNION Box 191 San Diego, CA 92112	Op-Ed Infrequent	Edward Pike	General interest.	Varies, call first.
San Francisco CHRONICLE 901 Mission St. San Francisco, CA 94119	Op-Ed 1 day/week	Templeton Peck	General interest.	650
San Francisco EXAMINER 110 Fifth St. San Francisco, CA 94103	"Commentary" Daily and Sunday	William Henson	Local, state, national, international.	800-1,000

Newspaper	Name/Frequency of Op-Ed Section	Editorial Page Editor	Subject Matter	Number of Words
Schenectady GAZETTE 332 State St. Schenectady, NY 12301	No name Daily (Obituaries face editorial page.)	John E.N. Hume III, Managing Editor	National, international, political. *Usually two syndicated columns on editorial page.*	800
Scranton TIMES Penn Ave. & Spruce St. Scranton, PA 18501	"Viewpoint" Sunday	Gar Kearney	Local, human interest.	Varies; call first.
Scranton The TRIBUNE 338 N. Washington Ave. Scranton, PA 18505	None	n/a	n/a	n/a
Seattle POST INTELLIGENCER Box 1909 Seattle, WA 98111	"Opinion & Analysis" Daily and Sunday	Charles J. Dunsure	Local, state, national, international, general interest. *Syndicated columnists and guest authors only.*	650-900
Seattle TIMES Box 70 Seattle, WA 98111	Op-Ed Infrequent	Herbert Robinson	General interest.	700
Tampa TRIBUNE Box 191 Tampa, FL 33601	Untitled Daily and Sunday	Wade Stephans	Political, business, social.	500-700
Troy TIMES RECORD 501 Broadway Troy, NY 12181	"Opinion" Sunday	Joseph A. Cooley	Local, state, human interest, social, medicine, education, general interest.	750

Newspaper	Name/Frequency of Op-Ed Section	Editorial Page Editor	Subject Matter	Number of Words
Washington POST 1150 15 St. N.W. Washington, DC 20071	Op-Ed Daily and Sunday	Meg Greenfield	Local, national, international, general interest. *Some days all staff written or syndicated, other days all submitted.*	800-900
Wilkes-Barre CITIZEN'S VOICE River & Market Sts. Wilkes-Barre, PA 18711	Op-Ed Infrequent	Editorial Page Editor	Local, state, national, political, human interest. *Usually syndicated columnists.*	500-700
Wilkes-Barre TIMES-LEADER Box 730 Wilkes-Barre, PA 18711	Op-Ed Infrequent	James F. Lee	Local, national, international, political, human interest. *Usually syndicated columnists and staff written.*	400-800

IMPORTANT SPECIALIZED MEDIA

Newspaper	Name/Frequency of Op-Ed Section	Editorial Page Editor	Subject Matter	Number of Words
CHRISTIAN SCIENCE MONITOR	5 times/week	Janet Domowitz	Political, social, law, economics, government, general interest.	700
WALL STREET JOURNAL	5 times/week	Tim Ferguson	National, international, political, business, economic, general interest, plus Leisure & Arts and The Americas columns.	750-1,500

THE MOST BANG FOR YOUR BUCK:
PICKING OUT THE PREFERRED MEDIA

It has become common practice to save time and public relations expenditures by concentrating placement efforts on the most prestigious media. These publications create the most bang for the buck: the most readership, the most important readership, the most recall, and the most cash register reaction.

Media placement specialists might bicker about which publications should be included on a preferred media list, but the following lists of twelve preferred and over forty secondary publications would be generally acceptable.

PREFERRED PUBLICATIONS:

Barron's

Business Week

Dun's

Forbes

Fortune

Industry Week

The New York Times

Newsweek

Time

U.S. News & World Reports

The Wall Street Journal

The Washington Post

SECONDARY PUBLICATIONS:

All airline publications

Atlanta Business Chronicle

Christian Science Monitor

Connecticut Business Journal

Corporate Report

Entrepreneur Magazine

Financial World

Harvard Business Review

Houston Business Journal Inc.

International Management

Journal of Commerce

Los Angeles Business Journal

The Market Chronicle

Nation's Business
New England Business
New York Daily News
Northern Ohio Business Journal
San Francisco Business Journal
The Stock Market Magazine
Texas Business
Wall Street Reports
The Wall Street Transcript
Westchester (New York State) *Business Journal*
The Wharton Business Journal
World Business Weekly
The Los Angeles Times
The Chicago Tribune
The Boston Globe
Newsday
The Philadelphia Inquirer
The Miami Herald
The Houston Chronicle
The Houston Post
The Dallas Morning News
Washington Report
Finance
Financier Magazine
Institutional Investor
Money
Venture

4

Radio and Television

Secrets of Working with the Electrifying Media

The electronic media are highly regarded public relations targets, and this trend is expected to continue as the national popularity of radio and television remains strong. More than 80 million American homes have radios and television sets (and, the quip goes, 78 million have flush toilets). Approximately 30 percent of these 80 million homes also have cable television, and the number of communities wired for cable is increasing rapidly. Credible estimates indicate that approximately 75 percent of all Americans rely solely on television for the news.

Electronic programming offers the public an ever-expanding variety of shows, from international events to local city council meetings to health symposia. There is a spot for almost any offering a public relations practitioner might have. Electronic placements can be dramatic, and the audience extensive; millions of viewers are reached in seconds, and the credibility of the electronic media is extraordinarily high.

A knowledgeable cadre of public relations people who specialize in electronic placement work is now in place, both on agency and corporate staffs. These practitioners have been drawn primarily from radio and television stations or networks, and they are proficient in all aspects of electronic story development and placement—news, feature material, and the production of video news tapes.

Electronic placement activity, while specialized, is not as challenging as many of this new cadre would have others believe. But the electronic placement specialty does involve an acquired knowledge that most public relations practitioners do not possess. A knowledge of how the electronic media work is required of electronic placement specialists, as is an ability for creating a story, knowing where and how to pitch it, and how to use a spokesperson most effectively.

SIX CLUES TO CREATING A WINNING ELECTRONIC STORY

Electronic placement skill starts with the creation of a story line. There are significant differences between story development for print and for electronic placement. For example, there are six elements to a good electronic story. All six elements do not have to be present to score a placement, but the more that are, the better the chances of getting some air time.

Keep the story simple. Strip all complicating factors out of the narrative. Keep it as excitingly basic and as basically exciting as possible.

Aim the story at the people in the street. The more your story interests Mr. & Mrs. Everyone, the better your chances of getting it aired. If you can talk about topics they are interested in—their health, money, jobs, kids, cars, homes, even their gardens—you have a good chance of making a placement.

Create a local angle. People are most interested in events that happen nearby.

Create a way for the program host to get involved in the presentation. Hoopla helps generate excitement that would not be present in the normal sit-and-talk routine.

Develop a prop. Props can vary from straightforward slides to cut-aways, working models, or actual demonstrations.

Make the story topical. For example, a story about an advanced automobile tire could become a story about the latest weapon in the battle to help control the nation's highway carnage.

All stories are not necessarily right for the electronic media. This is one reason why electronic placement specialists are helpful. They can assist by evaluating a story before inordinate effort is committed to its placement. Aside from the fact that some stories just do not lend themselves visually to electronic coverage, some cities are notably tough to score in, either because they have few outlets, or because of exceptionally high journalistic standards. New York City, Chicago, Los Angeles, Atlanta, Miami, Dallas, and Washington, DC, are tough electronic cities.

HOW TO PITCH AN ELECTRONIC STORY

Pitching an electronic story requires about two months, but if the story is solid, it can be done successfully in two days or even in two hours.

It is recommended that as much as eight weeks lead time be allowed if the most beneficial thought and effort are to be devoted to electronic placement opportunities, and if the greatest possible results are to be obtained. Starting a project early assures proper story evaluation and development, allows exploratory evaluations of scheduled events in target cities, and permits the development of props and the best editorial contacts.

Mailing pitch letters and story kits to radio and television stations at least three to six weeks in advance is standard practice. Television scheduling is much more complicated than that for print media. Time is important because a story must be scheduled, frequently it must be researched, visuals must be incorporated, shooting locations found, and a crew scheduled to shoot.

The Pitch Letter: It Can Make You or Break You

The pitch letter is the most important element in electronic placement activity. Similar to the general readership print media, the first few lines of the pitch letter can make or break a story. Start with a headline—or, as it is commonly called, a "sell head"—at the top of the page. Using short sentences and short paragraphs, explain, in as exciting a fashion as possible, your story. The fewer words, the better. The cover letter is meant to convince the reader that the story is worth covering. Supporting information can be attached.

A Proven-Effective Pitch Letter

An example of an effective pitch letter, to the host of a talk show that frequently airs health-oriented topics, is this epistle: short, simple, and offering the television journalist the chance to interview a patient and a doctor about a medical advance that could affect many viewers.

Asthma Sufferers Can Now
Lead Normal Lives

Dear Mr. _____:

We know a fifteen-year-old girl who loves to ice skate. But when she does, her heart pounds. She gasps for breath. Sometimes she passes out. She has asthma. Her condition is so bad she cannot lead a normal life.

Until last month. A new drug, developed by our client, (name of company) changed all that. Just a few deep breaths from an inhaler that she carries in her pocket, and she skates for hours.

Wouldn't her story interest other asthma sufferers? She could appear on your program during the week of April 6th with Dr. (name of doctor). He is a spokesperson for the drug company, and a noted allergist.

Attached is background information about the new drug, and about Dr. (name).

I will call next week to see if you wish to pursue this story. Thanks for your evaluation.

Sincerely,

Visuals are vital to electronic placements. Describe visuals and establish the credibility of the spokesperson in the pitch letter. Usually, spokespersons have visuals that could be important to making an electronic placement. They should be queried about this possibility.

One of the most important things about the pitch letter is to make it clear that the television producers are not only receiving a story idea, they are also receiving invaluable assistance in putting a story together. The spokesperson's availability, the shooting location, and visuals should all be described specifically, because they can make the difference between air time and no air time. Company files, industry associations and philanthropic organizations, should be consulted for supporting visuals before the pitch letter is composed.

THE MEDIA SPOKESPERSON: WHEN NOBODY CAN BECOME SOMEBODY

A spokesperson can be a famous athlete, a minister, a doctor or professor, a movie starlet, or somebody from the research and development facility of a corporation. A somebody or a nobody. The most significant concern in selecting a spokesperson is that he or she know the subject matter, be articulate and presentable, and be specially coached for the appearance or for the media tour.

The more prominent the spokesperson, the better the opportunity for placement. But a "name" is not essential. Many people who have never appeared on television but who know their subject and are well-trained, have made successful media tours.

All spokespersons should receive media training, preferably in a studio environment, prior to a media tour. Even television celebrities require training. They should be coached about the product, for example, and about the proper messages with which to present it. And, they should be coached regarding how and when to interject product mentions.

The Media Tour: Is It Worth the Expense?

While media tours are critically important to some publicity campaigns, such as consumer marketing campaigns, they can be expensive. Expenses for air fare, hotels, honorarium, limousines and rental cars, add up rapidly on a coast-to-coast tour. Media tours are, however, still inexpensive when compared to consumer advertising.

It is difficult not to support media tours, especially when all possibilities for exposure are considered: radio and television, daily newspapers, trade magazines, and even speeches. Costs can be reduced if the spokesperson travels alone (without a public relations representative) although this can backfire if the spokesperson is not completely familiar with the public relations effort. Not infrequently, a public relations representative serves the dual role of spokesperson. This helps hold down expenses and assures a targeted public relations effort.

Most media tours highlight television bookings and give rather strong emphasis to radio. The glamour and impact of the electronic media should not completely overshadow print opportunities, however. Local daily newspapers, trade and business publications, plus special interest media create additional opportunities that can add meaningful wallop to a tour.

Public relations agencies with electronic and print placement departments generally have excellent media tour planning and evaluation capabilities. The following forms are used by agencies to plan media tours and to evaluate

MEDIA TOUR MASTER SCHEDULE

DATE: _____ HOTEL THAT NIGHT: _____ SPOKESPERSON: _____

DAY: _____ ADDRESS: _____ SCHEDULED BY: _____

CITY: _____ PHONE: _____

Arrival Time for Interview	TV/RADIO/ PRINT/LIVE/ TAPE/INTER- VIEW TIME/ TIME ON AIR	Station/Newspaper Location, Show/Section, Phone Number	Contact	Interviewer	Comments and Special Instructions	AIR/PRINT DATE	AUDIENCE FIGURE

MEDIA TOUR SYNOPSIS–RADIO, TV, PRINT

SPOKESPERSON _____

MARKET _____

DATES _____

Total Interviews _____
Total TV _____
Total Radio _____
Total Print _____
Total Audience Reach _____
TV Reach _____
Radio Reach _____
Print Circulation _____
Total Air Time _____
TV Air Time _____
Radio Air Time _____

GENERAL ANALYSIS

_____

_____

_____

_____

_____

_____

_____

_____

_____

_____

_____

_____

_____

MEDIA TOUR EVALUATION FORM—RADIO, TV, PRINT

Station/Paper _____

Market _____

Show _____

Air/Print Date _____

Audience/Circulation _____

Interviewer _____

Evaluator _____

Checklist (List speaker's messages, by priority.)

Rating

Excellent _____

Good _____

Fair _____

Poor _____

Comments: _____

_____

_____

_____

_____

_____

_____

spokesperson and tour effectiveness. They also provide indispensable information for the preparation of management/client reports following tours.

WHERE TO PLACE A STORY

Placing a story can require the finesse of a specialist, for several reasons. A knowledge of television and radio stations is important; there are over 1,400 of the former, and more than 9,000 of the latter across the United States. Add to this approximately 4,500 cable television systems; a knowledge of the specialization in broadcasting is another factor that must be taken into consideration. There is AM (Amplitude Modulation) radio and FM (Frequency Modulation) radio. There are VHF (Very High Frequency) television stations and UHF (Ultra High Frequency) television stations. Some electronic outlets are referred to as "commercial," others are "public," "educational," or "noncommercial." Some radio stations have programming beamed to ethnic groups or minorities. Some have all-news formats, all jazz, all mountain music. Some attempt to offer something for everybody.

HOW THE NETWORKS OPERATE

A knowledge of how television and radio networks, network feeds, syndicators, and wire services work is essential to effective electronic media placement.

A network is the paternal member of the electronic media. Networks transmit material to affiliates across the nation. This material can be news, sports, special features, religious—anything. (If a local station is not a network affiliate, it is referred to as independent.)

Publicists must know where to place material with the television networks, which include CBS (Columbia Broadcasting System), NBC (National Broadcasting Company), and ABC (American Broadcasting Company). Radio networks include Mutual Broadcasting Co. and RKO Radio Network. There are several smaller networks for both radio and television, including those serving "public" outlets.

Network "feeds" are provided by the three major networks to their affiliates. Feeds include both news and feature material that are transmitted in addition to regular programming. Frequently, a story placed by a public relations representative will qualify for the feed when it will not be selected for a regular network item.

Syndicators, who sell their material to radio and television on an individual basis, seldom use public relations submissions, since they sell primarily entertainment features.

The two major wire services, Associated Press and United Press International, also offer placement opportunities. The wire services go directly into the newsrooms of television and radio stations.

Whom to Contact

A knowledge of how the electronic media is organized, how to approach the media, and whom to approach, can save countless hours and offer the best opportunity for placement success.

There are two parts to a radio or television station. The activities of one part are directed by the news director, the activities of the other by the program director. Although assignments can vary, these two staffers usually report to the station's general manager. The news director has responsibility for the station's newscasts; this individual is also responsible for local coverage of events that could be considered "newsy" in content, such as elections, business, or sports. The program director handles all non-news programming, including interviews, game shows, and musical shows.

The electronic publicist should be aware that these responsibilities can vary from station to station. Also, a program director can have several staffers reporting to him, such as a news director. Sometimes, assignment editors report to the news director. But, usually, the news director is responsible for news, and the program director is responsible for non-news programs.

At the network level, radio and television news operations are separate. One of the major differences between print and broadcast media is that the latter encourages publicists to provide pitch letters to several staffers at the network level. Because there are many levels of responsibility at the networks, there are many levels of interest in a story. There are producers, directors, assignment editors, managers, and other contact people. Personal contact with network staff people, and a continuing knowledge of who has left and who has joined the staff, is essential to highly productive placement efforts.

Insiders' Tips on Electronic Placement

There are other nuances that are important to electronic placement. For example, networks obtain almost all their programs, except for news and sports programs, from outside sources. Therefore, if placements are to be made, they are not made through the program director, but rather through the outside service that is providing the material.

All three of the major networks maintain regional offices across the United States, and the big three also all have offices in New York City and Washington, DC.

Other important tips include the fact that all network material is sent to all affiliates; there is no "regionalization." Also, network and local affiliate news staffs operate completely independently, so the publicists should supply both with material.

While it is generally agreed that, similar to print pitch letters, the fewer words the better, there is a departure between print and electronic when it comes to follow-up. Veteran publicists believe that persistent telephoning is a necessity if a story is to be given maximum opportunity for airing, because there are more steps involved in television story preparation than for print. If something goes awry at any stage, the publicist can save the story in stepping in and providing material, a spokesperson, or a location to assure that production work starts again.

CABLE TELEVISION: TAPPING AMERICA'S CENTRAL NERVOUS SYSTEM

Public relations people will spend increasing amounts of time becoming familiar with cable television during the 1980s. It is estimated that in 1985, more than 75 million Americans will be cable television viewers, and this number is expected to increase to the neighborhood of 120 million.

If television is "America's central nervous system," cable television is helping to sharpen the emotional impact of this medium. Cable is fostering a new dimension between viewer and programmer. In what has been commonly referred to as "narrowcasting," cable is offering programs for narrow slivers of audiences, not for mass consumption. There will be something for every taste—all-news programming, all-sports, all-opera—on the hundreds of channels soon to be available. This means that public relations people will be working differently with cable stations than they do with the major networks and their affiliates.

Insiders' Guidelines for Placing Your Story with Cable

The following tips apply to placing material with cable stations:

- Strive for quality of placement, not quantity of audience. Cable viewers generally are better educated and have more money than broadcast viewers. And, with the huge variety in programming, a public relations placement can split a hair in audience selection.

- Business and research-and-development news are more apt to be welcomed on cable than on broadcast television. So are good news pieces. Many cable viewers are seeking an alternative to broadcast television, and solid news pieces help cable programmers present something out of the ordinary.

- Slides and a working script are welcomed at cable stations when pitching a story. Stations vary in the type of slides they want (conventional or "chrome key," in which the picture is outlined). There are services in major cities that are familiar with cable and which can help public relations people submit exactly what each station requires.

- When deciding where to direct story material at a cable station, start by realizing that this task is difficult. Cable has not been around long enough to develop rigid job titles and classifications. Begin by contacting the marketing director, which every system has. Directories are being compiled that should help with the names and titles in cable systems.

VIDEO NEWS CLIPS: READY-TO-AIR MAY BE EASIER TO PLACE

An increasingly important method of generating television news about a product or service is the video news clip that is prepared, much like a case history news story for a print publication, and submitted to television stations for their use.

Video news features fill a definite need in the programming requirements of local broadcast news staffs. The material may not have an interesting enough message to warrant coverage normally, but if it has strong visual appeal or local importance, it could have enough popular appeal to air during the local news. For example, it might be a seasonal piece geared to late summer or early fall, about a heat conservation device for gas and oil-fired furnaces.

A ready-for-airing news feature should be sixty or ninety seconds in duration, never longer; the sixty-second version is favored by most news staffs. Generally, these features are evergreen in nature. They suffer from "instant stale" if tied to a specific event or date (although, with certain holidays such as the Fourth of July and Christmas, a solid holiday theme sometimes results in excellent pickup).

It is important that an agency with a capability for producing video news clips be employed for that purpose. They know how to accomplish filming, and how to include a brand name so it will not prove offensive to local news staffs. These specialists are also familiar with the appropriate degree of film refinement to use. The films should not be too spiffy, or they will not incorporate well with the film quality of most stations. There are many other tricks of the trade, including submitting a complete script so a station can localize the piece if desired.

Video news clip experts also possess mailing lists that combine large- medium- and small-city stations. By working with selected stations continually, these specialists get the best possible use of clips. Or, if a targeted product marketing effort is involved, these specialists can develop specific lists of stations in the cities desired. They also follow up to learn if and when a news clip was used, and provide a list of those stations using the material. And they can, for a reasonable cost, provide tapes of the news piece as it actually appeared on local news programs.

5

Spokesperson Training
How to Dress Them Up and Take Them Everywhere

One of the most predictable byproducts of the turbulent 1970s was the preparation of management to communicate effectively with corporate publics.

The secret had long been out that corporate executives were private people and notoriously poor at meeting the public. Now, however, management had to be prepared to speak out on heated issues that were being torched by fiery opponents. Wilma Soss and her Federation of Women Shareholders defied management at annual meetings. The Sierra Club defied management over plant emissions. Government defied management over safety and hiring practices. And the press scrutinized corporate activities as never before.

For the first time, management had to "go public." Communications responsibilities started at the very top of the corporate ladder and extended down to the plant manager. The chairman had to be ready to respond to audiences as broad as shareholders, consumerists, and customers, while a local manager might have to address an OSHA hearing or an environmental group. Many specialized organizations and public relations firms responded to the need to train management to be effective communicators.

TRAINING PROGRAMS:
FROM PRIVATE EXECUTIVE TO PUBLIC SPOKESPERSON

Training programs vary from three hours to two days in duration. A popular format combining public speaking, interviewing, and crisis management instruction is divided into two parts and is conducted over a two-day period. The public speaking portion includes exercises with impromptu and scripted speeches, and videotaping and playback to analyze the participant's progress. The second training phase concentrates on the interview, and includes all forms of popular media: radio, television, daily newspaper, and other print. Interview preparation, controlling the interview, and methods of dealing effectively with hostile reporters are important segments of instruction.

Preliminary work is essential for trainers. They must analyze problems and controversies within an industry, identify external pressure groups, and determine appropriate responses to external attacks.

Electronic devices such as closed circuit television and recording cassettes are used by most training organizations. These tools are important to the analysis of individual performances, and they document the progress of participants.

Spokesperson training seminars should be scripted to assure thoroughness, and to provide participants with study materials they can keep. All situations presented during training should be those the trainees might encounter during their professional careers. The degree of skill with which they handle real-life confrontation could well be determined in the video studio of a public relations agency.

The Most Effective Training Techniques

The most effective training techniques are dramatic, straight-to-the-point, conveying a strong educational message. Management trainees have responded in positive fashion to techniques including presentations by civil rights activists, simulated television and newspaper reports concerning disaster situations at company facilities, and appearances by business journalists who reveal their chief dislikes of businesspeople. Other effective instruction includes seminars designed to teach businesspeople how to handle spokesperson responsibilities, and confrontation situations involving possible corporate opponents such as labor unions, activists, and shareholders. Theatrics—provided they dramatize points of instruction—are effective.

Spokesperson training refers to the broad spectrum of public communications: electronic and print press interviews, public speaking, and crisis management. The training session can be large or small, basic or elaborate. One executive might be trained for one specific press interview, or an entire management corps of several hundred persons could be trained in basic interview or public speaking techniques.

Training sessions are exhausting. A lot of learning and a lot of experimentation in unfamiliar areas is crammed into a one-day format. One of the most disturbing aspects of these sessions is the recurring opportunity for executives to look bad—by giving inappropriate responses, becoming irritated with the training procedures, or performing poorly in front of their peers.

Not infrequently, executives will get cold feet and withdraw, sometimes the day the sessions are to occur. But while the training is unsettling because it involves the unfamiliar, most experienced training firms work the company executives into the instructional format naturally and easily. Usually, after an hour or two, executives enjoy the training and accept it as a challenge that they want to conquer.

EXCERPTS OF A TRAINING SESSION
AT A MAJOR NEW YORK CITY PR AGENCY

The training session introduction is important in reducing the trepidations of the trainees. The following comments, which were presented by trainers of one of New York City's major public relations agencies at the start of a training session for executives of a major oil company, are typically candid and reassuring.

Good morning, and welcome. Before we begin, I'd like to introduce some of the people who put this seminar together.

(INTRODUCTIONS)

Gentlemen, war-painted Indians no longer ride the American prairies, although many foreign visitors assume that they still do.

New York cab drivers don't all have Brooklyn accents. In fact, I can testify that some barely speak English.

And from what I've heard—repeat, "what I've heard"—ladies of easy virtue never have hearts of gold.

The point is that all of us, to some degree, are guilty of stereotypical thinking, especially concerning people and careers about which we know little.

And stereotypical thinking can hurt you in your dealings with the subjects of your misconceptions.

This morning we're going to be talking at some length about the media, both print and electronic. And all of us have our impressions of what it's like and how those in journalism think and operate—mostly wrong, I believe, because the news media has changed so radically and so quickly in recent years.

To begin this morning, I think it would be useful to look at these impressions, these stereotypes, through the medium of old movies.

"STEREOTYPES"—Four-minute film showing the "old" press.

If any of you have seen *All the President's Men,* the movie about Bob Woodward and Carl Bernstein, the *Washington Post* reporters who broke the Watergate case, the contrast should be apparent.

In many of today's newspaper offices, there are no manual typewriters on the desks, no green-eye-shaded, cigar-smoking editors with a pint of whisky in their drawers. No hot-lead composing rooms.

The typewriters are electronic; they type on computer tapes. To edit a story, the reporter or editor calls it up, page by page, on a computer CRT terminal, a television screen, and edits with a light pencil. A computer sets the type—offset, not hot metal—in a fraction of the time it used to take. And a whole front page can be changed, redone, in a matter of minutes.

The reporters are even more different. They're younger, for one thing, brighter, better educated. Most of them have masters degrees. There are few professional cynics—although skepticism is still the hallmark of the trade. And you won't find many "failed playwrights" or hard-drinking, middle-aged ne'er-do-wells.

They idolize people like Woodward and Bernstein—and I'm sorry to report, there aren't many who have anything good to say about business.

Television—where the money is in journalism these days—is even more different. You'll see what I mean as we go along this morning.

And there's a new philosophy in the field as well—it's called "advocacy journalism."

For nearly a century "objectivity" had been the reigning word in the list of journalistic imperatives. Young reporters were told that a story, first of all, has to be fair, to give both sides of a controversial issue and let the reader reach his own conclusions. That creed is under attack today by many journalists as unrealistic and simplistic. Important news, they say, is becoming far too complex for the reader to unravel for himself.

In George Bernard Shaw's famous play about the American Revolution, *The Devil's Disciple,* one of the characters asks the British General Burgoyne: "But, Sir, what will history say?"

Shaw, through Burgoyne, replies: "History, my dear fellow, will lie as usual."

The point is that truth—or history if you will—is what most people perceive it to be. And in our day and age, gentlemen, the perceptions of most people—bombarded with millions of words, thousands of images daily—are being manipulated as never before.

It's not enough anymore to just *give* the news to the press. You must make every effort to *interpret* that news, to make sure the reporter—and the public—understands it.

"If a businessman wants to have an impact, he had better get his facts together," says Irving Shapiro, ex-board Chairman of DuPont ... "We are not always right, but by God if we pull our facts together and tell our story, we'll come out okay because the basic facts of business are pretty good."

Are they?

It's up to management, like yourselves, to convince the American people of that. And according to some of the polls we've talked about earlier, you have a lot of convincing to do.

Let's take a look at how it's done.

You start with the basic assumption that no reporter, no matter how well informed, knows your business better than you do. You are the expert, and that expertise is the basis on which to build your media plan. But expertise is not enough. Just as the reporter has probably done some research and found out something about your company, you need to know something about him and his business. To even up the odds a little bit.

And that's what we're going to do now, give you some tips on meeting the press and dealing with reporters.

We've purposely taken quite some time this morning to look at the media to try to understand how and why it operates the way it does. For the rest of today, each of you will be asked to put yourselves in the role of corporate spokesmen.

Remember that in responding to media questions, you are speaking not to some gray audience vaguely called "The Public." Because everyone reads newspapers, listens to radio and watches television, you are addressing employees, shareholders, adversaries, the government, and customers—as well as the press itself.

In today's media environment, effective communication is the responsibility of every executive and each of you has the capability to be an effective communicator. This seminar is designed to capitalize on that capability. You'll have the opportunity to "live through" many communications experiences. We have found that the best way to learn is by doing not just sitting back and listening.

From time to time, we may be a bit rough on you. We think this, too, is a critical element. Consider this part of the experience, a sample of what might really happen and has happened to corporate spokesmen in the past.

We ask your attention, your lively participation, your thoughts, and your recommendations. In short, deal with the problems as if they were real.

I think you'll find the problems we've selected are real enough.

We're going to show you some corporate spokesmen today—some of them doing a good job, some not so good. Some of them speaking for your industry, some of them for other industries, but that doesn't matter so much as *how well they do the job.*

We're going to play some videotape, let you watch the other guy in the "hot seat," then ask what you thought of his performance. As the morning progresses, you'll get your own chance in front of the camera, in as realistic a setting as we can provide.

We'll record your performance on videotape, play it back so that you can criticize yourself, and we'll try to help you improve as we go along.

As for the issues we'll talk about, there are many controversial subjects in your company's operating areas these days: oil spills, price fixing, political contributions, cancer-causing chemicals, and environmental devastation.

We can't cover every aspect of every subject in one day, so we've had to pick and choose. We've chosen issues, not just because they're important to your company, but also because they present the most difficult and varied *communications* problems.

Let's get to work! And, let's have some fun!

ELECTRONIC AND PRINT PRESS INTERVIEWS: PUTTING TRAINEES IN THE HOT SEAT

Management communications training for press interviews is presented either in a standard format, or as a specialized course of instruction, customized to approximate situations that might actually occur to a particular company. The specialized approach is considered best. Participants respond most positively to hypothetical training situations reflecting the industry with which they are familiar. This stimulates trainee involvement and insight into the spokesperson's role.

Customized press interview instruction is also compatible with the many and varied interview situations that are encountered. Executives are trained for everything—annual meeting interviews, crisis situations, product marketing campaigns, and high-visibility television appearances.

Objectives of press interview training are broad. Executives should learn to:

• Evaluate the media before an interview.

• Gain important insights about the interviewer.

• Look and feel at ease in radio or television studio environments.

• Anticipate questions.

• Decide which questions to answer, which not to answer.

• Present positive and realistic answers.

• Control an interview, or portions of interviews.

- Present the essential points of their message.
- Maintain composure even during hostile interviews.

What to Expect During a Typical Press Interview Training Session

The most important and most common training sessions are those that involve training for print and electronic interviews. The following format is typical of what businesspeople experience during a characteristic press interview training session.

8:45–9:00	*Introduction* Training staff meets with trainees over coffee and crullers. Training activities are reviewed.
9:00–9:15	*Surprise Television Interview* "News team" rushes into training room to interview participants about activities at their company.
9:15–9:45	*Media Relations* Trainers, using video and slides, reveal interview techniques employed by the press and methods to deal effectively with press adversaries.
9:45–10:15	*Newspaper Interview* John Smith, Executive Vice-President for Operations & Administration, is interviewed by "columnist" of leading daily newspaper. Article is written for afternoon critique.
10:15–10:30	*Communications Objectives* Over coffee, trainers and trainees discuss communications objectives that would be most beneficial for the company.
10:30–11:00	*Television Interview* Thomas Brown, President, is interviewed on talk show. Interview played back and critiqued.
11:00–11:15	*Telephone Interview* Mr. Smith receives telephone call from a *New York Times* "reporter," regarding controversial new product the company is developing. Critique follows interview.
11:15–11:45	*Television Feature Interview* Mr. Brown is interviewed for television talk show. Interview videotaped, played back for critique.
11:45–12:10	*Critique, Newspaper Interview* "Columnist" who interviewed Mr. Smith returns with story. Smith's techniques of dealing with the press are critiqued.
12:10–1:15	LUNCH
1:30	Return to training studio.
1:30–2:15	*Television Interviews* Messrs. Brown and Smith are interviewed twice for television news shows. Trainers stress necessity to develop positive 15-second sound bites. Videotapes are played back and critiqued.
2:15–2:30	BREAK

2:30–3:00   *Television Business Interview*
Messrs. Brown and Smith interviewed individually for television business show. Playback, critique follow.

3:00–3:30   *Summary and Review*
Sessions reviewed in depth. Trainees' questions answered. Instruction given regarding how to best utilize training book that is provided at end of session.

A SAMPLE TRAINING MODULE FOR OIL INDUSTRY EXECUTIVES

Training modules are usually tailored to reflect the state of affairs in the industry that the participants represent. The following module, for example, which was used during a training session for oil industry executives, typifies those used for electronic and print interview instruction. All training sequences are videotaped, then played back on a television monitor and critiqued.

"The Hot Seat"
(EXECUTIVE PARTICIPANT ANSWERS TELEPHONE. TRAINER PLAYS ROLE OF CALLER.)
CALLER: "Hello, Mr. _____. This is Tim Smith of WHAM-TV. Nobody knows better than you that the Senate is debating an oil industry divestiture bill right now. If this succeeds, it will have a major impact on Texxon Oil Company and on our community, so we're doing a TV special to explain the issue. Could you, or one of your people, join us in our studio this Saturday at one o'clock? The show, as you probably know, is called "The Hot Seat." I think this will provide a great opportunity to get across Texxon's point of view."
(PARTICIPANT ANSWERS AND IS CRITIQUED BY GROUP.)

• Did participant know for certain who the caller was?
• Did participant commit without knowing all particulars?
• Does the participant know the format of the show? Does he/she know what he/she is getting into?
• Does participant understand exactly what will be discussed, and how it will be discussed?
• Should telephone requests for press interviews be accepted automatically?
• Who should the corporate spokesperson be, and was a spokesperson agreed upon with the caller?
• Exactly what should be discussed?
• What must be accomplished to prepare the spokesperson for the interview?
(DISCUSSION)

Following this preparatory module, the training session proceeds to the actual studio "interview."

MODERATOR: "Hello, Mr. _____. Good to have you with us. It's great to have a Texxon person on the show."
(SHOW BEGINS WITH INTRODUCTIONS BY MODERATOR.)
MODERATOR: "Good afternoon, ladies and gentlemen. Welcome to another edition of 'The Hot Seat.' Our guests this afternoon are Mr. _____ of Texxon Oil Company, and Mr. Ralph Raider of the Consumer's League. We're

here to discuss Senate Bill #2387, which is currently being debated. This bill, which could affect all of us, will come to a vote very shortly. This legislation would break up the big oil companies. The bill is entitled: 'Legislation to Restore and Promote Competition in the Oil Industry.'

"Mr. Raider, you told us before the show that competition simply does not exist in the oil industry. Is that correct?"

RAIDER: "That's exactly right. The top eighteen companies cited in the Senate Bill control over eighty percent of our gasoline. They conspire to fix prices to eliminate competition. The so-called independents used to be able to be a couple cents cheaper than the majors, but they're even charging the same price now."

MODERATOR: "You know, I've noticed that myself. The prices are all the same now. It seems to me that they also settle those price-fixing cases out of court. The oil companies plead 'no contest' or something like that. Doesn't that make you appear guilty, Mr. _____?"

(Response)

RAIDER: "Even with their bloated profits, the oil companies have virtually destroyed the small, independent dealers. Texxon lost a suit in New York a couple of years back. They tried to squeeze nearly 100 small dealers out of business. These were little guys who had worked 10, 20 years to build businesses in their communities. But, the little guys sued and won. Texxon had to pay them damages, although the total amount was peanuts to a giant like Texxon.

"Then, what Texxon did was to put in self-service stations. These places were staffed by people working for a bare minimum wage. This bare bones approach let Texxon sell gas a couple of cents cheaper than the local independent guy. Then, as the little guys went out of business, Texxon put the prices back up to where Mobil, Shell, Chevron, and the other giants were selling."

MODERATOR: "You know, I've seen that in my own neighborhood. We have several abandoned stations. The owners just couldn't match the tactics of the major oil companies. How do you explain all this, Mr. _____?"

(Response)

MODERATOR: "Well, we're running out of time. Mr. Raider, will you take one minute to summarize your views?"

RAIDER: "Yes, indeed. The major oil companies are the biggest monopolies in this nation. They fix prices, destroy independent dealers, and take huge profits. What we need today is Teddy Roosevelt. He would take up the sword on behalf of the American consumer. At the very least, the oil companies should be forced to divest of their marketing operations. But that won't happen. The politicians know where their financing comes from. A lot of it comes from big oil."

MODERATOR: "Mr. _____, would you please summarize your views?"

(DISCUSSION/CRITIQUE)

• What should the corporate spokesperson know before going on the show?

• Did the corporate representative put his/her points across at every opportunity?

• Did the spokesperson have one or two points to make? Were these points made at every opportunity? Were communications objectives obvious?

• Did the corporate spokesperson identify with Mr. and Mrs. America?

• Would anybody have handled themselves, and this interview situation, differently?

Thirteen Crucial Guidelines Presented During
Electronic and Print Press Interview Training Sessions

- *Understand the media.* How does the newspaper, magazine, television or radio station lean politically? What sort of person is the average reader or viewer? How do the media usually cover business news? A knowledge of the media permits a respondent to present his or her side of a question in a manner that would be acceptable to the readers or viewers.

- *Evaluate the interviewer.* Time permitting, check on the reporter assigned to interview you. What type of articles has he or she written recently? What are the reporter's political leanings? How has the reporter handled stories about the business community? Attempt to learn how your interview will fit into the overall story. Ask the reporter who else is being interviewed, what type of information and statistics will be used, how important the story will be. Also, attempt to find out why the reporter decided to do the story, or, if assigned, who assigned it and why.

- *Evaluate press queries.* Attempt to determine exactly what the media is after, and how your contribution would fit into the whole. If you believe the story is going to be totally negative, consider not participating.

- *Prepare your own objectives.* Go into an interview with a clear understanding of what you want to get across.

- *Remember, you are the expert.* You are being interviewed because you possess special and extensive knowledge about a company or a situation. You know more than the reporter will ever know about the interview topic, and you can use this knowledge to help "steer" the interview.

- *Attempt to "direct" interviews.* Be firm if a journalist attempts to rephrase a statement or to get you to say something the way he or she wants it said. Keep things moving straight ahead with comments such as, "No, that is not what I said. What I said was…" and, "Wait a minute. I think you have the wrong idea about what I meant."

- *Do not be distracted* by an interviewer who attempts to unnerve you, by the apparatus and behind-the-camera bustle of a television station, or by fear of unseen audiences—newspaper and magazine readers, television viewers, and radio listeners.

- *Anticipate.* Compile a list of questions that the reporter might ask; develop answers ahead of time. Also, develop a list of topics that you would like to discuss, in the event the reporter is unprepared or inexperienced. Assume a leadership role during the interview, if possible.

- *Be positive.* Try not to respond directly to speculative questions, but attempt to answer questions in a positive manner. This might require your rephrasing a reporter's question or declining to answer loaded questions.

- *Be emphatic.* Make your points up front, then offer substantiating information. Journalists want newsworthy information right away, corroborating information secondarily.

- *Don't think you have to answer all questions on the spot.* Honor a reporter's deadline, but also attempt to provide the reporter with the best possible information. Protect yourself, too, by going to people who are more familiar than you may be about certain aspects of corporate operations. If there are reasons why you cannot or should not answer a question, say so.

- *Stick to the truth,* or the interviewer may discover you are bluffing. This invokes a reporter's wrath, and destroys your credibility. Also, bluffing might cause you to lose track of the interviewer's line of questioning, and to become confused and indecisive.

- *Never answer "off-the-record" questions* unless you have developed a close and long-term association with a reporter. If you do, you may find "industry sources" mouthing your off-the-record comments in print.

You're on the Air: Tips from a Veteran Trainer on Making Every Second Count

Trainers usually spend considerable time instructing participants how to conduct themselves during interviews by the electronic media. These media are different. The scare factor is enormous, because there are microphones, lights and cameras, because respondents are instantaneously put face-to-face with millions of people, and because—since some interviews last only seconds—every word uttered has significance.

Margaret A. Warder, Warder Communications, 167 E. 82 St., New York City, a veteran electronic press trainer, tells her trainees:

Write your communications objectives down beforehand. If you're in a studio situation, there will be a lot going on around you. Your notes will help you stay on target.

Don't think negatively. You have more control over a broadcast interview than you probaby think you have. You will be off-balance, though, unless you are able to anticipate questions. So develop a list of questions ahead of time, and rehearse.

Half of the broadcast interview is yours. The questions belong to the interviewer. The answers are *yours.* During practice, sit down with a friend or co-worker and let him grill you. You'll be amazed at the issues and questions that will surface. And you'll be amazed at how quickly you can build confidence by anticipating questions and counteracting them.

Watch the program you will appear on ahead of time. Get to know a bit about the personality of the host. How does he like to work? What is his style?

Be alert and sensitive. Anticipate negative topics, and seize opportunities to turn potential negatives around with positive replies.

Believability is important. It should be pursued at all times. One way to be believable is to use the interviewer's name occasionally during the interview—but don't overdo. Anecdotes also play especially well on radio and television. These media have a high entertainment factor. If a story makes a good point for your side, use it.

Don't discount humor, either. If you are good at spontaneous humor, use it when appropriate. Include humorous stories and anecdotes or sayings. Humor can help you to establish warmth and credibility with your audience immediately.

Always remember that the electronic interview is "capsulized." A taped, ten-minute interview could be cut and aired in one or two minutes, sometimes only a few seconds. So it's essential that you learn to crystallize your thoughts. Use short, hard-hitting sentences. Eliminate wasted verbiage. Use key words. And always use simple, everyday words. Evaluate the language that's used in your industry. Should you use simpler language when dealing with the public?

Above all else, be positive. Because the electronic medium is capsulized and because it edits abundantly, you must be continually positive or it could end up on the cutting room floor. If you end each sentence or thought positively, you can beat the editor at his own game.

Arrive at the studio early. They will want you early, but be even earlier. Walk around. Observe. You will build confidence as the strangeness wears off.

Once you're seated at the set, try not to be distracted. Look your host or hostess right in the eye, and make believe you're in your own living room having a private conversation. Relax ... feel confident, and be enthusiastic about your business. Be natural, and smile when appropriate. If you start to get some challenging questions, lean close to the interviewer. It's tough to fight with someone who's close and confidential.

Don't play to the camera. It's the director's job to put the correct picture on the screen. Don't try to outguess him.

And, it is important to dress properly. Men should wear business suits and soft, solid blue shirts. Studio lights are bright and hot; white clothing reflects light and makes people look pale. Burgundy neckties are popular. They add an acceptable flash of color, and they pep up conservative business suits.

Women should avoid black, white, or red apparel. These colors provide too great a contrast for color television. Also stay away from large, jangling jewelry and clothing with geometric designs that could flash back on camera.

A Helpful Pre-Interview Analysis Form

It is best to jot basic notes down during the pre-interview analysis. The procedure requires only a few minutes, and it helps to bring the event into sharp focus. The pre-interview analysis should include the following facts.

PRE-INTERVIEW ANALYSIS

1. Subject of interview _____

2. Purpose of interview _____

    _____

3. Why was I selected? _____

    _____

4. Who else is being interviewed? _____

    _____

    _____

5. Interviewer's/reporter's style _____

_____

_____

6. Political/social leanings of media involved _____

_____

7. Manner of previous business coverage by same media _____

_____

_____

8. Why is this feature being done? _____

_____

9. Who assigned this feature and why? _____

_____

10. Is there any reason why I should not participate in this feature? _____

_____

11. What are the primary points I want to make? _____

_____

12. Time (broadcast daily, weekly, monthly?) _____

_____

13. Geographic spread _____

14. Total number readers/viewers/listeners _____

15. What is the public's knowledge and interest about my industry and company? _____

_____

_____

_____

15. What is the public's knowledge and interest in the feature's subject? _____

_____

_____

16. What recent events could the public, or the interviewer/reporter, relate to my company or

organization? _____

_____

_____

_____

INTERVIEW FORMAT

<u>Television</u>

1. Type of interview:

News _____

Face-to-face/Talk Show _____

"Meet the Press" _____

Press Conference _____

Face-off _____

Call-in _____

2. Location (studio or remote) _____

_____

3. Program length _____

4. Live or pre-taped (playback date) _____

_____

5. Will it be edited? _____

Newspaper/Magazine

1. Location (physical environment) _____

_____

2. Photograpy? _____

3. When will story appear? _____

4. Importance of story _____

Radio

1. Type of interview:

   News _____

   Face-to-face/Talk Show _____

   Call-in _____

   Telephone interview/Phoner _____

   Face-off _____

2. Location (studio, telephone, remote) _____

_____

3. Program length _____

4. Live or pre-taped (playback date) _____

_____

5. Will it be edited? _____

PUBLIC SPEAKING TRAINING: HOW TO CONTROL YOUR AUDIENCE

Public speaking trainers strive for a balance and an understanding of the three elements common to all communications: the message, the speaker, and the audience. Instruction includes the basics of selecting interesting topics (perhaps with an aura of urgency to hold an audience's attention), effective techniques of delivery, "working with" an audience—in short, understanding how to motivate and to persuade.

Objectives of speaker training programs are:

- To develop individual "speaking personalities."
- To help break down barriers to effective communications: fear of crowds, feelings of inadequacy, reliance on script.
- To instill confidence.
- To develop understanding of the requirements of different speaking engagements: small and large groups, dinner audiences, auditoriums and small rooms, with press or without.
- To explain methods of "analyzing" an audience and of anticipating audience reactions.
- To instill appreciation of tactics employed by speakers to help insure success.
- To condition spokespersons regarding effective methods of projecting a message through words, humor, voice.
- To learn how to anticipate audience questions.
- To develop a sense of pride in accomplishment.

WHAT TO EXPECT AT A SPEECH TRAINING SESSION: A SAMPLE FORMAT

Speech training formats have become standardized, with trainers incorporating other people's methods into their own formats. A typical format might be like the following:

8:45–9:00	*Introduction* Over coffee, training staff reviews the day's activities, answers trainees' questions.
9:00–9:15	*Effective Speechmaking* Trainer discusses good speechmaking tactics (slides). Components include knowledge of audience and speaker, effective speech organization, competent delivery techniques.
9:15–10:00	*Extemporaneous Speech Training* Extemporaneous speechs, 2 to 3 minutes, videotaped for critique.
10:00–10:15	BREAK
10:15–11:45	*Speech Delivery* Trainees deliver 10 to 12 minute speeches from notes or scripts, whichever is favored. Speeches videotaped for critique.
11:45–1:00	LUNCH
1:00–1:30	*Audiovisual Aids and Presentations* Trainers explain benefits of speech delivery incorporating audiovisual aids: slides, video tape, flip charts, film.
1:30–2:30	*Script, Audiovisual Delivery* Trainees deliver scripted slide presentations. Videotape critique follows.

2:30–3:00   *Question-Answer Training*
Instruction regarding fielding of questions following a speech, how to parry hostile questions, how to reason with questioners, how to figure questioner's objectives.

3:00–3:15   BREAK

3:15–4:00   *Question-Answer Training*
Role-playing exercise. Trainees challenged by questions from floor. Critique follows videotape review.

4:00–4:30   *Conclusion*
Trainers review entire session, answer questions.

Two Keys to Public Persuasion: Audience Analysis and Speaker's Tactics

If a public speaking trainee completes formal training with a reasonably polished delivery, a knowledge of how to analyze an audience and to devise speaker's tactics, the instruction can be considered successful. A basic but effective method of analyzing audiences and devising speaker's tactics includes:

I. AUDIENCE ANALYSIS
1. Number of attendees
2. "Typical" attendee: age, sex, education, work, salary, political leanings, marital status, leisure pursuits, etc.
3. Attendee's knowledge of speech topic.
4. Type of presentation anticipated by the audience.
5. Anticipated audience reaction to speech topic:
   a. Emotional
   b. Professionally interested
   c. Neutral
   d. Detached
   e. Hostile
   f. Amused
6. Audience attitude toward speaker, his or her organization, and speech topic:
   a. Undecided
   b. Supportive
   c. Adversarial

II. SPEAKER'S TACTICS
1. What facts should audience be presented with?
2. What is most effective method of presenting topic?
   a. Inform
   b. Persuade
   c. Motivate

   a. Humor
   b. Straight
   c. Combination

   a. Film/Slides
   b. Verbal delivery
   c. Verbal and visuals

3. What are speaker's two (or more) most important communications objectives?

a. _____

b. _____

Perhaps the most profound revelation imparted in speaker's training is that presenters must be able to *persuade* an audience—to convince them that he or she is presenting an important and credible message. Methods of accomplishing this include: providing real-life examples; refraining from offering personal opinions, which invite disagreement; relating incidents by using terms and examples that the audience can appreciate; using analogies that are clever and—if appropriate—humorous; reinforcing positions with statistics, quotes from reliable authorities; and by structuring answers in a logical, concise manner.

COMMITTEE HEARINGS: PUTTING PR TO THE ULTIMATE TEST

One of the most difficult public speaking training sessions is for a committee hearing, be it Congressional, or a forum before a regulatory body or a unit of state, county, or municipal government.

The sanctity of the polls does not apply to hearing rooms, where partisan audiences frequently cheer, jeer, and wave placards and banners. Committee members, usually politicians, grill and wheedle witnesses, and play many situations—at the expense of inexperienced witnesses—to gain favorable attention.

The physical surroundings at hearings are equally distracting. It is difficult for witnesses to maintain a central focus because there are several interviewers, such as committee members and unidentified staff. There is an anonymous factor, also, about hearings, which are usually conducted in sprawling auditoriums or similar facilities. Nameless people (special interest attendees, the curious, and the media) are in constant motion. As committee members and staff disappear and reappear, notes are mysteriously passed back and forth, and whispered conversations provide a buzzing backdrop.

Hearings are probably the most difficult adversarial situations that corporate people face—not only for the reasons already mentioned, but also because the initiative at hearings is created, maintained, and manipulated by politicians. Control rests with the chairman and the committee, not with the witness.

Success or failure at hearings is measured differently than that of any other public activity that businesspeople are called upon to participate in. The most important consequence of a public hearing is not positive press. It is how proposed legislative action is influenced. The committee always has the final say.

How to Prepare for a Hearing: Before, During, and After

Although hearings are usually difficult at best, trainers offer the following advice for those who must prepare for them.

BEFORE THE HEARING

- *Receive specialized spokesperson training* developed specifically for the hearing room. This instruction should be administered by training organizations that understand the atmosphere of the hearing. Most spokesperson training firms lack this expertise.

- *Obtain advance copies of the testimony* of all witnesses. This material is made available by the committee at least one day before a witness' appearance.

- *Carefully study all testimony.* Be sure legal counsel monitors the hearing and all testimony, and that counsel is available to brief you at all times.

- *Study your key points* intently. Prepare yourself by organizing and memorizing a list of the primary points you want to make. Read the list aloud many times, or until you can recite it in less than the time you have been allowed to testify. This might ingratiate you to committee members—who have probably already read your submitted testimony—and it could allow time for extra questioning during which you could reinforce your primary points.

- *Carefully follow all media coverage* prior to testifying. This will give you an indication of which way the hearing is going.

DURING THE HEARING

- *Rivet your attention* on the committee's general counsel, wherever he is seated, and on the chairman. These are the members who developed both the witness list and the line of questioning that is being followed.

- *Anticipate interruptions* during your testimony. Also, do not expect to testify on schedule. There is nothing sacred about the chronology of witness lists. New lines of questioning are common. Verbal meanderings can put your testimony off to another day. Or, you may be informed that the committee desires only 5 minutes of testimony, not the fifteen originally scheduled.

- *Have a substitute available* to testify in the event you are unavailable due to sickness or a corporate emergency. The substitute should know the hearing topic as well as you do. This person should also be as well rehearsed as you would be.

- *Engage an expert*—perhaps a scientist, accountant, engineer, or business consultant—to accompany you to the witness table. A question that is difficult for you could be easy for an expert.

- *Have an aide available* to handle unexpected tasks, such as committee requests for printed materials or other information. The aide's responsibility would be to fill requests promptly.

- *Have your testimony written—or, at least reviewed and edited—by an expert* who knows how to make the points that must be made in the time allowed. The language must be forceful and persuasive. Truth is sometimes sacrificed to make points and to win favor at hearings, especially where emotional issues such as the environment and nuclear power are concerned. It should never be recommended that a corporate witness intentionally lie, thereby risking damage to both his or her effectiveness and to the cause espoused. But all witnesses should be apprised of the fact that others might present mistruths. And, they should be instructed that the best way to combat untruthful witnesses is to make sure that their testimony is prepared in as powerful and convincing a manner as possible. In short, make your points. At the end of your testimony, summarize your points.

- Although the committee is always the main focus of a hearing, the media is important. The press is the only unbiased line of communication to the public during a hearing.

- A copy of your testimony and a news release concerning it can be disseminated. And, public relations staff should be prepared—up to, through, and after your appearance—to implement media strategies outside the hearing room if you are facing a stacked deck inside.

- For example, committee staffs frequently schedule witnesses to appear late enough to miss major media deadlines after serious allegations have been leveled. If this ploy is suspected, it is appropriate to release a statement before testifying. It is not wise, however, to take a case outside the hearing room unless there are extraordinary circumstances. The media can present your views, but the committee has the final say on a course of action.

AN EXCERPT FROM AN ADVERSARIAL TRAINING SESSION

Following is an example of the type of adversarial training given by specialized firms prior to a witness' committee hearing. This is an actual segment of training given secretly before several oil company executives were to appear before a Congressional Committee investigating the feasibility of recommending legislation that would require the breakup of large, vertically integrated (petroleum production, refining, transportation, and marketing) oil companies.

TRAINER

No one here has to be reminded of what happened to the seven oil company executives who went before Scoop Jackson's Senate hearings on the energy crisis. The Exxon vice president who couldn't remember his company's dividend has become something of a symbol to image-makers around the country.

The Gulf President who participated became so incensed that he issued a press release which began, "We are not cheaters and gougers, and we resent any implication that we are."

The point is, public committee hearings always hold the possibility of antagonism—perhaps especially so for oil companies in recent years, but also for any business organization. Public hearings are not called except for very important measures and controversial issues. They are frequently covered by reporters and broadcasters. Frankly, some hearings are held for the primary purpose of gaining exposure and support for a bill, and not to air arguments on issues.

Politicians, since they are human—a little more human than most of us, some would argue—do not underestimate the value of national TV exposure during hearings. There are some who say that the Jackson hearings were actually the campaign kickoff for the Senator's run for the presidency, which, quite interestingly, followed.

To take the other side for a minute, politicians are also generalists. Few have any specific knowledge of the petroleum industry. Veteran legislators will tell you that specialist witnesses at public hearings are necessary, but that they are also, many times, difficult to understand. They speak in technical jargon or in-house language ... their arguments are often arcane ... and they sometimes argue many different points on the same day, confusing the situation.

That is exactly the spot we are going to put you in today during training. Senator Hearthstone, the chairman of the committee holding hearings on the breakup of big oil, has been listening to you and your opponents testify on Senate Bill 2387 for three days. Now, we're at the end of the third day. The Senator is in a state of nearly total confusion. He is tired, irritated, and short-tempered. He wants to get out of the stuffy hearing room, and head for liquid refreshment at the Monocle Restaurant across the street.

The Senator is not certain he understands the main arguments in opposition to divestiture. He turns to you. A desperate look in his eye, he demands you summarize your position. Present three or four main points that even a tired, confused Senator—one who needs a drink—can understand.

Mr. _____ and Mr. _____, let's see if you can provide the answer. Will you come to the front of the hearing room, please. I will be Senator Hearthstone. And, I'll be joined by my colleague here, who we will say is Senator Humbug from South Dakota.

SENATOR HEARTHSTONE

Mr. _____, the Committee appreciates the fine testimony you have provided for the record. As you have indicated, this is a matter of vital importance. I want to assure you that the Committee takes your input with utmost seriousness. After three days of testimony, though, I must say there are still many questions in my mind; doubts, pro and con.

One of my doubts has to do with competition. Your firm, as an independent refining-marketing company, repeatedly complains about the monopolistic practices of the integrated petroleum companies on the matter of crude supply. Your president testified to that effect before the Senate Antitrust Subcommittee not long ago. You have admitted in your testimony that your company would be the least affected of the eighteen firms named in the bill. And, you admit that divestiture would probably increase competition. Why are you against the bill?

EXECUTIVE IN TRAINING
(Response)

SENATOR HUMBUG

I'll tell you why you're against the bill. You're trying to become an integrated company, just like the oil majors. You have invested huge sums of money in crude oil production. Most of it overseas, of course. Not in the United States, where it would contribute to energy independence and the national security. You have invested in Nigeria ... Canada ... Iran ... Venezuela ... even in Bangladesh. You claim jobs will be lost if the majors are forced to divest. I say to you, sir, those jobs have already been taken away from Americans!

EXECUTIVE IN TRAINING
(Response)

SENATOR HEARTHSTONE

Mr. _____, you suggest an alternative to divestiture. You claim that the industry should adopt functional accounting procedures. Report profits and return-on-investment for each phase of activity. Do you do that now? And, since the whole purpose of this bill is to foster competition and to reduce prices to consumers, how would your proposal help accomplish this?

EXECUTIVE IN TRAINING
(Response)

SENATOR HEARTHSTONE

Now, Mr. _____, you contend that vertical integration is better for the consumer. The picture you present is one of your company's oil flowing from your wells into pipelines and barges...to your refineries, and from there to your own service stations. The implication is that any breakup of this orderly flow would bring in costly and unnecessary middlemen, and thus increase the price to consumers. Isn't it true that all the oil companies are integrated, anyway? Integrated by reason of contractual relationships? Isn't it true that you *share* the risks of drilling in joint ventures? That you *share* the ownership of pipelines? That you bid *jointly* on Federal offshore lease sales? That you freely *exchange* gasoline and other products with other companies ... and that you sell it under your own brand name? Isn't what we're looking at here just a plain, old-fashioned, industry-wide monopoly?

EXECUTIVE IN TRAINING
(Response)

(Then, discussion about how the executives-in-training have performed.)
• How many points made?
• How quickly?
• Effectiveness of major arguments.
• How could they have been managed more effectively?

MODERATOR

Thank you, gentlemen. Now, we'll adjourn for lunch. But, to summarize this morning's instruction, whether you're in front of a TV camera right here, or in a witness chair at an actual hearing, the basics are the same. You must:
• Be prepared;
• Be brief;
• Be candid;
• Never "wing it";
• Always keep your cool;
• And—above all else—get your points across at every opportunity.

CRISIS MANAGEMENT TRAINING: AN IMPORTANT NEW WEAPON IN THE PUBLIC RELATIONS ARSENAL

Crisis management training is arduous. It is difficult to anticipate crisis with complete accuracy, so the training tends to be subjective. Additionally, it is sometimes troublesome to convince management that crisis situations could, in fact, overtake their company. But crisis management training is important and has become an accepted strategem in the public relations arsenal.

Thorough crisis management instruction should include:

- The development of crisis-reaction plans, and guidance pertaining to the anticipation and the evaluation of crisis
- Information regarding methods of identifying potential crisis situations
- Counsel concerning the coordination of the legal, public relations, human resources, and industrial relations disciplines in a crisis situation
- Coaching on dealing with an investigative press
- Instruction regarding how and when to disseminate news
- Counsel with regard to communicating on a personal level—with employees' families, for example—and with news media simultaneously
- Advice regarding working with the authorities
- Information about methods of restoring public confidence following a crisis

The major deficiency in crisis management training formats is that they almost uniformly concern themselves with teaching management how to respond to the press *after* a crisis has occurred. Scant if any attention is focused on anticipating a crisis or on preliminary preparations to help cope with a crisis if one should arrive.

The logical steps involved in crisis communications include:

- Evaluating crisis.
- Anticipating a crisis.
- Preparing for a crisis.
- Communicating during a crisis.

Evaluating Crisis

A basic understanding of crisis is necessary for managers to appreciate a crisis situation thoroughly and to employ appropriate strategies to cope with these predicaments.

It is widely agreed that there are three types of crisis: disasters, which come in the form of accidents or acts of God; societal involvement crises, or events (such as the nuclear accident at Three Mile Island) that the general public gets involved in; and potentially controllable crises, such as salmonella contamination in food.

Companies most vulnerable to these misfortunes, such as airlines and other transportation firms, are expected to have disaster plans. But most other companies do not, even tough floods, explosions, fires, and industrial calamities are not uncommon. Disasters, though hideous when they occur, can be the least difficult crises to handle. The human community usually bands together after a disaster, and the primary communications task is to provide the public with information as quickly and as honestly as possible. Also, disasters tend to hit a company hard and fast and, despite possible lawsuits and governmental investigations, dissipate rather swiftly.

Societal involvement dilemmas, however, present management with long-lasting challenges. Crises such as the Bhopal, India poison gas leak not only have the potential of causing widespread death and destruction, but they also can ignite public crusades that could last for years and result in incalculable damage both to an individual corporation, and to an entire industry.

A potentially controllable crisis can also result in lawsuits and in governmental investigations. These debacles are usually more harmful to a company than disasters, though, because they frequently result from carelessness or from unanticipated circumstances that should have been taken into consideration. The public—notably customers and consumers—tends to have a long memory when it comes to corporate ineptitude.

Anticipating Crisis

With advanced data accumulation and with other analytical techniques, it is possible to identify trends as disparate as political issues, societal mores, and industrial troubleshooting, at an early stage. When applied to the art of crisis management, evaluation of potential problem areas significantly minimizes management insecurities regarding those issues to be treated with greatest concern. Few companies, however, appear to be making efforts to anticipate crises. When a crisis does develop, management is usually too stunned to respond with introspection and cool reserve.

How to Develop Your Crisis Management Plans

If most managements do not make an effort to anticipate crises, neither do they endeavor to develop an organized procedure to deal with a crisis should one arise. Confusion and poor response frequently result. This is inordinately damaging, because the public reacts swiftly and emotionally to a crisis. The public's first and instantaneous reaction is to think, "What are all the facts?" Next, "Why didn't we get information quicker?" And, last, "Why did that company permit this to happen?"

Development of a crisis plan, similar to strategies to defend against a corporate takeover attempt, should be accomplished by a special task force appointed specifically for the purpose of preparing for a crisis, or, in the event that misfortune strikes, of activating strategies to deal with it.

The chief executive officer should head the crisis task force. The public expects communications to emanate from the very top in calamitous situations; there should be no compromise with this presumption. The other obvious members of a crisis task force come from departments that would be involved in the crisis: legal, industrial relations, public relations, human resources, plus a safety coordinator if the company has one.

The crisis plan should be committed to paper. This document should spell out courses of action for each type of crisis—disaster, societal involvement, or potentially controllable. The plan should also indicate the responsibilities of each member of the emergency team. A communications center should also be designated. All team members should know the center's location and should be in possession of a copy of the crisis plan.

Large corporations with far-flung divisional operations should devise both corporate and divisional crisis management plans. Local plant or divisional managers should serve as co-spokespersons, along with the chief executive officer, in the event of a crisis at a divisional operation.

Companies whose operations call for detailed crisis management plans—airlines, railroads, chemical and mining concerns, for example—tend to keep them confidential. The reason for this secrecy is that admission of the existence of these plans would be interpreted as acknowledgment that calamities are not only imminent, but episodic.

A Lesson in Crisis Management from Duke Power Company

Probably the best source of information for public relations people interested in developing crisis management plans is an industry which has been fatality free: the nuclear power industry. Despite the clamor of anti-nuclear groups and the smudge of Three Mile Island, the nuclear power industry has proven to be both safe and open about its operations, including its crisis management plans.

Duke Power Company, headquartered in Charlotte, North Carolina, operates one of the most reliable nuclear power complexes in the United States—Oconee Nuclear Station in southwestern South Carolina. The crisis management plan for this station contains eighty-six pages. The document was originally developed with input from local and federal authorities, and the press.

The Best Crisis Management Plan in the Electric Utility Industry and How It Works

In specific detail, the Oconee Crisis Management Plan lists the responsibilities of all Corporate Communications Department personnel who would be on duty in the event of an emergency. These duties include, among other things: establishing an emergency response facility at one of two pre-designated locations; notifying local, regional, and national electronic and print media of the emergency; coordinating activities with the media during the emergency; notifying and working with local, state, and federal elected officials as well as local, county, and state authorities.

Once a year, as with other nuclear facilities in the Duke system, the Oconee Crisis Management Plan is put into action with a drill that involves, to some degree, the Nuclear Regulatory Commission, the South Carolina Department of Health and Environmental Control, police, county, and other officials. Each drill, which lasts from a few hours to a few days, costs as much as $200,000 in salaries and other direct expenses. Activities in the Crisis News Center involve sixteen staffers of the Corporate Communications Department.

The Oconee Crisis Management Plan, which is considered the best in the electric utility industry, is continually updated. The plan contains office and residence telephone numbers for all press, government, and industry representatives to be contacted in the event of an emergency, as well as numbers for all Duke Power Company personnel who would be involved. The plan also includes an analysis of population and population densities within the Emergency Planning Zone around the power plant, a summary of evacuation times and conditions, and diagrams of the plant's nuclear steam supply system.

Development of an effective crisis management plan requires leaving nothing to assumption. Any voids in a plan would slow response time and cause confusion should an emergency occur. The Oconee plan, a few parts of which follow, is logical, well thought-out, and has no loopholes. Mary Cartwright, General Manager–Media & Community Relations for Duke Power, is the individual most responsible for the company's Crisis Management Plan. J. Kenneth Clark is Duke Power's Vice President–Corporate Communications, whose department is responsible for the plan's execution. (Material used by permission.)

CRISIS NEWS CENTER PRIMARY AND BACKUP

Primary CNC

As described in Figure 11, p. 61, the primary CNC for Oconee Nuclear Station is the Keowee-Toxaway Visitor Center. Access to the facility is as shown in Figure 12, p. 62.

The CND, PS, and Monitor will take up positions in the Recovery Manager's office as shown in Figure 13, p. 63.

Alternate Location

It is possible that during an emergency, the crisis news organization would be moved to another off-site location. That location for the Oconee Nuclear Station will be the town of Liberty.

The crisis management organization will relocate to the Liberty retail office. The Crisis News staff would occupy a portion of the display area toward the front of the building.

The news center, where media would congregate, is the Liberty Town Hall, a short distance from the retail office. Position functions for all Crisis News Center personnel will remain the same.

Each person is responsible for transportation to the primary/alternate Crisis News Center.

The State Law Enforcement Division (SLED) of South Carolina will be involved in limiting access into the general Oconee area to those people who are directly involved in the station emergency. In order to assist you in passing through roadblocks, please place the large yellow card on your car dash and wear the smaller card around your neck.

Routes to Liberty from Oconee Nuclear Station:

Route 1 – South on SC-130 to US-123; left (east) on US-123 to intersection with US-178; left on US-178 (north) to Liberty.

Route 2 – East on SC-183 to Pickens intersection with US-178; right (south) on US-178 to Liberty.

Oconee Crisis News Center Organization

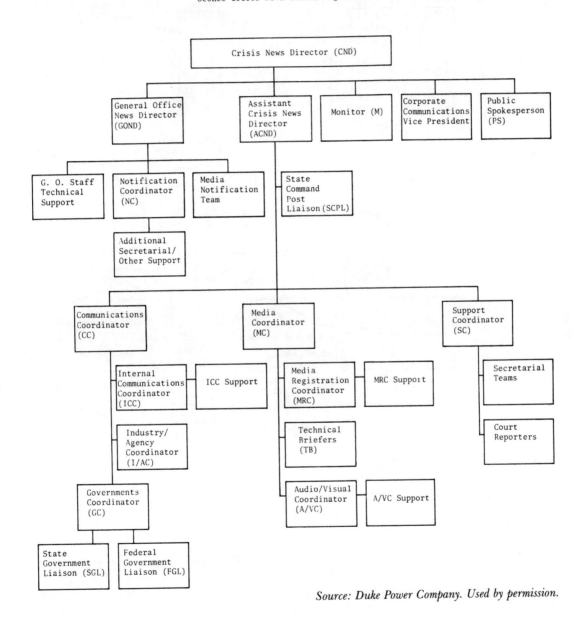

Source: Duke Power Company. Used by permission.

DUKE POWER COMPANY
EMERGENCY RESPONSE FACILITIES
OCONEE NUCLEAR STATION

NEARSITE CRISIS NEWS CENTER
KEOWEE-TOXAWAY VISITOR'S CENTER (UPPER LEVEL)
MEDIA AREA-NEWS CONFERENCES, PHONES

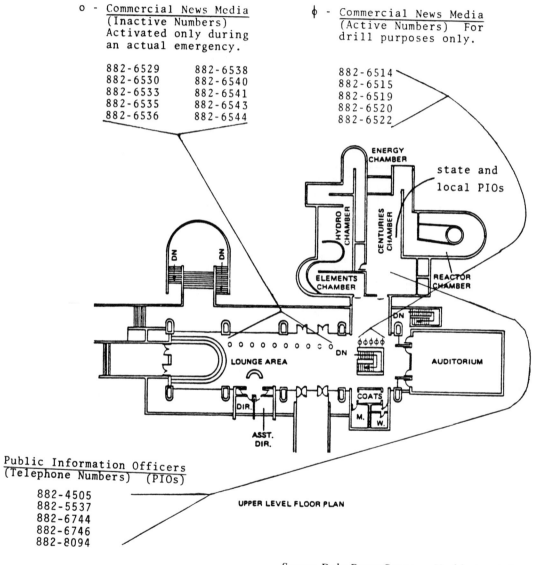

o - Commercial News Media
(Inactive Numbers)
Activated only during
an actual emergency.

882-6529	882-6538
882-6530	882-6540
882-6533	882-6541
882-6535	882-6543
882-6536	882-6544

φ - Commercial News Media
(Active Numbers) For
drill purposes only.

882-6514
882-6515
882-6519
882-6520
882-6522

state and
local PIOs

ENERGY CHAMBER
HYDRO CHAMBER
CENTURIES CHAMBER
ELEMENTS CHAMBER
REACTOR CHAMBER
DN
LOUNGE AREA
DN
AUDITORIUM
COATS
M. W.
DIR.
ASST. DIR.

Public Information Officers
(Telephone Numbers) (PIOs)

882-4505
882-5537
882-6744
882-6746
882-8094

UPPER LEVEL FLOOR PLAN

Source: Duke Power Company. Used by permission.

DUKE POWER COMPANY
EMERGENCY RESPONSE FACILITIES

OCONEE NUCLEAR STATION

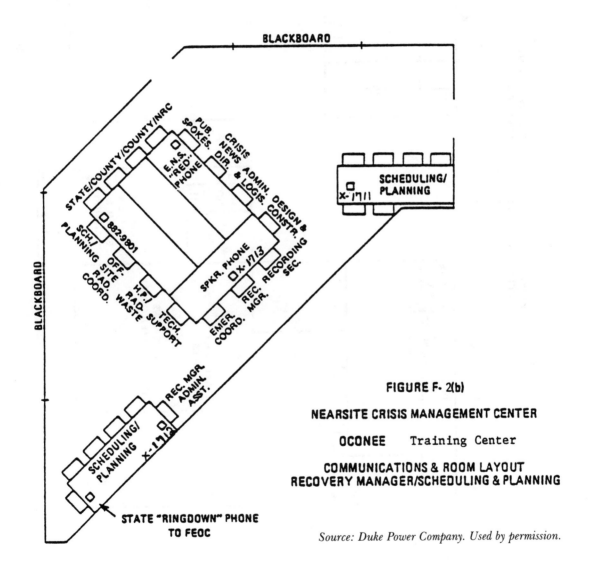

FIGURE F· 2(b)

NEARSITE CRISIS MANAGEMENT CENTER

OCONEE   Training Center

COMMUNICATIONS & ROOM LAYOUT
RECOVERY MANAGER/SCHEDULING & PLANNING

Source: Duke Power Company. Used by permission.

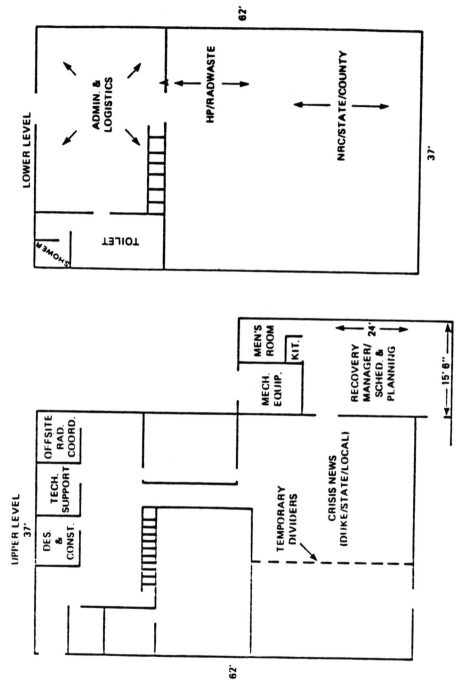

LIBERTY RETAIL OFFICE
LAYOUT

DUKE POWER COMPANY CRISIS MANAGEMENT PLAN
OCONEE NUCLEAR STATION BACKUP CMC
UPPER LEVEL

Source: Duke Power Company. Used by permission.

Crisis Management Organization Emergency Activation Message

This sheet is to be used by persons making notifications to other members of the Crisis Management Organization, to ensure that all pertinent information is passed on to the staff before their departure to their General Office Staging Area or Near-Site Crisis Management Center.

Your name _____.

Person who contacted you _____ your group _____.

Persons you contacted with this message (if any) _____

Message Format

1. This is _____ (caller's name).

2. I am notifying you of a drill/actual emergency at _____ Nuclear Station, Unit No. _____.

3. At this time, the class of emergency is: _____ Alert _____ Site Area Emergency _____ General Emergency.

4. You are to activate your portion of the Crisis Management Organization and have them report to _____ your G.O. staging area _____ the nearsite CMC _____ backup CMC.

5. Specific Instructions (if any): _____

   _____

   _____

   _____

6. Please return a copy of this completed format to the Emergency Response Coordinator, Charlotte, N.C.

Additional information to be obtained from Duty Engineer:

1. The initiating condition causing the emergency is as follows _____

   _____

   _____

   _____

2. Release of radioactivity _____ is taking place _____ is not taking place.

3. Corrective measures being taken at present are as follows _____

_____

_____

_____

News Release Format

FROM: Corporate Communications Department
Duke Power Company
422 South Church Street
Charlotte, North Carolina 28242

THIS (IS/IS NOT) A DRILL

Oconee Nuclear Station—Duke Power Company reported an (alert/site emergency/general emergency) at its Oconee Nuclear Station located near Walhalla, S.C. at (time) on (date).

Preliminary information indicates (give nature of problem).

_____

_____

_____

_____

The status of the accident situation is (stable/improving/degrading/not known).

A release of radioactivity (is/is not) taking place. (Specific information if release is taking place.)

_____

_____

_____

_____

Additional details will be provided as available.

THIS (IS/IS NOT) A DRILL.

For further information, call Corporate Communications in Charlotte at (number).

NOTE: A news center is being activated at the Oconee Visitor Center near the station. Facilities will be made available at the center for media representatives. The news center phone number is (number) (Oconee: Take route 123 to Seneca. At Seneca take route 130 north. Follow signs to Keowee-Toxaway Visitor Center.)

THIS IS A DRILL

April 6, 1983
10:30 am

FROM: Corporate Communications Department
         Duke Power Company
         422 South Chruch Street
         Charlotte, North Carolina 28242

THIS IS A DRILL

Oconee Nuclear Station -- Duke Power Co. reported a site area emergency at its Oconee Nuclear Station near Walhalla, SC this morning.

At 9:55 am a plane crashed into the Oconee Unit 3 containment building. This building houses the reactor, steam generators and nuclear steam supply system.

Preliminary information indicates that there was damage to the personnel access area. A storage tank that holds a reserve supply of water for refueling and fuel core cooling systems was also damaged.

No release of radioactivity is indicated at this time. Radiation monitoring teams have set up around the plant and will provide regular updates.

Additional details will be provided as available.

For futher information, call Corporate Communications in Charlotte at 704/373-2328, 373-5584 or 373-8138.

THIS IS A DRILL

NOTE: A news center is being activated at the Oconee Visitor Center near the station. Facilities will be made available at the center for media representatives. The news center phone number is 803/882-0601. (Oconee: Take route 123 to Seneca. At Seneca take route 130 north. Follow signs to Keowee-Toxaway Visitor Center.)

FUNCTIONAL RESPONSIBILITIES

A. Crisis News Director (CND)

CRISIS NEWS DIRECTOR	Office Telephone	Home Telephone	Time Called
Shift 1 -			———
Shift 2 -			———

Reports To: Recovery Manager

Supervises: Crisis News Group, Figure 1, p. 31-35.

Basic Functions:

1. Activate the primary/alternate Crisis News Center (CNC).

2. Manage all activities at the CNC for duration of the crisis. (Any event declared more serious than an unusual event.)

3. Be the final arbiter on all decisions to be made with respect to operation of the CNC.

4. Upon notification of a crisis, determine degree of activation for CNC staff.

5. Call news conferences to order, introduce spokesperson and close the news conference.

Primary Responsibilities

1. Contact the Notification Coordinator and indicate nature of the emergency, staffing requirements, and information to be released to the news media. (See Figure 2, p. 36, for message format for news group calls and Figure 3, p. 37, for calls to the media.)

NOTIFICATION COORDINATOR	Office Telephone	Home Telephone	Time Called
Shift 1 -			———
Shift 2 -			———

2. Contact Public Spokesperson and direct individual to report to CNC. If unavailable, call Recovery Manger to determine who PS will be.

PUBLIC SPOKESPERSON	Office Telephone	Home Telephone	Time Called
Shift 1 -			———
Shift 2 -			———
			———

RECOVERY MANAGER

3. Call NRC Region 2 office in Atlanta to notify Public Information Officer (PIO) of nature of emergency, including plans for public dissemination of information.

PUBLIC INFORMATION OFFICE	Office Telephone*	Home Telephone	Time Called
			_____
			_____

4. Contact the South Carolina Governor's Press Secretary or designee and brief individual on the emergency and location of the CNC.

	Office Telephone	Home Telephone	Time Called
Primary:			_____
Alternate:			_____

5. Call vice president, corporate communications, Duke Power Company, Charlotte, N.C., and indicate nature of the emergency.

VICE PRESIDENT CORPORATE COMMUNICATIONS	Office Telephone	Home Telephone	Time Called
			_____

Vice president, corporate communications, ensures G.O. staff is in place and assists G.O. or CNC as appropriate.

6. Call ACND and request individual to report for duty at appropriate location and to set up news center with storage items and materials that have been reserved for such an event.

ASSISTANT CRISIS NEWS DIRECTOR	Office Telephone	Home Telephone	Time Called
Shift 1 -			_____
Shift 2 -			_____

Because of the travel time required, the ACND will call ahead to News Center personnel at Oconee who will assist in setting up facilities in advance of first shift arrival.

	Office Telephone	Home Telephone	Time Called
			_____
or			
			_____

In order to accommodate media that arrives before CNC is operational, as soon as someone is in place at the Visitor Center, call ahead to security to let them know the Visitor Center is staffed. Security at Checkpoint 1 will allow media through without formal registration.

*After hours, calls are automatically transferred to Bethesda Operations

Crisis News Director (CND)

Primary Responsibilities (cont'd)

Leave instructions with (staffers' names) and brief entire staff on event.

In addition, ACND will call:

	Office Telephone	Home Telephone	Time Called
Shift 1 -			_____
Shift 2 -			_____

They will provide assistance as directed by the ACND.

7. Proceed to the area requested by the Recovery Manager and await further instructions.

Public Spokesperson (PS)

Basic Functions/Primary Responsibilities

Of all positions, the PS is the most important from the standpoint of presenting consistent, accurate and factual information and as such is the *only* member of the Crisis News Team, once arriving on site, who is authorized to speak for Duke Power Company while the crisis continues. The PS will address *only company actions* and *will not* discuss state or local activities.

This individual, once informed by the CND that an emergency exists, will immediately go to the CNC so as to be prepared for subsequent public pronouncements. The PS, while assigned to the CNC staff, will be located in the Recovery Manager's office during most of the time on duty. The PS needs to be up-to-date on the event so that there is less chance for faulty communications during news briefings.

It is expected that at least three news conferences per day will be held, more if necessary. The PS will work with the CND in determining news conference times and what visuals may be needed and what is to be covered. The PS and CND also will *determine the nontechnical language* to be used during media briefings.

Other team members are encouraged to attend news conferences so as to better understand the events surrounding the crisis in order to transmit information to others who may ask questions or need clarification on an issue.

News conferences will be conducted in the auditorium of the Keowee-Toxaway Visitor Center.

All news releases and public announcements will be approved by the CND and the Recovery Manager. News releases must be reviewed by the NRC site team manager. Assistance in developing the various public announcements will be provided by the PS.

Media Registration Coordinator (MRC)

Basic Function

This individual will work closely with all media representatives, making sure that they are registered upon arrival at the CNC. The MRC and staff will make the media aware of what facilities are available, will maintain a record of the media covering the crisis, issue press kits, news releases, and will coordinate with federal and state representatives when they arrive at the CNC.

Information representatives from the utility industry, trade associations and government agencies are directed to the Industry/Agency Coordinator (I/AC).

Primary Responsibilities

1. Upon notification by the NC that the CNC is being activated, the MRC will call:

	Office Telephone	Home Telephone	Time Called
Shift 1 -			___
(Section Head)			
			___
			___
Shift 2 -			___
(Section Head)			
			___
			___

These people will operate from the News Room and will issue press kits, any news releases that may be applicable and advise media on available facilities (tables, typewriters, telephones, paper, etc.).

2. Proceed directly to CNC and prepare for arrival of media. Position staffer as soon as possible at road entrance to facility.

3. Will set up news conferences and will, to best of ability, inform media of next scheduled news conference.

4. If necessary, and after consultation with CND, will utilize services of ICC for assistance in media registration and will post current news releases in the registration trailer.

5. One member of each shift will assist security by identifying and registering media representatives (including information representatives from the utility industry, trade associations and government agencies) arriving at the station. Registration will consist of media and information representatives providing some type of identification upon entering the Crisis News Center. Upon confirmation a badge will be made and given to the individual for the duration of the emergency. In the event that a site emergency is declared where

Media Registration Coordinator (MRC)

Primary Responsibilities (cont'd)

nonessential personnel evacuate the site, media and information representatives are required to have an identification made in a special facility on Route
73, near the construction entrance that leads to the Crisis News Center.
Upon site evacuation, a member of this shift will move to the special trailer to
assist security in registration.

Once the ID is made, the media and information representatives would be
allowed to proceed past the various checkpoints to the Crisis News Center.

6. MRC will make sure all news releases are posted in trailer and that copies are
given to the Emergency Coordinator in the Technical Support Center.

7. MRC will function throughout duration of crisis.

Governments Coordinator (GC)

Basic Functions

This individual will be responsible for notifying the State Government Liaison
(SGL) and the Federal Government Liaison (FGL) and elected officials in the
Emergency Planning Zone (EPZ) of the crisis and the progress that is being
made. The SGL and FGL will contact elected officials on a state and federal
level who represent the affected area.

The GC and the two liaisons will make periodic calls during the crisis as
developments change, and should make contacts even if the situation is
unchanged. They will brief the officials, inform them they are the contact for
future reports and make arrangements to locate them on a regular basis for the
duration of the crisis.

The GC also will assign two people from the Charlotte Division whose job will be
to monitor and tape as many radio and TV news programs as possible (within
division) that deal with the emergency during the course of the crisis. The audio
tapes will provide a permanent record of what was said in the area. The audio
tapes should be sent the Manager, News Services, Corporate Communications,
at the conclusion of the crisis. More importantly, by monitoring, the individuals
will be able to pick up on rumors or other flagrant inflammatory statements.
These statements should be orally communicated as soon as possible to
General Office News Director (704/373-8138) who will then confer with the
CND to determine if a rebuttal is necessary.

The GC and two liaisons should be aware that the executive branches of
government are being notified by Duke Power through other avenues, and that
appropriate local, state, and federal agencies dealing with public health and
safety have already been informed of the crisis.

Primary Responsibilities

1. Upon notification by the NC that the CNC is to be activated, the GC will
contact those persons listed in Figure 8, p. 55-57, Governments' Coordinator
Call List.

Governments Coordinator (GC)

Primary Responsibilities (cont'd)

2. Report to (staffers' names) in Corporate Communications. The GC will monitor crisis developments, make update reports to SGL and FGL and then continue to keep EPZ officials updated on developments.

Federal Government Liaison (FGL)

Basic Functions

The FGL will contact elected officials on a federal level who represent the affected area, informing them of the crisis and the progress that is being made and make periodic calls to them even if the situation remains unchanged.

The FGL will brief the officials, inform them that he is their contact for future reports and make arrangements to locate them on a regular basis for the duration of the crisis. This individual is not required to go to the CNC since the following contacts can be accomplished from the normal work place or from home.

Primary Responsibilities

1. When contacted by the GC that the CNC is to be activated, the FGL will contact those persons in Figure 10, pp. 59-60, FGL Call List.

2. Repeat the calls every 3 to 4 hours or as warranted by the situation.

State Government Liaison (SGL)

The SGL will contact members of the state legislative delegation from the EPZ counties informing them of the crisis and the progress that is being made and make periodic calls to them even if the situation remains unchanged.

The SGL will brief the officials, inform them that he is their contact for future reports and make arrangements to locate them on a regular basis for the duration of the crisis.

The SGL is not required to go to the CNC since the following contacts can be accomplished from the normal work place or from home.

Primary Responsibilities

1. When contacted by the GC that the CNC is to be activated, the SGL will contact those persons in Figure 9, p. 58, SGL Call List.

2. Repeat the calls every 3 to 4 hours or as warranted by the situation.

Seven Pointers for Successful Crisis Communications

What the nuclear power industry has done so effectively in its crisis management training is to involve the public, the press, and government in its communications, and to involve them with all possible speed. Additionally, this industry is completely candid in its disclosures and attempts to be as thorough as possible. Spokesperson trainers attempt to get these messages across.

Fires, explosions, airplane crashes, civil disobedience, oil spills, and many other calamities have been targeted by trainers, and the necessity for honest, timely communications has been appropriately drilled into the minds of thousands of corporate managers. The chaotic interviewing conditions and extreme aggressiveness of the press following a calamity are also duplicated during training sessions. Corporate representatives have learned to expect a contentious atmosphere during a crisis.

The communications pointers most often advanced by crisis management trainers include the following:

- *Divulge crisis information as fast as possible.* A crisis attracts immediate attention, and if management does not immediately respond to the public's need to know, the void will be filled by the press, or by rumor and speculation.

- *Communicate honestly and completely.* Disseminate as much news as possible as quickly as possible, and be squeakily candid about it. There is no way to minimize crisis news, so do not try.

- *Communicate on a recurring basis.* Facts change quickly in a crisis situation. Put "new" news out as fast as it is verified, even if it supersedes facts divulged only moments before.

- *Involve all publics in your communications.* The general public, employees, shareholders, the financial community, government agencies and legislative bodies, customers, and suppliers should all be notified of crisis facts if they in any way effect their relationships with a company. Receiving crisis news directly from a company, rather than from an outside source, builds credibility with a company's publics.

- *Establish liaison and cooperate with the authorities.* Immediately coordinate activities with police, fire, or other authorities who might be involved in a crisis. This is especially important in dealing with the families of any employees who may have been injured or killed.

- *Inform the press of corporate contacts.* Let the press know immediately who they should contact within the company for up-to-date crisis information. Make certain that 24-hour lines are available.

- *Place corporate observers at the scene of a crisis.* This assures that accurate information is relayed to corporate spokespersons immediately. If telephone contact is impractical, arrange for radio contact.

HOW TO RATE MEDIA TRAINING

Many spokesperson training organizations make it a standard practice to rate each training session. This practice lends an element of professionalism as far as the participants are concerned. It also provides a measurement regarding successful and unsuccessful training techniques. The forms used for training seminar evaluations are uncomplicated, and may resemble the following.

MEDIA TRAINING SEMINAR EVALUATION FORM

A candid appraisal of the media training seminar you have just completed will help us evaluate the program's content, and plan future seminars. You may return this form anonymously. Thank you for your assistance!

SUBJECT	Excellent	Good	Fair	Poor	COMMENTS
Value of seminar overall					
Understanding media					
Television interviews (A.M.)					
Newspaper interviews					
Radio interviews					
Radio editorial					
Bloopers					
Community relations problem					
Television interviews (P.M.)					
Leave-behind materials					
Quality of instruction					
Knowledge obtained					

6

Management Speaking Tours

Solving the Mysteries of the Corporate Road Show

The management speaking tour is a natural extension of spokesperson training. While a high percentage of top executives continue to shun public attention, it is not uncommon for enlightened higher-ups to stump for the recognition of important publics such as shareholders, academics, customers, and the financial and business communities. In situations where corporate activities are not compelling enough to warrant an audience, a common practice is for management to present positions on contemporary social, economic, and political issues. Topics including corporate morality, age and sex discrimination, pollution control, and trade with Communist nations have been presented.

The management speaking tour—which attracted substantial attention during the 1970s as a method to help restore damaged corporate reputations—should be carefully evaluated before implementation. Preliminary work should include: the development of objectives and methods of utilizing the program in support of other corporate public relations objectives; selection of appropriate speaking engagements; arranging publicity opportunities; and the scheduling of individual executives.

OBJECTIVES AND STRATEGIES OF MANAGEMENT SPEAKING TOURS

While the objectives of management speaking tours vary depending upon corporate strategies, several commonly applied objectives include:

- Projecting a company as a leader in its industry.
- Presenting management as innovative and enterprising.
- Building a recognition of management strategies and corporate/technological/marketing progress.

- Creating awareness of the company as a socially active and socially constructive enterprise.

- Helping to create the perception of a company as a good citizen, dedicated to contributing to the social and economic advancement of the community and the nation.

When objectives for a speaking tour are established, an operational strategy must be devised to assure success. Developing a strategy involves answering questions such as:

- What specific audiences are targeted?

- Precisely what are our messages?

- Why these messages?

- Will these messages influence the most possible people in a positive manner?

- How can publicity be maximized?

- How can the program be best dovetailed with existing programs (such as corporate advertising, public relations and financial relations) to assure maximum benefits?

Who Should Speak?

Corporate speakers can be selected after a comprehensive strategy has been developed. Primary considerations in speaker selection include title, availability, effectiveness, and professional assignment within the company. If an aggressive program is desired, a half-dozen or more corporate executives could be pressed into service. However, some top national forums require that guest speakers be chief executive officers.

There are two tiers of management speaking engagements. Tier I involves a company's top officers and the most prestigious corporate and financial rostrums in the nation. Tier II involves speaking engagements in plant communities, and presentations by division heads and plant managers.

What Should Speeches Emphasize?

Speeches should concern issues of contemporary interest. Looking within a theme for a theme should be routine practice in the development of speech topics. For example, a topic such as "The Reindustrialization of America" might seem old hat. But something like "The Laser's Potential for Keeping Employees on the Payroll During the Reindustrialization of America," might provide enough spark to ignite interest, especially if the laser is pertinent to the company involved.

Speech writers are engaged next. It is their responsibility to develop emotional as well as professional rapport with the executives with whom they will work. To avoid mistarts, it is essential that writers prepare speech outlines, and that these briefs be agreed upon up front. The executive corps should be continually involved in the speech preparation process. This assures a targeted effort. Two or three drafts are usually required before a speech is in final form.

Selecting Your Audience: From the Underwear Association to the Flying Funeral Directors of America

A company's public relations representatives should approach selected audiences many months in advance of the desired dates for executive appearances. Some Tier I audiences book speakers over one year in advance. These platforms offer the largest and most prestigious audiences, and this helps attract publicity.

There are more than 10,000 associations in the United States, and their professional affiliations are boundless. There is the Association of Drilled Shaft Contractors, for example, as well as the Flying Funeral Directors of America, the Gift Wrappings and Tyings Association, the Underwear Association, Cereal Institute, Brewers Yeast and Grains Council, National Clay Pipe Institute, and the National Liquor Stores Association. Research texts are necessary to help zero in on the organizations that offer the most appropriate forums. One research publication, *Business Organizations & Agencies Directory*, edited by Anthony T. Kruzas and Robert C. Thomas, and produced by Gale Research Company, is especially valuable. The book provides association names, addresses, telephone numbers, directors' names, numbers of staffers, names of publications produced by each association, and the groups' objectives. Additionally, the *Business Organizations & Agencies Directory* provides information regarding more than two dozen other categories of American business and industry, such as chambers of commerce, labor unions, business libraries and information centers, conference and convention centers, data banks and computerized business services, etc.

Essential Information About Some of the Most Prestigious Associations in the Nation

This list does not include all Tier I forums, but it contains a high percentage of the organizations that public relations people contact when attempting to arrange executive speaking engagements on some of America's finest platforms.

These associations are located in the nation's most populous metropolitan areas, which include:

New York	9.5 million people
Chicago	7.0 million people
Los Angeles	6.9 million people
Philadelphia	4.8 million people
Detroit	4.4 million people
San Francisco	3.1 million people
Boston	2.9 million people
Dallas/Ft. Worth	2.6 million people
Houston	2.6 million people

St. Louis	2.3 million people
Pittsburgh	2.3 million people
Cleveland	2.0 million people
Atlanta	1.9 million people
New Orleans	1.1 million people

The leading speaking platforms in each location include:

Atlanta
Atlanta Chamber of Commerce
Kiwanis Club of Atlanta
Rotary Club of Atlanta

Boston
Executives' Club of Greater Boston Chamber of Commerce

Chicago
American Bar Association
American Dental Association
American Hospital Association
American Medical Association
The Commercial Club
Economic Club of Chicago
The Executives' Club of Chicago
Lions International
National Association of Women Lawyers
National Health Federation
Rotary International

Cleveland
City Club of Cleveland

Dallas/Ft. Worth
Dallas Chamber of Commerce
Dallas Citizen's Council
Dallas Economists' Club
Ft. Worth Chamber of Commerce
Ft. Worth Export-Import Club

Detroit
Economic Club of Detroit

Houston
American Institute of Banking

Financial Executives' Institute

The Houston Club

Kiwanis Club of Houston

National Association of Business Economists

North American Society of Corporate Planning

Rotary Club of Houston

Los Angeles

Los Angeles Chamber of Commerce

Town Hall of California

New Orleans

Chamber of Commerce of the New Orleans Area

New York

American Institute of Certified Public Accountants

American Management Associations

American Society of Travel Agents

The Conference Board

Economic Club of New York

Edison Electric Institute

Joint Council on Economic Education

National Association of Manufacturers

National Association of Purchasing Management

National Foreign Trade Council

National Retail Merchants' Association

New York University, Graduate School of Business Administration

Sales Executives' Club of New York

Sales & Marketing Executives International

Philadelphia

Philadelphia Chamber of Commerce

Poor Richard Club

Pittsburgh

Economic Club of Pittsburgh

Greater Pittsburgh Chamber of Commerce

Pittsburgh Rotary Club

St. Louis

Optimist International

San Francisco

Commonwealth Club of California

Washington, D.C. area

American Association for the Advancement of Science

American Association of University Women

American Automobile Association

American Bankers' Association

American Gas Association

American Iron & Steel Institute

American Newspaper Publishers' Association

American Psychological Association

American Society for Public Administrators

Chamber of Commerce of the United States

Council of Administrative Women in Education

League of Women Voters

National Association of Broadcasters

National Business Education Association

National Business League (minorities)

National Education Association

National Federation of Business & Professional Womens' Clubs

National Federation of Press Women

Ripon Society

U.S. Conference of Mayors

Young Democratic Clubs of America

Young Republicans' National Federation

A DIRECTORY OF SIXTY-THREE HIGH-VISIBILITY SPEAKING PLATFORMS IN THE UNITED STATES

AMERICAN ASSOCIATION FOR THE ADVANCEMENT OF SCIENCE
1515 Massachusetts Avenue, N. W.   (202) 467-4400
Washington, DC 20005

Represents all scientific areas. Over 120,000 members represent about 300 scientific societies, other professional organizations. Annual convention.

AMERICAN ASSOCIATION OF UNIVERSITY WOMEN   (202) 785-7700
2401 Virginia Avenue, N.W.
Washington, DC 20037

Almost 200,000 members. Conducts study-action programs, has biennial convention.

AMERICAN BANKERS ASSOCIATION   (202) 467-4000
1120 Connecticut Avenue, N.W.
Washington, DC 20036

Membership of over 13,000 commercial banks. Annual convention in October draws 11,000–15,000; 20 regional meetings annually. Outside speakers technical, financial leaders. Lead time 6 to 8 months for annual, less for regional meetings.

AMERICAN BAR ASSOCIATION   (312) 947-4000
1155 East 60th Street
Chicago, IL 60637

Membership 300,000 lawyers, people in related fields. Two major meetings annually, attracting up to 18,000. Outside speakers are usually prominent attorneys, not necessarily practicing law. Topics are "issue oriented"—run-away children, death penalty, unemployment. Lead time, one year. Many journalists attend meetings.

AMERICAN DENTAL ASSOCIATION   (312) 944-6730
211 East Chicago Avenue
Chicago, IL 60611

Approximately 125,000 dentists belong to ADA, which promotes public health and dental science. Prints mounds of dental health, education materials. Convenes annually.

AMERICAN GAS ASSOCIATION   (703) 841-8400
1515 Wilson Boulevard
Arlington, VA 22209

Excellent speaking opportunities at annual June Executive Conference, and at October annual meeting. Audience at latter is 11,000; 300 at former.

AMERICAN HOSPITAL ASSOCIATION   (312) 645-9400
840 North Lake Shore Drive
Chicago, IL 60611

Membership consists of almost 30,000 hospitals and other health care facilities. Supports better health care. Convenes annually.

AMERICAN INSTITUTE OF BANKING   (713) 222-1717
801 Travis
Suite #1717
Houston,, TX 77002

Membership consists of 12,500 local bankers. Training seminars, annual meeting held. Biweekly forums have guest speakers.

AMERICAN IRON & STEEL INSTITUTE   (202) 452-7100
1,000 16th Street, NW
Washington, DC 20036

Speakers are booked for annual Communications Conference. Audience 100–200. Schedules six months in advance. Annual meeting in New York, with almost no outside speakers.

AMERICAN MANAGEMENT ASSOCIATIONS   (212) 584-8100
135 West 50 Street
New York, New York 10020

Has about 60,000 executives from government and business. Annual convention always in New York in September. Some speaker possibilities.

AMERICAN MEDICAL ASSOCIATION   (312) 751-6013
535 North Dearborn Street
Chicago, IL 60610

Approximately 175,000 physicians are members. Provides information regarding drugs, food and nutrition, therapy and research. Informs membership of national, state medical and health legislation, and represents the medical profession to Congress, governmental agencies.

AMERICAN NEWSPAPER PUBLISHERS ASSOCIATION   (202) 620-9500
The Newspaper Center
P. O. Box #17407
Dulles International Airport
Washington, DC 20041

Holds annual convention in different city each year. Attendance 2,000, mostly newspaper management. Convention speakers selected by arrangement committee. Lead time one year. Speakers are highly visible government, business leaders.

AMERICAN SOCIETY OF ASSOCIATION EXECUTIVES   (202) 626-2723
1575 Eye Street, N.W.
Washington, DC 20005

Annual convention attracts 3,000–5,000 of total 10,000 membership; 60 regional seminars yearly, attendance 20–200. Schedules government, business, academics one year ahead.

ATLANTA CHAMBER OF COMMERCE   (404) 521-0845
1300 North Omni International
Atlanta, GA 30303

Guest speakers arranged for early morning, night sessions concerning business topics. Audience: 20–80.

BUSINESS ROUNDTABLE   (212) 692-6370
200 Park Avenue
Suite # 2222
New York, NY 10166

Membership includes 195 *Fortune* 500 companies. Participation mandatory for member CEOs. Annual meeting June, New York. Outside speaker is economist or politician.

CHAMBER OF COMMERCE OF THE NEW ORLEANS AREA (504) 524-1131
P. O. Box #30240
New Orleans, LA 70190

Business people from over 2,000 companies constitute membership. Annual meeting mid-December. Also sponsors monthly luncheons except during June, July, Aug. Outside luncheon speakers have audiences of 175–400.

CHAMBER OF COMMERCE OF THE UNITED STATES   (202) 659-6000
1615 H Street NW
Washington, DC 20062

Represents 4,000 trade associations and chambers. Outside speakers address local meetings and annual convention. Audience at convention, always held in Washington in spring, is 3,000. Speakers are scheduled three months in advance.

COMMONWEALTH CLUB OF CALIFORNIA   (415) 362-4903
681 Market Street
San Francisco, CA 94105

Luncheon meetings Fridays, Sheraton Palace Hotel. Attendance 250–1,000. Special meetings sometimes arranged by study groups; 13,000–15,000 members, students, executives, professionals. Lead time 3 months. Proceedings published for members, libraries, schools; 130 radio stations provide coverage. Public affairs topics. Excellent publicity.

THE CONFERENCE BOARD   (212) 759-0900
845 Third Avenue
New York, NY 10022

Irregular meetings. Location, attendance varies. Membership: 4,000 business, trade associations, government, labor, academe. Topics: latest business trends.

DALLAS CHAMBER OF COMMERCE   (214) 651-1020
1507 Pacific Avenue
Dallas, TX 75201

Over 4,000 business firms in chamber. Annual meeting held in May. Audience: 1,500. Chamber also conducts seminars jointly with Southern Methodist University. Noted speakers, frequently government representatives.

DALLAS CITIZENS' COUNCIL   (214) 653-1031
607 Adolphus Tower
Dallas, TX 75202

Members include 250 CEOs, executives of local corporations. Fall annual meeting attracts outside speaker. Audience: 600–800.

DALLAS ECONOMISTS CLUB   (214) 238-2562

Membership includes 40 economists, financial executives. Meets monthly. Guest speakers discuss economic, financial topics. Books several months in advance.

ECONOMIC CLUB OF CHICAGO   (312) 726-1628
105 West Madison
Chicago, IL 60602

Dinner meetings held October, December, February, April at Palmer House. Luncheon meetings held November, January, March, May. Approximate attendance: 800–1,000 business, professionals for dinner, 300–400 for luncheon. Committee chooses business and government speakers in June; lead time 6–12 months.

ECONOMIC CLUB OF DETROIT   (313) 963-8547
920 Free Press Building
Detroit, MI 48226

Luncheon meetings held every Monday, September–May, generally at Cobo Hall. Members include 3,300 top executives, 60 percent automotive. Lead time 3–12 months. General business topics. Speeches aired on WCAR radio.

ECONOMIC CLUB OF NEW YORK   (212) 840-3450
522 Fifth Avenue
New York, NY 10036

Meets four or five times each year in the Grand Ballroom, Waldorf Astoria. Dates flexible to accommodate speakers. Attendance: 1,000–2,000. Speakers must be internationally prominent. Guest speakers from government, business also address black-tie dinners of 10–15 top CEOs.

ECONOMIC CLUB OF PITTSBURGH   (412) 355-3101
5th Avenue and Wood Street
Pittsburgh, PA 15122

Membership approximately 500 from business, academe. Monthly luncheons at William Penn Hotel draw 150; 500 attend annual dinner. Speech topics wide open. Well-known politicians, chairmen, economists are speakers. Arrangements made final in September.

EDISON ELECTRIC INSTITUTE   (202) 828-7400
1111 19 Street NW
Washington, DC 20036

Annual meeting June. Audience: 2,000. Speakers recruited six to seven months in advance.

EXECUTIVES' CLUB OF CHICAGO   (312) 263-3500
20 North Wacker Drive
Room 2045
Chicago, IL 60606

Luncheon meetings every Friday, last week in September through first in May. Average attendance: 500. Membership: 3,000–3,500 business people, professionals. Lead time six months. Speakers through Thanksgiving confirmed in June. Topics vary. Strong publicity opportunity.

EXECUTIVES' CLUB OF GREATER BOSTON CHAMBER OF COMMERCE
                                            (617) 426-1250

125 High Street
Boston, MA 02110

CEOs frequent guest speakers. Meets monthly, Copley Plaza Hotel. Audience: 600–700.

FINANCIAL EXECUTIVES' INSTITUTE   (212) 953-0500
633 Third Avenue
New York, NY 10017

Membership 12,000, primarily corporate, financial. Average attendance October annual meeting 1,200. Also six area conferences. Speakers from government and business. Arrangements nine months ahead.

FORT WORTH CHAMBER OF COMMERCE   (817) 335-2491
700 Throckmorton Street
Ft. Worth, TX 76102

Guest speakers address December annual meeting, and outlook conference held during first quarter. Guests also address irregularly scheduled business conferences.

FORT WORTH EXPORT-IMPORT CLUB   (817) 625-2111
P. O. Box #17372
Ft. Worth, TX 76102

Membership consists of air freight, shipping, petroleum executives. Meets monthly, has after-dinner speakers. Books three months in advance.

THE FORUM CLUB OF HOUSTON   (713) 749-3226
c/o University of Houston
Central Campus
Houston, TX 77004

Monthly luncheons attended by 300–500 of total membership of 1,300 business, academic, civic, government people. Speaking arrangements minimum six months ahead. Topics vary, speakers from all walks.

GREATER PITTSBURGH CHAMBER OF COMMERCE   (412) 392-4500
411 Seventh Avenue
Pittsburgh, PA 15219

Executive luncheons held up to four times yearly. Attendance 300–500, depending upon speaker. Membership: 1,000 firms, 2,000 individuals. Lead time: maximum eight weeks.

HARVARD BUSINESS SCHOOL CLUB OF NEW YORK   (212) 575-0982
27 West 44th Street
New York, NY 10026

Monthly, annual meetings in New York. 2,000 members. Maximum 100 at monthly, 200 at annual meetings. Speech topics vary, also speakers: business executives, artists, politicians. Lead time: six months.

THE HOUSTON CLUB   (713) 225-1661
811 Rusk
Houston, TX 77002

"Men's forums" held weekly, usually Tues. Attendance: 200–600. Lead time, maximum eight weeks; 3,000 members, mostly Houston businessmen.

KIWANIS CLUB OF ATLANTA
2509 Peachtree Center Office Tower
Atlanta, GA 30303

Meets Tuesdays, 12:15 P.M., Top of Merchandise Mart. Books two months in advance. Audience: over 200.

KIWANIS CLUB OF HOUSTON   (713) 522-3434
1934 West Gray
Room #208
Houston, TX 77019

Meets Wednesdays, 1:00 P.M., Whitehall Hotel. Luncheon speakers booked several months in advance. Audience: 250.

LEAGUE OF WOMEN VOTERS OF THE UNITED STATES (202) 296-1770
1730 M Street, N.W.
Washington, DC 20036

Voluntary organization with over 140,000 members. Promotes political responsibility. Biennial meeting has speakers.

LIONS INTERNATIONAL   (312) 986-1700
400 22nd
Oak Brook, IL 60521

Organization has 26,800 local clubs in 150 nations. Members are business people and professionals. Promotes community service, international understanding. Speakers scheduled six months in advance. Has annual meeting (June) and convention. Three keynote speakers at annual meeting, with audience potential 12,000.

LOS ANGELES CHAMBER OF COMMERCE   (213) 629-0711
404 South Bixel Street
Los Angeles, CA 90017

Active group. Annual Business Outlook seminar well-attended. Occurs in fall, 1,000 attend.

NATIONAL ASSOCIATION OF BROADCASTERS   (202) 293-3500
1771 N Street, N.W.
Washington, DC 20036

Membership represents radio and television stations and networks. Supports acceptable programming and advertising practices, combats discriminatory legislation, and advocates freedom of the press. Annual convention.

NATIONAL ASSOCIATION OF BUSINESS ECONOMISTS (713) 759-0940
(Must use local secretary's number)   Ask for Kathy Smith

Unusual group of 125 business economists, corporate planners and financial analysts. Meet monthly at either The Houston Club or the Hyatt-Regency. Audience: 40–60.

NATIONAL ASSOCIATION OF HOME BUILDERS   (202) 452-0200
15th and M Streets, N. W.
Washington, DC 20005

Annual convention Jan., has drawn 50,000; 120 educational seminars held annually, attended by up to 1,000. Large press contingent attends convention, seminars. Lead time: 6–12 months.

NATIONAL ASSOCIATION OF MANUFACTURERS   (202) 626-3700
1776 F Street, N.W.
Washington, DC 20006

Annual meeting Mar. Speakers from the association or government. Approximately 16 smaller meetings annually. Members are 12,000 U.S. manufacturing corporations. CEOs and major officers attend annual meeting, board meetings.

NATIONAL ASSOCIATION OF PURCHASING MANAGEMENT (212) 626-3700
11 Park Place
New York, NY 10007

Membership includes about 20,000 corporate, educational, and government agency purchasers. Conducts purchasing seminars at Harvard, Michigan State, University of North Carolina, Cornell, and Stanford. Annual convention in May.

NATIONAL FEDERATION OF BUSINESS & PROFESSIONAL WOMEN'S
CLUBS   (202) 293-1100
2012 Massachusetts Avenue, N. W.
Washington, DC 20036

Large organization with about 175,000 members from 700 different occupations. Charter is to advance professional opportunities for women through educational activities. Annual convention always in July.

NATIONAL FOREIGN TRADE COUNCIL   (212) 581-6420
10 Rockefeller Plaza
New York, NY 10020

Annual convention November, New York City. Members: manufacturers, exporters, importers, banks, foreign investors, transportation, insurance, communications, publishing, advertising agency executives. Topics: American foreign trade and investment, common markets, export controls, balance of payments, trade barriers, etc.

NATIONAL PRESS CLUB   (202) 737-2500
529 14th Street, N.W.
Washington, DC 20045

Membership 5,000 working press. Weekly luncheons attract 300–400. Most speakers from political, business, media backgrounds. Topics varied. Lead time: two to four months.

NATIONAL RETAIL MERCHANTS' ASSOCIATION   (212) 244-8780
100 West 31 Street
New York, NY 10001

Several speaker possibilities at annual meeting, where eight business disciplines are represented: financial executive, sales promotion, operations, traffic, personnel, merchandising, information systems, and credit management. Each discipline selects speakers. Audience: 200, sometimes more. Scheduling requires four to five months.

NEW YORK UNIVERSITY   (212) 285-6000
Graduate School of Business Administration
100 Trinity Place
New York, NY 10006

Key Issues Lecture Series draws prominent speakers: top corporate executives, government leaders, university professors. Series runs October to May, audience averages 200.

OPTIMIST INTERNATIONAL   (314) 371-6000
4494 Lindell Boulevard
St. Louis, MO 63108
June annual meeting has three guest speakers. Audience: 3,500–4,000.

PHILADELPHIA CHAMBER OF COMMERCE   (215) 568-4040
Suite # 1960
1617 John F. Kennedy Boulevard
Philadelphia, PA 19103

Approximately 2,200 companies represented. Poor for speaking engagements. Occasional seminars on executive skills draw 20–60.

PITTSBURGH ROTARY CLUB   (412) 471-6210
203 William Penn Hotel
Pittsburgh, PA 15219

Meets Wednesday, 12:15 P.M., William Penn Hotel. Leading corporate executives
from the region are speakers. Audience: 120–200.

POOR RICHARD CLUB   (215) 735-5914
1319 Locust Street
Philadelphia, PA 19107

Poor Richard Club is a good platform. The organization is oldest advertising/
journalism club in the nation, with 1,000 members in advertising, journalism,
public relations, printing, television and radio in the Philadelphia area. Many
noted guest speakers have appeared at Poor Richard's weekly meetings.

ROTARY CLUB OF ATLANTA   (404) 522-2767
235 Peachtree Street, N. E.
Suite #1612
Atlanta, GA 30303

Club has over 400 members, meets Monday, 12:15 P.M. at Top of the Merchandise Mart. Books two months in advance. Audience: over 200.

ROTARY CLUB OF HOUSTON
1145 San Jacinto Building
911 Walker Street
Houston, TX 77002

Club meets Thursday, 12:15 P.M., at the Shamrock, outside of town. Audience:
400–500.

ROTARY INTERNATIONAL   (312) 328-0100
1600 Ridge Avenue
Evanston, IL 60201

Approximately 800,000 members around the globe. June annual meeting,
usually four sessions, each with a guest speaker. Audience: as large as 14,000.

ROTARY/ONE   (312) 644-7070
505 North Michigan Avenue
Chicago, IL 60611

Maximum 400 members attend weekly meetings at noon at Ratisson Hotel.
Businesspeople, professionals. Lead time: at least six weeks. Any timely topic
possible. Wide diversity of speakers.

SALES EXECUTIVES' CLUB OF NEW YORK   (212) 689-5117
Hotel Roosevelt
New York, NY 10017

Over 3,000 corporate executives interested in improving marketing/selling
techniques. Holds weekly luncheon meetings, monthly seminars.

SALES & MARKETING EXECUTIVES INTERNATIONAL   (212) 986-9300
380 Lexington Avenue
New York, NY 10017

Approximately 23,000 sales, marketing, and general corporate executives make
up membership which seeks advancement of the state of the art. Sponsors Sales

Management Institute, Salesmens' Workshops, clinics, seminars. Annual convention in May has guest speakers. Audience: 6,000–7,000. Schedules at least six months ahead.

TOWN HALL (213) 628-8141
523 West Sixth Street
Los Angeles, CA 90014

Luncheon meetings every Tues., usually at Los Angeles Biltmore Hotel; 2 meetings per month in other locations. Average attendance: 75–150. Membership: 5,500–6,000, varied pursuits. Lead time: maximum six months. Speakers from government, business, academe. Topics current, controversial. Proceedings appear in *Town Hall Journal* and are aired nationally on radio.

UNITED STATES CONFERENCE OF MAYORS (202) 293-7300
1620 I Street, N.W.
Washington, DC 20006

Approximately 750 mayors of towns with more than 30,000 population belong to USCM. Charter is to help improve municipal government by fostering cooperation with state and federal governments. Provides research and counseling. Annual convention in June.

WHARTON BUSINESS SCHOOL CLUB OF NEW YORK (212) 867-7458
161 East 42nd Street
New York, NY 10016

Membership 2,000 Wharton graduates; some University of Chicago, Harvard. Weekly meetings, Union League or Harvard Clubs, attract maximum 100. Speakers from business, topics business-oriented. Lead time three months.

What the B-Schools Can Offer You

The business schools of some major universities also regularly sponsor guest speakers, and these sessions offer important forums for the business community. For example, the Yale University School of Public and Private Management has an outsider's speaking program, as well as an annual conference on contemporary management themes. The Columbia University School of Business conducts a Distinguished Leaders Lecture Series, where top corporate executives and government officials discuss the national economy. Members of the university's student body, its faculty, and administration attend these informative sessions.

Some Additional—and Underused—Speaking Platforms for Tier I Presentations

Tier I presentations also include meetings with representatives of the financial community. Depending upon a company's financial relations objectives, these presentations could be company-hosted affairs at company facilities, appearances before any of the more than fifty analyst societies in the United States and Canada, or appearances before specialized analyst splinter groups.

Tier I forums usually require speakers with credentials, especially where major associations are concerned. Large American corporations regularly place executive speakers at their podiums. There are other influential platforms, however, that offer potential for the messages of both large and small companies. The thousands of trade, business, and professional associations offer speaking opportunities in all specialized areas: business and commercial; agricultural; legal and government; military; scientific and technical; educational; health and medical; religious; athletic; public affairs; labor unions, and others.

A few of the thousands of diverse and important organizations representing these varied pursuits include:

AMERICAN ASSOCIATION OF UNIVERSITY WOMEN   (202) 785-7700
2401 Virginia Avenue, N.W.
Washington, DC 20037

Biennial convention, spring. Membership: 190,600. Fifty state groups, almost 2,000 local groups. Conducts study-action programs.

AMERICAN DAIRY ASSOCIATION   (312) 696-1880
6300 North Riber Road
Rosemont, IL 60018

Membership 200,000 dairy farmers. Annual meeting attracts 600–700. Outside speakers from industry, government; speech topics related to dairy industry. Lead time can be years.

AMERICAN MINISTERIAL ASSOCIATION   (717) 854-5216
P. O. Box 1252
York, PA 17405

Annual convention, September. Membership: 76,000 independent, inter-denominational ministers, other church representatives. Forty-three state groups, 352 local groups; sponsors charitable programs.

AMERICAN PHARMACEUTICAL ASSOCIATION   (202) 628-4410
2215 Constitution Avenue, N.W.
Washington, DC 20037

Convention April. Membership: 56,000 pharmacists, wholesale and manufacturing firms, importers, teachers, researchers and others.

RETAIL JEWELERS OF AMERICA   (212) 489-0023
1271 Avenue of the Americas
New York, NY 10020

Semi-annual convention February (conference) and July (convention), always Chicago. Forty-four state groups. Membership: 17,000 jewelry retailers.

Tier II Speaking Platforms: "Let Your Fingers Do the Walking"

Tier II speaking platforms include organizations with both local and national chapters. Sometimes, such as with Rotary, Kiwanis, and Lions, large-city chapters are Tier I, smaller chapters are Tier II. It is beneficial to write an organization's national headquarters to obtain a list of local chapters and other specifics regarding speakers. In some instances, such as with Rotary, the organizations will provide such information only to members.

CHAMBER OF COMMERCE OF THE UNITED STATES   (202) 659-6000
1615 H Street, N.W.
Washington, DC 20062

LIONS CLUB INTERNATIONAL   (312) 986-1700
300 22nd Street
Oak Brook, IL 60570

ROTARY INTERNATIONAL   (312) 328-0100
1600 Ridge Avenue
Evanston, IL 60201

OPTIMIST INTERNATIONAL   (314) 371-6000
4494 Lindell Boulevard
St. Louis, MO 63108

NATIONAL BUSINESS LEAGUE   (202) 829-5900
4324 Georgia Avenue, N.W.
Washington, DC 20011

KIWANIS INTERNATIONAL   (312) 943-2300
101 East Erie Street
Chicago, IL 60611

LEAGUE OF WOMEN VOTERS OF
THE UNITED STATES   (202) 296-1770
1730 M Street, N. W.
Washington, DC 20036

NATIONAL FEDERATION OF
BUSINESS AND PROFESSIONAL WOMEN'S CLUBS   (202) 293-1100
2012 Massachusetts Avenue, N. W.
Washington, DC 20036

AMERICAN BUSINESS WOMEN'S ASSOCIATION   (816) 361-6621
9100 Ward Parkway
Kansas City, MO 64114

AMERICAN ECONOMIC ASSOCIATIONS   (707) 762-0137
1313 21st Avenue, South
Nashville, TN 37212

AMERICAN ASSOCIATION OF UNIVERSITY WOMEN   (202) 785-7700
2401 Virginia Avenue, N. W.
Washington, DC 20037

Tier II speaking engagements are available literally by consulting a telephone book. If you were looking for speaking engagements to help build support for a controversial public program in, say, Patchogue, Long Island, New York, a glance at the Suffolk County telephone book would reveal a wide diversity of possibilities: St. Sylvester's Senior Citizens Club, East Patchogue Civic Association, Patchogue Chapter of Hadassah, St. Peter's Episcopal School PTO, Patchogue Golden Age Club, NAACP Islip Branch, Patchogue Village Republican Club, American Association of University Women, Parents without Partners, Knights of Pythias, Loyal Order of Moose, League of Women Voters, and Soroptomist International.

MEETING PUBLICITY OBJECTIVES:
HOW TO HAVE YOUR CAKE AND EAT IT TOO

There is frequently an opportunity to achieve publicity when corporate executives make speaker's appearances. In some cases, the sponsoring organization assists with publicity. This is helpful, since the organizations deal continually with the local press and have a thorough understanding of reporters and placement requirements.

If an executive has a Tier I engagement, the sponsoring organization will be of such stature that publicity could be an easy task. If the executive has especially pertinent or important remarks, this will help assure air time and ink.

Depending upon the significance of a speaker's remarks, placement efforts should start at the top of the media spectrum. Publicity opportunities include all local radio and television stations, and daily newspapers. They should all receive a news release together with a copy of and—very importantly—a summary of the speech. Major national business media should be approached. Obvious possibilities include *Business Week, Fortune, The Wall Street Journal, Forbes,* and *Vital Speeches.*

If a speech has person-in-the-street appeal, top media such as "The Today Show" (NBC-TV) or "Good Morning, America" (ABC-TV) are placement possibilities. Op-ed articles are also feasible if the executive's speech is distilled to about 700–1,000 words. (There are about fifty op-eds in U.S. daily newspapers that do not share competitive distribution territories.) The trade press should always be included in publicity plans. And speech reprints should always be disseminated—as rapidly as possible, even before the speaking engagement for trade media with long lead times—to as many targets as are deemed important.

7

Employee Relations
New Tactics for an "I-Oriented" Environment

Not since the Industrial Revolution has the American work place faced changes as profound and deep-seated as those that are presently shaking the very framework of the ways we work and manufacture products. The reindustrialization of America has started, however modestly, as the first of the nation's "factories of the future" go on line. Simultaneously, the deindustrialization of America continues, as blue-collar manufacturing jobs decrease, while professional and service-oriented opportunities increase.

Adding to the disorder in America's changing industrial environment is the fact that the retraining of blue-collar workers will be essential to maintaining smooth operations in the nation's factories, but that no authorities, including the Bureau of Labor Statistics, can yet accurately predict what kinds of new jobs will be created and in what numbers.

But public relations practitioners are already involved in America's changing industrial work place at the most basic, and most meaningful level—on the plant floor. Public relations people are communicating change to a changing work force, with dramatic new attitudes and personal objectives.

To a lesser but still important degree, there are new corporate attitudes, too. There are new work rules, new ideas pertaining to management-worker relationships, and there are new terms: "job enrichment," "quality-of-work-life," "participative management," "nonadversarial relationships," "psychology of entitlement," "self-acutalization."

What these new terms suggest is that the traditional adversarial relationship of the work place, a legacy from the Industrial Revolution, is crumbling. In its place there is evolving a more solicitous and open environment, one in which the worker is treated as an individual with individual rights; as a person with exercisable options; as an individual whose professional and personal needs must be met to an appreciable degree if the employee is to be a competent and productive contributor to corporate growth.

The influences that fostered these changes are understood. But there is little comprehension regarding how significant a modification in employer-employee relationships will result from these changes, and there is little common understanding of what specifically should be done to improve these relationships.

WHO IS THE "NEW AMERICAN WORKER"?

The influences that spawned the "New American Worker" were born of the permissive society that granted freedoms of individual expression heretofore unknown in the nation's history. Self-fulfillment became an overriding consideration in the search for a rewarding life. At the same time, the fear factor—fear of the stigma of being fired, of not having employment and a source of income—lost much of its influence. Two-salary households comprise about sixty percent of the American work force, and benefits such as severance pay, unemployment and supplemental compensations, provide security in the event employment is terminated.

To today's American worker, the search for personal fulfillment, which is difficult to obtain when automation can reduce a worker's participative role to less than that of a robot, is considered more important than receiving a pink slip. Also, money and the work ethic have lost much of their relevance in American society. Money will always be important, but inflation has obliterated much of the materialistic advancement that people once associated with hard work and salary increases.

The work ethic has significantly lost its grasp on the minds and hearts of American workers. Implicit in work ethic is the belief that, if an individual honestly and diligently applied himself, he would be rewarded professionally and materialistically.

Also implicit in the work ethic is a measure of self-sacrifice and subordination to something considered more important than the individual. But self-sacrifice is not a contemporary motivator. American workers survey a century of industrialization and find fear and repression, unionization and a refinement of adversarial management-labor relationships, meaningful monetary gains for workers, but also a lifetime commitment of loyalty and subservience to a company and to a machine—scant appeal for a worker born into an era of introspective self-fulfillment with few ethical restraints. What stimulates growing numbers of American workers is personal fulfillment; acquiring personal fulfillment usually requires being "an individual." And, if being self-fulfilled requires quitting or attempting to reshape a job, more and more American workers will take those routes.

Today's workers' ethics and social values are unique in the history of the American labor force. And today's workers are also better educated and more vocal about what they perceive as legitimate on-the-job demands than were those who preceded them. This situation, plus the fact that high energy costs, inflationary pressures and international competitive confrontations are putting economic strains on American corporations, are forcing concessions on the parts of both management and labor.

What Business and Labor Should Know About Today's Work Force

The questions that business and labor are attempting to answer concerning the contemporary work force are:

1. What do the workers want?
2. What can be done to increase worker motivation and job interest?

Most studies indicate that American workers believe they are fairly compensated for their labors. But, research also indicates that worker alienation has been steadily increasing for decades. This problem is not unique to the United States. It is a problem familiar to most industrial nations in the world. The demand for self-expression and a changing role on the job is most acute in the United States, though, because this nation pioneered industrialization and has developed the phenomenon to a degree that is more advanced than any other nation.

So, today's American worker is intelligent, I-oriented, committed to living a life replete with personal rewards, and not necessarily committed to anything "larger"—be it God, country, or company.

What Personal Rewards Do Workers Seek?

1. Workers desire the opportunity for self-expression, for the opportunity to recognize their own personal contributions to the manufacture of a product or to the advancement of corporate goals.
2. Workers desire dignity and recognition through the granting of incentives such as sabbaticals, flextime, and informal job schedules.
3. Workers desire increased job challenge, including participation in the decision-making process, and nonadversarial working relationships on the plant floor.
4. Workers desire good pay and benefits, and enough free time to pursue personal interests.
5. Workers desire precise and timely interpretation of corporate objectives and progress, and they want to know how their local plant or division fits into overall corporate strategies.
6. Workers desire candid and timely communications.

The second question regarding America's changing work force and its influence on an industrialized society—"What can be done to increase worker motivation and job interest?"—is difficult to answer. Many companies are wrestling with the problem, and experimentation will continue through the 1980s or longer.

The "flattening" of management responsibility, and the meltdown of formal job structures will continue. The various concepts that will be employed to help involve employees in the management process, and to provide the opportunity for self-expression among a work force that is increasingly self-oriented, include the following.

PRODUCTION CONTROLS:
PROVIDING OUTLETS FOR SELF-EXPRESSION

Self-expression on the job has been one of the primary demands, stated and unstated, of the new breed of American worker. One effective method of providing self-expression is permitting individual work crews to establish their own production requirements based on plant-wide objectives instituted by management. Inherent in the establishment of employee production goals are decisions regarding what and how many hours will be worked, and, on occasion, terminating peers for infractions such as malingering, poor attendance and shoddy workmanship.

Programs such as this provide the added benefit of permitting employees to pursue self-fulfillment activities outside the plant during increased periods of free time. Negatively, it is impossible to institute these programs in many facilities because there is not enough flexibility in work schedules to permit selection of staggered work hours by all crews.

Quality-of-Work-Life (QWL):
Can Participatory Management Work?

QWL is still very much an experimental approach to participatory management, and it is still questionable whether it will survive the decade of the 1980s. Despite the fact that major corporations such as General Motors, Honeywell, Xerox, American Telephone & Telegraph, and Sperry believe in QWL programs and have implemented them, the concept is a difficult one to make work at all levels of the corporate chain-of-command.

The primary objectives of QWL are to increase productivity and product quality by creating an environment in a manufacturing facility, or in an entire company, of mutual involvement in the manufacturing process. Quality circle groups of hourly workers hold regular meetings, usually with management representatives, to respond to matters as diverse and as important as capital expenditure requests, individual's work or production routines, product inspection and general quality control practices, operating profit responsibility, grievances, recreational pursuits and other topics.

While QWL can instill in a work force feelings of self-esteem and worthy involvement in a company's operations, the practice is difficult to implement. The psychology of an entire company's management must change from one that is authoritarian and dominant in approach, to one of mutual involvement and cooperation. All management representatives must support the QWL principles, and actively participate in the program.

Changing the mindset of managers whose only corporate experience has been of the superior-subordinate school is a difficult task. Perhaps even more difficult, though, is the question of the first-level manager, for QWL renders much of the responsibility of the supervisor redundant. Additionally, the supervisor is being asked to relinquish power to subordinates. Corporations must develop new roles for their first-level managers, new roles that emphasize responsibilities such as instructing, coordinating, helping to draw the innovative qualities out of his or her assignees. Sometimes, QWL programs are instituted using specially-trained supervisory personnel at the first manager level.

Quality Circles: Gaining a Foothold in Today's Work Place

More than 200 American companies have implemented quality circles. This concept will find application in many more firms during the 1980s, and will make substantial contributions to changing the American workplace.

Quality circles are actually one component of QWL. Quality circles are groups of workers with the assigned responsibility of evaluating product quality and, if deficiencies are noted, of recommending corrective procedures. The concept is readily adaptable and has received enthusiastic support from workers, who crave a sharing of management responsibilities.

Socio-Technical System: Uniting Management and the Work Force

STS originated in England and has been successfully applied in several industrial facilities in the United States. The concept combines sociological and technical considerations for job improvement. Usually, hourly production workers and representatives of salaried disciplines such as engineering or manufacturing, combine talents to improve production and working environment. Both the human and economic realities of the work place are involved.

Usually employed in the design of new plants and/or new production lines, STS is also occasionally used in the redesign of facilities. STS has proven to be extremely effective at breaking down the traditional adversarial relationship between management and the work force, at effecting cost-saving techniques on production lines, and at winning the emotional and professional commitments of the workers involved in the planning and decision-making processes.

Problem-Solvers: The Corporate "A" Team

Another tool of the work innovation movement that is easily administered is the Problem-Solvers concept. This simply means that a team of employees continually addresses itself to solving problems as they arise. The problems can be in any area, operational or human. They can involve grievances, manufacturing, engineering, design, shipping, or discipline. The Problem-Solvers team is usually supplemented by additional hourly and management representatives as problems change and require diverse disciplines to solve.

Incentives: Appealing to Personal Interest

Employees are also requesting and receiving more incentives than ever before in the history of the American workforce. The incentives usually preferred are flextime, extra vacation time, sabbaticals, informal job schedules, and leisure recreational sports at or near the place of employ.

Incentives such as these mesh with changing social values and lifestyles that demand self-expression and individual fulfillment. More and more incentives will be offered to members of the work force during the 1980s, and this will cause production scheduling problems for industrial companies. The type of enterprises that initially granted incentives such as flextime, sabbaticals and informal work schedules were insurance companies. Clerical duties and clerical employees are easily assigned tasks on uneven schedules, without the difficulties inherent in maintaining production levels for manufactured products while coping with frequently changing work schedules.

FEEDBACK: HOW TO OPEN UP
COMPANY COMMUNICATION CHANNELS

The participatory process in the American plant is also spawning appeals for candid and timely communication with management, both from the top down, and from the bottom up.

Corporations are answering these appeals in different ways. Communications practices often reflect the personality of the plant manager or other management representative responsible for them. Some plants have frequent get togethers of the "town meeting" sort. Others employ strategically placed hot lines to carry the news. Still others advocate shirtsleeve meetings between first-line supervisors and employees to keep communication channels open. Regardless of the methods employed, the trend toward open communications will continue to expand. And, there are many methods of insuring that employees are receiving information promptly and candidly, and in a manner they trust and believe. The time-honored method of using front-line supervisors as communications conduits will probably be used extensively in the future, however, for workers place more credence in communications from supervisors than they do in any other method.

Why are supervisors considered a company's most important communications tool? First, they are accessible to employees during the entire work day. Also, since supervisors have a personal working relationship with employees, they have a unique opportunity to develop both professional and emotional rapports with their co-workers. Also of consequence is the fact that front-line supervisors have the important opportunity of sounding out workers regarding potential problems.

NEW JOB INNOVATIONS YOU CAN EXPECT TO SEE—AND USE

The 1980s will experience a revival of job innovations. These practices could be the brainchildren of industrial relations experts, or, as has occurred frequently in the past, of individual plant managers or production people. Successful innovations include merit pay standards, in which employees are remunerated according to their productivity, and pay increases for work innovations that make an employee's job less labor intensive and more productive.

Other successful innovations include assigning total responsibility to individual workers—total responsibility for the manufacture and assembly, for example, of a product or a certain part of a product. This means responsibility not for a single piece, but for at least a recognizable unit, so the worker can identify his or her efforts with a significant entity.

HOW PUBLIC RELATIONS PEOPLE CAN WIN EMPLOYEE COMMITMENT: A FOUR-POINT PLAN

Public relations communicators must assume an active role in helping to structure the new American work place effectively. For, it is unanimously agreed by industrial relations experts that employee willingness to help achieve corporate or plant objectives is critically important during this adjustment period. Without employee support, corporate progress will wane. Communications are the vehicle by which management will win or lose an employee's loyalty and commitment to corporate goals and objectives.

How should public relations people respond to this challenge?

1. First, a company's communicators must determine whether management is properly relating to the everyday concerns of the rank-and-file. Audits must be undertaken of both management and workers to ascertain whether hourly and salaried are pulling together or pulling the fabric of corporate coexistence apart. The audits should be undertaken with the assistance of the Industrial Relations and Human Relations Departments, and recommendations should be made to correct deficiences. The full cooperation and mandate of both top management and plant managers should be obtained prior to starting these projects.

2. A communications audit should be conducted to assure that corporate and divisional communications tools and practices are as effective as possible. House organs, bulletin boards, newsletters, audio-visuals should be evaluated—preferably with the assistance of an outside consultant with authority to criticize openly and honestly—and a media system should be recommended to achieve clearly documented communications objectives.

   Outside consultants are recommended for internal communications audits, because they possess the specialized talents required to obtain and evaluate information and to develop communications programs that specifically address problems. Also, they are familiar with the technicalities of installing and programming audiovisual systems.

3. Key communicators should receive concentrated training in management-employee dialogue. This training should also be conducted by outside authorities and should include communications techniques for crisis response, for making presentations and handling meetings, and for creating dialogue with hourly workers.

4. Communications with front-line supervisors should be fine-tuned. These are the individuals who are going to contribute the most to a successful communi-

cations program. Public relations personnel should provide communications training for supervisors, with emphasis on techniques to assure meaningful dialogue on the plant floor. Here are four proven methods to increase the proficiency of supervisor communications:

- *Create a beneficial environment*
  An honest, open, friendly environment is critically important to both the giving and the soliciting of information. Supervisors should understand the importance of a mutually beneficial environment, and how to create it.

- *Maintain dialogue with section leaders*
  Supervisors should maintain continual dialogue with section or department leaders in order to keep them informed of important company news, and to sound them out regarding employee attitudes.

- *Provide sounding boards*
  Basic sounding boards such as regularly scheduled shirtsleeves meetings and the interpretation of scuttlebutt, are important to both the hourly staff and to management. Grievances can be aired before they are blown out of proportion, and workers can sound off about topics that may be disturbing them.

- *Be a buddy*
  The companionship of front-line supervisors and their employees should be encouraged. The most natural way of doing this is for supervisors to involve themselves, even if infrequently, in off-the-job social or athletic events. Personal relationships encourage a smoother working rapport and engender trust and confidence.

Effective corporate communications programs require the active participation of top management, plus the Industrial Relations, Public Relations, and Human Relations Departments, and key managers, department heads, supervisors, and hourly workers. Any weak link in the corporate chain can destroy a program.

HOW TO SET UP ECONOMIC EDUCATION PROGRAMS

Economic education programs are one of the most frequently implemented employee relations strategies, especially in capital intensive manufacturing industries. Sometimes, industry associations provide counsel regarding how individual member companies can conduct these programs, with or without outside assistance. Typical of these programs is one provided by the Aluminum Association, Washington, DC, to its membership.

It was designed, to give employees a better understanding of the economic considerations that ultimately affect their job security and earnings potential. These economic considerations range across the entire spectrum—from worldwide, to U. S., to (this industry), and on down to the employee's company, plant, work area, and finally his or her own individual job.

These campaigns are usually conducted in three phases:

1. *Survey phase.* Work force is surveyed to learn employee understanding and misconceptions about economic facts pertaining to their nation, industry, company, and themselves.
2. *Program phase.* Communications program is developed to counter problems uncovered in the survey.
3. *Re-survey phase.* Second survey is conducted to determine positive effects of the communications phase, and to change the program's emphasis if necessary.

The questionnaire for the Aluminum Association's economic education program was extensive. It contained over eighty questions, and had elaborate instructions for its implementation. Participation by the entire work force was recommended:

> By making your survey a census—surveying all employees in your work force—
> ...you avoid the appearance of favoritism (implying to any employees that their views don't count). The greater the percentage of employees covered, the more factors you can analyze. For instance, with a census you can compare attitudes of new employees with veteran employees, male with female, hourly with salaried, or you may choose to examine survey returns by job classification or age if such comparisons are important to you.

The instructions recommend that, if a sample of employees is selected rather than a census, "it must be random to be valid." Selecting the name of every fourth employee is recommended.

When looking for an opinion research firm to conduct the employee survey, they are more apt to be found under the heading "Market Research Firms" in the Yellow Pages than under "Public Opinion Research." Also, there are two directories that list these organizations:

American Association for Public Opinion Research
P. O. Box #17
Princeton, NJ 08540
(609) 924-8670

The Green Book
New York Chapter, American Marketing Association
420 Lexington Avenue
New York, NY 10017

A SAMPLE LETTER AND QUESTIONNAIRE
FOR IMPLEMENTING ECONOMIC EDUCATION PROGRAMS

The questionnaire for the Aluminum Association survey was administered to groups of twenty-five to fifty employees in company cafeterias or training rooms. However, when plant managers resisted this approach for fear of production losses, the questionnaire was mailed to employees' homes. This substantially reduces the number of completed questionnaires received, though.

The economic education program and the employee survey should be announced in advance to assure maximum understanding and participation. The following letter was sent to employees with the questionnaire in the metals industry survey.

Dear (address employee by name, if possible):

As you know, (name of company) is planning a new program of employee communications. With the new program, (name of company) hopes to keep you better informed of the financial and economic aspects of your job, your plant and the company as a whole—how they are interrelated and how they fit into the national economy. You probably remember learning about our plans for this new communications program (tell how the plans for the program were publicized: the company newspaper, bulletin board, employee meeting or other means).

To carry out the survey, we ask you to fill out the enclosed questionnaire. But before you go to the questionnaire, let's cover an important point: The questionnaire is *not* a test. There are no "right" or "wrong" answers. Instead, the questionnaire offers a means of you telling us what your financial and economic interests and opinions are. You can help us achieve this aim by responding to each item in the questionnaire as frankly as possible.

Before you start marking your responses, quickly look over the questionnaire and refer to it as you read the rest of this letter. First of all, notice that you are not asked to put your name anywhere on the questionnaire. The idea is to keep your responses anonymous and thus preserve confidentiality.

Now look at the beginning, Part A of the questionnaire. You'll find a list of subjects that may or may not be of interest to you. Put a checkmark alongside each subject in one of the four columns that comes closest to describing your level of interest. Notice that the columns are headed "very interested," "interested," "already receive enough information," and "not particularly interested."

Now skip to Part B on page 5. There you'll find a list of statements that you may currently be hearing or reading. Check one of the columns after each statement to show whether you think it is "true," "usually true," "usually false," "false," or you are "undecided."

In Part C on page 7, you are asked to tell whether you "agree strongly," "agree," "disagree," "disagree strongly," or are "undecided," in your reaction to a series of statements. Here—as in Part B—you are asked to check the "undecided" column only as a last resort.

Part D on page 9 asks for information about yourself. Here again, to keep the information confidential, don't print or sign your name.

Part E on page 10 asks you to select one of several possible answers in response to each of several questions.

Part F, at the end of the questionnaire, asks for your comments—both on the survey questionnaire and on the proposed new program of communicating financial and economic facts to employees.

Work through the questionnaire as quickly as you can and then please return it to us in the enclosed, stamped, self-addressed envelope.

We plan to report the results of the survey to all employees just as soon as we can. Please remember, though, it will take time to collect the questionnaires from all over the company. Once we have them, all the responses will have to be collated and analyzed before a meaningful report can be made.

(Tell just where the employee should look for a report on the survey—a letter, bulletin board notice, company newspaper or other.) Meanwhile, we want you to know we appreciate your cooperation in the conduct of this survey.

Sincerely yours,

(signed)

Survey Administrator

Enclosures

Part A

The following questions were asked in the employee survey.

Subjects	Very Interested	Interested	Already Receive Enough Information	Not Particularly Interested
1. Who are the biggest customers for the products we make here?	( )	( )	( )	( )
2. Who owns the company?	( )	( )	( )	( )
3. Where does my plant fit into (name of company's) overall operations?	( )	( )	( )	( )
4. What products do our competitors make?	( )	( )	( )	( )
5. How do government regulations and policy affect my job?	( )	( )	( )	( )
6. How does (name of company) use its profits?	( )	( )	( )	( )
7. Who benefits from productivity increases at this plant?	( )	( )	( )	( )
8. What is (name of company) doing to make my job more secure?	( )	( )	( )	( )
9. What is (name of company) doing to make this plant more efficient?	( )	( )	( )	( )
10. What new business plans is (name of company) preparing for the future?	( )	( )	( )	( )
11. How high are (name of company) profits?	( )	( )	( )	( )
12. What plans does (name of company) have for this plant?	( )	( )	( )	( )

Subjects	Very Interested	Interested	Already Receive Enough Information	Not Particularly Interested
13. What does the ownership of the company matter to me and my job?	( )	( )	( )	( )
14. Who benefits most from business profits in the U.S.?	( )	( )	( )	( )
15. How tough is competition in our industry?	( )	( )	( )	( )
16. How can I help reduce waste?	( )	( )	( )	( )
17. How can I help to increase output?	( )	( )	( )	( )
18. How can I help to make my job more secure?	( )	( )	( )	( )
19. Who is responsible for inflation?	( )	( )	( )	( )
20. What can (name of company) do about stopping inflation?	( )	( )	( )	( )
21. Information about the company's wage and salary policies.	( )	( )	( )	( )
22. New products (name of company) has under development or consideration.	( )	( )	( )	( )
23. Do other companies compete with the products we make here?	( )	( )	( )	( )
24. Where the company stands on important public issues, such as energy, the environment, government regulations, etc.	( )	( )	( )	( )
25. How government legislation affects our business.	( )	( )	( )	( )
26. How our products are used by our customers.	( )	( )	( )	( )
27. How the U.S. economy works (supply and demand, profits, inflation, etc.)	( )	( )	( )	( )
28. What I can do to help reduce inflation.	( )	( )	( )	( )
29. How does (name of company) compare with our competition?	( )	( )	( )	( )
30. How my job fits into the overall operations of the company.	( )	( )	( )	( )

Subjects	Very Interested	Interested	Already Receive Enough Information	Not Particularly Interested
31. Financial results and goals of the company.	( )	( )	( )	( )
32. Is this plant profitable?	( )	( )	( )	( )
33. How important is this plant to overall activities of (name of company).	( )	( )	( )	( )
34. What's the outlook for our metal in the (name of the industry your company or division makes products for).	( )	( )	( )	( )
35. Is (company) in this business for the long term?	( )	( )	( )	( )
36. How high are U.S. business profits?	( )	( )	( )	( )

Part B

Below are some statements you might hear on any given day. Please give us your evaluation of how *true or false* they are by checking off the appropriate box. We request that you use the "Undecided" column *only if no other answer seems appropriate.*

	True	Usually True	Usually False	False	Undecided
37. "A good way to substantially reduce *inflation* long term is to impose mandatory *wage and price controls*."	( )	( )	( )	( )	( )
38. *"Competition* is wasteful because it means too many companies are making the same thing."	( )	( )	( )	( )	( )
39. "A good way to curb *inflation* is for the government to reduce unemployment."	( )	( )	( )	( )	( )
40. "Our *standard of living* here is higher than in other countries because our *productivity* is higher."	( )	( )	( )	( )	( )
41. "(Name of company) pays more in taxes than it does for the materials it buys."	( )	( )	( )	( )	( )
42. "Of every dollar of sales, more goes to the owners of a business than goes to the workers in wages and salaries."	( )	( )	( )	( )	( )
43. "One of the causes of our inflation is that people are being laid off."	( )	( )	( )	( )	( )

	True	Usually True	Usually False	False	Undecided
44. "Workers in the U.S. earn more than in other countries because the equipment and machinery they use allows them to produce more than workers in other countries."	( )	( )	( )	( )	( )
45. "The surest way to raise the country's standard of living in the long run is to limit profits and increase wages."	( )	( )	( )	( )	( )
46. "The number one problem we have at this plant is product quality."	( )	( )	( )	( )	( )
47. "Because (name of company) is so big and so diversified it can generally charge any price it wants for its products."	( )	( )	( )	( )	( )
48. "Generally, I get a straight answer whenever I ask my supervisor a question about our business."	( )	( )	( )	( )	( )
49. "Government spending is the most important reason why we have high inflation."	( )	( )	( )	( )	( )

Part C

We'd like to know your reactions to the following statements—whether you Agree Strongly, Agree, Disagree Strongly or are Undecided. Please check off your response to each statement in the appropriate column below. And again, please use the "Undecided" response only as a last resort.

	Agree Strongly	Agree	Disagree	Disagree Strongly	Undecided
50. My supervisor keeps me well informed about what's happening at the plant.	( )	( )	( )	( )	( )
51. One of the most important causes of inflation today is that business is making too much profit.	( )	( )	( )	( )	( )
52. Over the years, as factories install more efficient machinery, there are more and more jobs for people.	( )	( )	( )	( )	( )
53. All things considered, (name of company) is as much a victim of inflation as I am.	( )	( )	( )	( )	( )

	Agree Strongly	Agree	Disagree	Disagree Strongly	Undecided
54. The surest way for (name of company) to continue to stay in business is to modernize its equipment—even if it means the loss of a few jobs.	( )	( )	( )	( )	( )
55. No one asks me for ideas about how we can improve our production rates here.	( )	( )	( )	( )	( )
56. The government should take over and operate unprofitable companies rather than let them close down and put people out of work.	( )	( )	( )	( )	( )
57. Automation may have helped business increase profits but has seriously hurt American workers.	( )	( )	( )	( )	( )
58. One of the problems businesses face today is raising enough money so that they can expand and grow.	( )	( )	( )	( )	( )
59. Money invested in new machinery and equipment has benefited the owners of the business more than the workers.	( )	( )	( )	( )	( )
60. An unprofitable company is usually a poor place to work.	( )	( )	( )	( )	( )
61. Generally, the information I get from top management of the plant is accurate and reliable.	( )	( )	( )	( )	( )
62. Management at this plant is very concerned about reducing waste.	( )	( )	( )	( )	( )
63. The Government should change the tax laws to make it easier for business to invest in new machines and plants.	( )	( )	( )	( )	( )
64. The country would be a lot better off if the government put a tight lid on the percentage of profit any business can make.	( )	( )	( )	( )	( )

	Agree Strongly	Agree	Disagree	Disagree Strongly	Undecided
65. Companies must be able to earn profits if the American economic system is to survive.	( )	( )	( )	( )	( )
66. The average working man or woman would be better off if the Government owned and ran big business.	( )	( )	( )	( )	( )
67. Most companies charge fair prices for their products.	( )	( )	( )	( )	( )
68. Most companies in the United States can afford to raise wages 20% without raising prices.	( )	( )	( )	( )	( )
69. Somehow the American economic system does not work for me.	( )	( )	( )	( )	( )
70. I feel well informed about the new products my division introduces.	( )	( )	( )	( )	( )
71. Over the last two years, (name of company) has made substantial gains over its competitors.	( )	( )	( )	( )	( )

Part D

We would like to get some background about you. Please check the appropriate category. Remember—do not sign your name!

72. Age

_____ 20 or under   _____ 41–55
_____ 21–30   _____ over 55
_____ 31–40

73. Length of service

_____ 1–7 years
_____ 7–15 years
_____ Over 15 years

74. Education (please select highest level reached)

_____ 11th grade or less   _____ College graduate
_____ High school graduate   _____ Some postgraduate work
_____ Some college or vocational/technical   _____ Postgraduate degree

75. <u>Job Category</u>

    _____ Hourly   _____ Plant Management
    _____ Clerical/Secretarial/Administrative   _____ Division Management
    _____ Foreman/Supervisor   _____ Other (please specify)
    _____ Sales/Marketing   _____ _____

76. <u>Sex</u>

    _____ Male   _____ Female

<u>Part E</u>

77. If sales of our (*name of your main type of product*) products grow next year it will be because (select one):

    _____ The (*name of your market*) is booming.
    _____ The market for (*name of your main type of product*) products is growing.
    _____ We'll have to take the business away from our competitors.
    _____ We're the leader in the aluminum (*name of your main type of product*) field.

78. Competition in the (*name of your main type of product*) business, compared to 10 years ago, is:

    _____ Greater
    _____ Less
    _____ About the same
    _____ Don't know

79. The biggest market for our product is:

    _____ (*Name of one market*)
    _____ (*Name of a second market*)
    _____ (*Name of a third market*)
    _____ Don't know

80. My main source of information here is:

    _____ My supervisor
    _____ The bulletin board
    _____ The union
    _____ The grapevine
    _____ The plant newspaper or magazine
    _____ Other (please specify) _____

81. The most believeable source of information here is: (please rank from 1 to 5, with 1 being the most believeable, and 5 being the least believeable).

    _____ My supervisor
    _____ The bulletin board
    _____ The union
    _____ The grapevine
    _____ The plant newspaper or magazine
    _____ Other (please specify) _____

Part F

If you have any comments, please write them out here:

_____

_____

_____

_____

Thank you for participating.

(Name of responsible company,
official, and location.)

KEY REQUIREMENTS OF ECONOMIC EDUCATION PROGRAMS

Economic education programs must be carefully organized if they are to be successful. They require:

- Top management support.
- Long-term commitment.
- Honest answers to employee's personal concerns, such as job security and pay.
- Straight answers, without corporate propaganda.
- Management acceptance of criticism from employees, and honest responses to same.

Management support for an economic education campaign is especially important. By engaging in activity of this type, even by conducting an employee survey, management is expressing interest in change, in making the corporate system work better. Employees expect no less.

The results of the employee survey should be divulged to the work force as soon as possible. This shows that management is interested in employees' opinions and in establishing a more productive relationship.

Normally, supervisors present the survey findings, frequently after receiving training regarding the best way to field questions and to outline the economic education program that will follow. Survey results are sometimes also commited to paper and mailed to employees with a letter explaining the significance of the findings.

It is best to contract with a professional organization—a public relations agency or management consulting firm—for the execution of economic education campaigns. This is a specialized field, and most internal staffs do not have the expertise required to conduct effective programs. Tools that specialists use for economic education programs include house organs, newsletters, correspondence, section meetings, slide shows, contests, and bulletin boards.

8

Employee Motivation

A Master Plan for Getting Top Efforts Out of a Troubled Work Place

The implementation of employee motivation techniques to help instill an appreciation for craftsmanship and productivity is gaining acceptance almost of necessity, as personnel, economic and competitive problems combine to erode America's strength as an international industrial competitor.

Today's employees are not as loyal to their employers as their fathers and uncles before them were. Nor do they work as hard, or take as much pride in the products they produce.

"I can sum up what is happening in the American work force today in a single phrase," comments Daniel Yankelovich, a leading authority on worker attitudes, in a by-lined article in *Industry Week* Magazine. We have "a growing mismatch between incentives and motivations. The incentive system does not work as well as it used to. Formerly, management had the tools to motivate people strongly enough to insure ever-increasing productivity. This is no longer true. People's values and attitudes have changed faster than the incentive system—creating a mismatch."

Compounding the problems of mind and emotion are challenging economic and competitive issues. The capital/labor ratio, or the measurement of the tools with which the nation produces goods, is falling as the average age of American industrial plants increases. And there are other serious problems, such as the productivity growth of trading partners such as Japan and West Germany, growing trade deficits, dramatically decreased expenditures for research and development, and rapidly rising expenditures for everything from energy to raw materials.

Complicating the situation further is the fact that management, trained in skills such as the law, engineering, production and finance, is finding it difficult to anticipate and to respond to elusive qualities of human behavior; management is finding it difficult to "read" the work force, to find out what is on workers' minds, to communicate.

HOW THE PR FUNCTION CAN MOTIVATE EMPLOYEES

This is where the public relations function gets involved. And, this is also where the public relations function is sometimes misunderstood, for the area of employee motivation is new and, to most corporations, untried. The public relations practitioner should not pretend to be something he or she isn't: an industrial psychologist, industrial relations expert, personnel or human relations practitioner. Public relations expertise is applied to employee motivation work because communications is an important element of these programs, and because public relations approaches are essential to helping win the commitments of labor.

While relatively new, employee motivation work is winning recognition as a legitimate contributor to increasing production-line efficiency and product quality. Employee motivation can be likened to the hyping of a sales force with new objectives, new goals, and new incentives each year. While sales traditionally has its tires pumped up every year, and while management's performance is rewarded with bonuses and other incentives, the people on the plant floor have traditionally not received motivational attention. This was partly the result of complacency—American workers were loyal, productive, and produced high-quality products—and partly the result of a blue collar/white collar mentality that slotted plant employees as "different" than white-collar staffs in the areas of compensation and incentives.

Companies practicing enlightened employee motivation methods, however, today conduct plant motivation programs every eighteen to twenty-four months. Experience indicates that performance improvements attained during a motivation program tend to decrease starting approximately six weeks after the conclusion of a program, but not to drop to pre-program levels. Successive programs, therefore, tend to keep productivity and efficiency on the upswing, and they also contribute to a positive worker mentality.

There are six important segments to an employee motivation program:

1. Receiving a mandate
2. Conducting an audit
3. Establishing objectives
4. Planning the program
5. Conducting the program
6. Finishing the program on an up note such as with a Family Day

Step One: The Mandate

A mandate is usually critically important to the success of a motivation program. It is essential that plant, divisional, and corporate management support motivation programs, or the response of employees will be dulled by the lack of enthusiasm from white-collar ranks. The most important mandate is that of the plant manager. This is the individual who is involved in the effort on a daily basis; the success or failure of a program sometimes hinges on this person's support.

Public relations practitioners responsible for conducting employee motivation programs must be fully apprised of conditions within a plant before a program is undertaken. This includes labor-relations balance, productivity, product quality, materials waste, absenteeism, lost-time accident rates, housekeeping, and employee turnover. Any indicator of employee morale, loyalty or pride should be evaluated at the outset.

"Problem" plants are usually targeted for employee motivation programs. The most conspicuous problems are union-management difficulties, poor product quality, low production, and high employee turnover. Frequently, management selects an unprofitable or marginally profitable plant for employee motivation attention.

Public relations people should also seek the approval and support of the Personnel and Industrial Relations Departments at the outset. While Personnel support is usually routine, Industrial Relations representatives sometimes react with professional concern when the Public Relations or Communications Department becomes involved in the "training" or "motivation" functions, which are usually IR domain.

It is recommended that a member of top management, possibly the executive vice president for administration or the president, explain to the vice president for industrial relations that public relations was selected for the motivational assignment because of their communications expertise. The corporate executive should also enlist the professional assistance of Industrial Relations for the project, perhaps with information pertaining to the history of union relations and productivity at the facility.

Step Two: Conducting the Audit

An audit of plant personnel, including hourly (line and first-stage supervision), salaried (plant and office), and management should be conducted before program objectives are drafted. Audits require anywhere from a few days to many weeks, depending upon the number of employees and the complexity of the operations. Sometimes, especially in large plants or divisions, research is used with the audit.

Objectives of the audit and/or research would be to determine what problems exist, what is causing the problems, and to offer solutions. Plant management can steer auditors to employees they think would provide the most candid insights into operations. It is also recommended, however, that auditors interview other employees at random to assure the validity of findings. Focus group sessions may also help to shed light on operations. Two groups are recommended, with employees in one, and management and first-stage supervisors in another. The results should be compared.

The most competent organizations engaged in employee motivation work also include about six to twelve customers in the audit phase. Synergenics, a Burson-

Marsteller affiliate specializing in employee motivation work, explains—when pitching a new account—that, when these programs fail, one of the reasons is because "They treat the internal environment and ignore the external environment." Other major reasons for failure include:

- "There is too much theory ... not enough practicality."
- "They fail to address real issues."

Synergenics stresses that these programs must focus on the "external environment" as well as the internal, or the "dedication of your people to the needs, wants, and desires of your customers" will be overlooked. Many enlightened organizations are stressing customer orientation in day-by-day operations, too. "This company is market-driven, not technology-driven .... We want every employee to think of himself or herself as being on the customer's payroll."

"MARKET AFFILIATION": THE SECRET INGREDIENT FOR EFFECTIVE EMPLOYEE MOTIVATION PROGRAMS

When auditing customers, interviewers attempt to learn how close a relationship exists between manufacturer and customer, how the manufacturer is generally perceived in the marketplace, why and how business could possibly be lost, and what the primary purchasing considerations are.

The Synergenics flip chart presentation says (and they are probably right) that what is missing from most employee motivation programs is "Market Affiliation." In questionable English, Market Affiliation is described thusly:

> Programs, or approaches based on internal perceptions consistently fail to establish the high performance/achievement climates that are desired.
>
> Structuring internal programs against the backdrop of the real world environment in which a company operates (the marketplace) adds a dimension to such activities that
>
> — establishes commonality of goals
>
> — leads to increased entrepreneurism and professionalism at all levels
>
> — encourages creativity
>
> — achieves the desired results.

How to Review Audit Reports with an Eye Toward Results

A written audit report should be reviewed with management, and objectives for the employee motivation program should be developed.

Following the preparation of the written audit, a decision should be reached about whether to go with the project or not. The program's objectives should be reviewed with union officials. It would be unusual to encounter union problems. Occasionally, however, unions voice dissatisfaction over advanced motivation efforts, because previous programs have been successful to the point of creating a "family spirit" at a plant.

When the written audit is reviewed, any negative factors should be evaluated. Dr. Frederick Herzberg, who has gained wide attention as a psychologist, professor and consultant, is one of the deans in the area of employee motivation. In his book, *Work & the Nature of Man,* Herzberg explains his terms "hygiene factors" and "motivators;" these elements should be carefully evaluated with the written audit. Hygiene factors include, according to Herzberg, "company policy and administration, supervision, interpersonal relations, working conditions, salary, status, job security, and effect on personal life." Motivators include items such as "achievement, recognition, work itself, responsibility, advancement, and possibility of growth."

The public relations people conducting employee motivation programs will attempt to impress employees with motivators, while hygiene factors—let's say, unduly restrictive company policies, low wages and deplorable working conditions—are usually out of the public relations domain. In fact, if hygiene factors combine to embitter a work force, a motivation program should be questioned.

While public relations people should generally stay away from hygiene areas, these areas should be evaluated during audits. The extent that any negative or positive hygiene factors have on the work force should be presented in detail.

Working relationships between employees and management should be evaluated if plant problems appear traceable to a breakdown in communications or working rapports. It is possible, for example, to have a work force reacting negatively to the leadership practices of first-line supervisors. The plant manager, however, might be unaware of the situation, or he may not understand the degree of hostility between supervisors and hourly workers.

Consultants charged with implementing motivation programs should evaluate the reasons for poor working relationships. They could stem from the most basic, and damaging, of all causes—frustrations born of highly structured bureaucratic organizations that grind individualism to dust, encourage dependency and "Yes, sir," "No, sir" responses, and which are inflexible regarding change, even though today's worker finds it increasingly difficult to be productive in an adversarial relationship. Fear, inefficiency, and waste usually result. Consultants should encourage management to consider corrective procedures before undertaking an employee motivation program. If participative employee roles are not encouraged, motivation programs can be negated.

Employee motivation programs have sometimes been maligned as "rah-rah" during an era when employees do not respond to such cheerleading tactics. There is no question that many of these programs are rah-rah. And, some employees do not respond to them, but this has always been the case.

The fact is, most employees respond favorably to contemporary motivation programs, especially when the corporate environment encourages their participation, and when they understand and believe in program objectives.

Step Three: Establishing Objectives

Objectives would naturally mirror the situation existing in a particular plant. However, plant problems can usually be categorized as, for example, problems with productivity, craftsmanship, morale, lagging deliveries. Likewise, objectives of employee motivation programs are frequently similar. Typical objectives include the following.

- Impress upon employees that they, as individuals, are basic to product quality, production, and the company's reputation with customers.
- Emphasize the importance of teamwork among all departments and work units.
- Help create employee understanding of the problems and the opportunities confronting their plant specifically, and the company generally.
- Increase productivity.
- Reduce product defects.
- Reduce waste.
- Improve communications.
- Improve the individual's pride in performance.

Effective employee motivation programs should be challenging, educational, and entertaining. And they should have a motivational theme. A theme of "Yes, We Can!" has been used not only for motivation programs, but also for other activities such as the local blood drive, for the plant's bowling and baseball teams, and for other events.

In order to assure a program's success, it is imperative that a reasonable goal be established and kept in front of the employees at all times. If the major problem in a facility is waste, for example, an appropriate goal would be a reduction of "x percent" waste in the manufacturing process. If the major problem is tardy shipments, the goal could be 100 percent on-time shipments.

MEASUREMENT: THE ONLY WAY TO MEET YOUR MOTIVATION OBJECTIVES

Measurement is essential to a successful program. It should be coordinated with a method of rewarding employees for participating in the program in a constructive and purposeful manner. For example, each month a plant could set a goal of shipping a certain percentage of product on time or ahead of schedule. Each department within the facility would then set its own goals to help support overall goals. Individual department goals help create peer pressure. A system of incentives (discussed later in this chapter) assures that individuals who work hard to make the program work are rewarded for their efforts.

Measurement should include percentages that can be applied to production or waste reduction, and it should be possible to equate these percentages to a total amount of dollars saved over the course of a year. This could be a percentage increase of boilers shipped during the year, or of additional income to the division. Or the measurement could be a decrease in scrap materials or an increase in plant operating efficiency which translates to an annual saving.

Departmental and overall measurement devices contribute several benefits to a motivation program. They allow public relations practitioners to pinpoint progress made as a result of the program. Measurement devices also provide program implementors with the ability to measure the enthusiasm and dedication of individuals and of departments, and to implement corrective procedures if necessary.

A simple, and very common, measurement device involves waste. For example, if a plant is operating at 96 percent efficiency with 11 percent waste, and the cost of the waste is known, the following equation (goal) could be drawn:

4.5% waste/96% plant operating efficiency
equals
$58,000 annual savings

A more involved measurement tracks increases in productivity, and improvements in response to service calls, as documented on the chart on page 219.

Measurements should be decided upon when audit results are reviewed with management. Usually production and waste measurements are part of the normal, daily operations in a plant, and require little or no alteration for the employee motivation program. It is also important to have large, billboard-type replicas of the forms on the walls in various parts of the plant. Goals and progress to date should be reported on these billboards, so employees will have a running account of accomplishment.

Steps Four, Five and Six: Planning, Conducting, and Concluding the Program

Involving an industrial psychologist in the planning phase of an employee motivation program is recommended. While this professional would not be expected to understand communications practices, he or she could contribute important evaluations of the methods the public relations people devise to achieve program objectives. A psychologist can also judge the effectiveness of the various program elements at stimulating employee participation.

SIXTEEN PROVEN-EFFECTIVE PROGRAM FEATURES

Some common program elements that have proven effective include the following:

TASK TEAM. Should be selected before program is launched, and should involve the local facility's personnel director and plant manager. The Task Team provides credibility because it is composed of employees—approximately 12 members of the work force, although size will vary according to plant complexity and numbers of employees—who represent a cross section of men, women, minority groups, company-oriented workers, "neutrally oriented" workers, machine operators, sweepers, old and new hands. The Task Team should consist primarily of dedicated employees who are considered loyal to the company. But, a few underachievers—employees with better than average abilities who have not aggressively pursued job recognition and achievement—are also frequently included. Underachievers are often motivated by a prestigious assignment, and their future job performance improves accordingly.

The Task Team's responsibility is to conduct the motivation program as directed by public relations personnel. The Task Team interfaces with outside public relations counsel, if used, and the employees. The Task Team's role is to implement all the elements of the program, to report progress and problems, and to provide the spark necessary to assure an enthusiastic response from the workforce. The Task Team should meet with agency management representatives at least every other week, and every week as the program draws to a conclusion.

BUTTONS, BANNERS, DRIVE-TIME RADIO. Whether a Teaser Campaign (explained next) is employed to stimulate employees or not, activities should be kicked off in an exciting manner. It is important to get the employees' attention and to drive home a simple, positive message. The message should involve the program theme, be it improved quality, increased production, or waste reduction.

The element of surprise can be used effectively in presenting the program theme. The Task Team, for example, could hang banners and posters overnight, and have large buttons presented to all employees as they punched in for first shift. More elaborate efforts could involve an extravaganza such as majorettes and buglers parading through plants distributing buttons and handing out literature concerning the program.

Drive-time radio is an effective method of introducing employee motivation programs. Humorous radio spots featuring employees are effective methods of presenting messages. Additionally, drive-time radio provides an element of pride that employees usually take to their jobs.

TEASER CAMPAIGNS. Teaser Campaigns alert employees to the fact that a program is imminent, and they assure that activities will be launched with enthusiasm. Teasers usually start with large banners and posters displayed on bulletin boards and in other prominent locations. Proclamations are visually straightforward: "We are Number 1," "You are the First Team," "Yes, We Can!" Buttons announcing the theme are distributed to all employees by the Task Team. And, on the final day of the three-to-five-day Teaser Campaign, department managers gather employees and explain the forthcoming program. Flipcharts should be used as aids. Managers should already have been briefed on the program by public relations and management personnel.

"CURRENCY." Some type of currency is important to employee motivation programs. Currency provides a reward system for employees who make the program work; it also provides a measurement system for program supervisors to gauge the level of employee participation. Currency is presented monthly to employees as goals are attained in the plant generally, and by individual departments and single employees specifically. Major accomplishments are rewarded with the greatest amount of currency. The currency is redeemable at the end of the program, on Family Day, where it may be traded for major awards such as refrigerators, bicycles, and television sets.

DEPARTMENT GOALS. Goals are instituted after several weeks, when employees have an awareness of the spirit and the intent of the program, plus an understanding of overall objectives. Goals should be customer-related, measurable, and related to program objectives.

The Task Team should review all goals with department members; goals should be realistic, and express a genuine commitment on the part of department members to participate in the program. The Task Team should also work with public relations counsel to devise charts that track the progress of individual departments in meeting monthly goals.

NEWSLETTER. An inexpensive newsletter, usually with a four-page format, is an important element in employee motivation programs. Newsletters are intended only for the life of the program, and should not carry news that house organs normally carry. The publication should very directly and specifically chart the progress of the program, highlight the positive activities of individuals who are excelling in program activities, and reinforce primary messages.

The newsletter should have a frequency of every two weeks, and should appear every week during the last month, as anticipation for Family Day builds. The publication should be mailed to employees' homes, and should involve employees' families in every way possible.

DOLLAR-A-DAY. This module is designed to encourage employees to consider ways to routinely save the company money during their normal work patterns. Employees are requested to submit ideas for saving at least a dollar a day by improving work practices. Employees who suggest valid ideas are rewarded with currency.

LET'S TALK. This program module is another suggestion device, and is aimed at improving plant communications. Employees are rewarded for providing ideas regarding the improvement of communications, and to explain how improved communication would benefit plant operations generally or program objectives specifically.

OPPORTUNITY CALLING. A family involvement module, Opportunity Calling provides the chance to involve employees' families in the motivation program and it provides a device to measure the degree of employee enthusiasm.

Each day, for approximately one month, several random telephone calls are made to employees' homes. Family members are asked to respond with "pass words" about the program, as provided previously to all plant employees. Correct answers are rewarded with a $25 savings bond. This is an easy method of measuring employee involvement in a motivation program. Correct answers by about 70 percent of respondents are indicative of enthusiastic program support.

WHAT'S MY WORTH? Conducted as Family Day nears, this module is an extension of Opportunity Calling. The telephone respondent is asked how much the certificates of the family member who works at the plant are worth at that time. A $25 savings bond is the reward for a correct answer.

A MEASUREMENT EXAMPLE: HOW TO SHOW EMPLOYEES THE RESULTS OF THEIR EFFORTS

	November			December			January		
	Scheduled	Actual	%	Scheduled	Actual	%	Scheduled	Actual	%
1. Pumps on time	100	80	80	200	150	75	150	150	100
2. Parts on time	1000	500	50	1000	750	75	1000	800	80
3. Field service calls (24-hour response)	150	150	100	100	100	100	100	75	75
4. X Factor							100	80	80
	Monthly pct.	76%				83%			83%
	Cumulative	7.6				15.9			14.2

Definitions:

1. Pumps on time: Compare number of pumps promised vs. pumps actually shipped.
2. Parts on time: Compare promises vs. actual parts shipped on time.
3. Field Service: Compare all service call requests for 24-hour response vs. over 24-hour response.
4. X Factor: Select most critical department goals and compare projection vs. actual.

Note: Each month (after the first month) the average percentage is added to the previous month. For example:

76%
83%
159% = 15.9

THE RED TAG. This module is designed to directly influence an individual worker's pride in performance. The tag follows a manufactured product's route through production; every worker involved with the quality of the product signs the tag. The tag contains a pledge of adherence to high quality standards. When the product is shipped, the tag is mailed to the individual at the customer company who placed the order. A letter from the Task Team accompanies the tag. In addition to drawing the customer's attention to the manufacturer's quality standards, the tag serves to increase the sensitivity of production employees to quality and customer needs.

POSTER CONTEST. This contest is also keyed to family involvement, with employees' children attending grades one through twelve participating. The youngsters produce posters involving their family and its dedication to manufacturing quality products. Local art teachers serve as judges. The youngsters and employee family members receive certificates of participation, and winners are announced on Family Day. Savings bonds are the rewards.

CUSTOMER DAYS. These are among the most important employee motivation activities. They involve employees directly with customers and help condition workers to customers' needs.

Objectives for customer days include:

- Present the company as genuinely concerned about the customer's business.
- Introduce customers to employees, and explain customer's dependency upon their craftsmanship.
- Reinforce concept that individual employees are vitally important to quality control.
- Provide sales and marketing personnel with opportunity to strengthen relationships with customers.

Preliminary planning for a customer day is important, and should involve the following points:

- Important customers—new ones, or those generally supportive of the manufacturer's products or services—should be selected.
- Sales management should help select participants.
- The general manager should extend the letter of invitation. It should stress that the program is being conducted to further quality control and employee identification with customer needs. The general manager should also contact the customer personally, and explain the customer's participation.
- The customer should receive complete instructions once a mutually convenient date is agreed upon. A schedule of events should be included. The customer should be carefully briefed on his role as spokesperson for his company.

Normally, customers arrive the evening before the event, and have dinner with the general manager and/or sales personnel. A typical customer day schedule includes:

9:00 A.M.	–	Pick-up at hotel.
9:15 A.M.	–	Meeting with general manager.
9:30 A.M.	–	Introduction by general manager to Task Team. Task Team presents customer with gift to commemorate plant visit.
10:00 A.M.	–	Plant tour.
10:45 A.M.	–	Customer meets workers on plant floor, addresses group briefly. Remarks concern importance of quality control, on-time delivery.
11:15 A.M.	–	Customer meets with top Dollar-A-Day suggestion producers, congratulates group, explains how their efforts help him.
11:30 A.M.	–	Supervisor/manager briefing by customer.
12:00 Noon	–	Lunch with Task Team, supervisors/managers/sales/marketing personnel.
1:30 P.M.	–	Return to plant. Customer leaves or conducts other business.

The local press is sometimes interested in these events. Company photographers photograph the activities, and provide coverage as soon as possible after the event. The customer should also be asked whether his company's public relations group would be interested in coverage. And a photo album should be presented to the customer by the general manager shortly after the event.

CUSTOMER DAYS IN REVERSE. A customer day turned around requires the customer to invite the Task Team and/or sales/marketing personnel to his plant to see their products on line. These events provide the opportunity for the customer to explain the consequences should production line equipment fail. Near large cities, these events are sometimes followed by attendance at a sporting event.

QUALITY OF WASTE CONTROL. To impress upon employees the necessity for quality or for waste reduction, six-person teams are assigned each week to inspect their plant and to report both deficiencies and progress. This has proven to be a major aid in efforts to establish a mindset against waste and shoddy work ethics.

FAMILY DAY/BLIND AUCTION. Family Day with the popular Blind Auction is the highlight of an employee motivation program. There is no set formula regarding whether a Family Day should be held, or what it should consist of. But it is essential that the affair be reasonably elaborate and that family entertainment be highlighted.

Family Days have been conducted at amusement parks rented out exclusively for that purpose, at municipal park facilities, and in plant parking lots. They can be successful events regardless of where they are held, if the organizers know how to create an entertaining event.

The objectives of Family Day should be threefold:

- To end a motivation program on a positive note, and with a spirit of accomplishment and camaraderie.

- To help cement the major messages of the motivation program, so that they will influence employees' performance in the future.

- To help unite management and workers by creating a "good feeling" about the company, the future, and their plant.

Food, music, gifts and humor are the mainstays of Family Day. Hot dogs, hamburgers, roast pigs, beer and soda pop are examples of the food most frequently served at these affairs. There are Dixieland bands and kids' rides and photographers to take family portraits and horse shoes, baseball, sack races, and father-son events.

The Blind Auction is the highlight of Family Day. It is both a humorous event—Santa Claus has conducted a Blind Auction in August—and an event where those who made the program a success are rewarded for their efforts. The auction, which requires about one hour, is termed "blind," because employees do not know what item they are bidding for unless they guess a clue provided by the auctioneer. The auctioneer might say, "With this unit, you really will be able to tell if the grass is greener everywhere else in the world" to start bidding on a color television set. The personnel director works with the auctioneer to assure that those employees with the most certificates bid for and win the major prizes.

The Blind Auction is not recommended by all industrial psychologists. Some think awards should be made strictly according to how many certificates an employee has. But the Blind Auction introduces an element of excitement and mystery that appears to be universally appreciated by Family Day participants.

The plant manager should introduce Family Day festivities with a short (less than five minutes) speech, in which upbeat remarks alluding to the positive attitude of the work force are made. The auctioneer is then introduced.

A Kid's Store is a popular addition to Family Day activities. Youngsters who have won certificates by participating in program modules such as the Poster Contest can "spend" certificates at the store for items such as frisbees, balls, helium-filled balloons, kites and jump ropes.

A rain date should be established, along with a telephone number for employees to check on whether the event is to be held if skies are threatening. Also, the Task Team is responsible for duty such as parking lot attendants, guides, checkers and spotters during the auction, athletic contest umpires and referees.

A typical schedule of events for a Family Day would include:

11:30–Noon	Arrival at parking area, roving Dixieland band playing.
12:00–12:30	Food and beverages available.
12:25	Loudspeaker summons attendees to stage for opening remarks and start of the Blind Auction.
12:35–12:40	Congratulatory remarks by plant manager.
12:45	Introductory humorous remarks by auctioneer. Explanation of rules for Blind Auction.
12:50–1:50 (approx.)	Blind Auction.
1:50–5:00	Food and beverages available. Music by roving Dixieland band.
2:00–4:00	Kids' Store open.

3:00–5:00	Kids' and adults' contests.
4:30	Wild card drawing for two major prizes, generally color television sets.
5:00–5:30	Departure.

These parameters and modules are typical of those used in a basic employee motivation program. If a follow-up program is to be developed eighteen to twenty-four months following an initial program, a second audit should be conducted to assure that an appropriate approach is employed for Phase II.

EMPLOYEE MOTIVATION PROGRAMS: PHASE II

Phase II of employee motivation programs frequently involves plant communications. These programs usually hone in on front-line supervisors, since these individuals are the most important people in the plant communications process. The front-line supervisor is important to the company, also, because he or she is in a position to evaluate employee thinking and morale.

Frequently, the second phase program is tailored to increase the momentum generated by the first program. The second program should create the opportunity for increased management visibility among both the supervisory groups and hourly employees. Bargaining units should have major participation in the program, because these units have the singular opportunity to spot and attempt to alter anti-company attitudes that may exist on the plant floor.

Objectives of follow-up programs are: to capitalize on the benefits achieved during Phase I; to strengthen and reinforce Phase I objectives; to emphasize two-way communications between departments, employees and the division itself; to help establish a team spirit and pride in workmanship; and to help build employee understanding of the problems and opportunities confronting their plant and their company.

Phase II programs should concentrate on information of prime importance to employees, such as management policies and procedures, job security, corporate objectives and strategies, and how these relate to their plant and/or department, training and educational opportunities.

Supervisors should be instructed in the necessity for good communications within their work units, as well as the tested methods of establishing communications links with the workers under them; encouraging an open atmosphere, listening to employee comments pertaining to their work, instituting scheduled meetings, paying attention to grievances, and establishing a relationship with the Personnel Department.

New Modules You Can Add to Phase II Programs

New elements should be added to Phase II. These modules frequently include supervisor presentations about where the division is at the present time and where it is heading, the demands of the marketplace, and the importance of the individual to quality and profitability.

Other modules could include a newsletter and paycheck-stuffer campaign highlighting topics such as, "The Role of the Individual," "How Customers See Us," "Talking to the Market," and so on. Employee updates in the form of meetings with supervisors could be held. And modules aimed at increasing understanding among supervisors and department heads could be added. These modules could include quarterly updates, and theme meetings at which supervisors take turns leading discussions concerning in-plant topics.

Forms that provide employee anonymity and which provide the opportunity to comment openly on anything affecting the work place could be made available, and a suggestion program could be instituted. Shirtsleeve meetings, with no-holds-barred comments, could be held between hourly employees and their supervisors. These meetings would stress open communications, team building, and brainstorming.

The Red Tag and Customer Days could also be featured in Phase II. And family involvement practices, such as contests and Family Day should be instituted.

The question is frequently asked, "How long should an employee motivation program run?" The answer is open-ended, but it usually lasts from three to six months. The most important consideration regarding duration of motivation programs is that they run long enough to accomplish objectives but not to bore. Six months is generally maximum, and during a program of this duration, the Task Team would undoubtedly sense "peaks and valleys" of employee enthusiasm.

One element that helps carry programs at high levels of commitment is stressing the fact that employees are responsible for the program's success or failure. It is their program, they are executing it, and they are responsible for making it work.

A TYPICAL TIMETABLE FOR AN EMPLOYEE MOTIVATION PROGRAM

Ideally, these programs start in winter, when employees are generally not vacationing or pursuing outdoor activities. They end during spring when weather favors an outdoor Family Day. (Indoor Family Days can also be successful, though, if facilities such as an armory are available.) The following schedule is typical.

Dec. 29, 19xx	:	Public relations agency meets with Task Team, provides Task Team with banners, buttons, posters, reviews program in depth.
Jan. 3	:	Overnight display of theme in all shops and offices. Buttons distributed. Newsletter #1 mailed.
Jan. 16	:	Public relations agency meets Task Team, reviews employee reaction to program.
Jan. 16	:	Newsletter #2 mailed.
Jan. 20	:	Customer Day.
Jan. 23	:	Supervisors' communications meeting. Customer Day in Reverse.
Jan. 24	:	Supervisors' "theme" meeting.

Jan. 30	:	Management meeting with supervisors. Theme: shipments and quality goals. Newsletter #3 mailed.
Feb. 5	:	Initiate "News Center." Supervisor/employee meeting. Theme: same as management meeting of Jan. 30.
Feb. 8	:	Employee update.
Feb. 12	:	Initiate paycheck-stuffer program.
Feb. 13	:	Public relations agency meets with Task team, reviews progress.
Feb. 14	:	Newsletter #4 mailed.
Feb. 15	:	Initiate employee hot line.
Feb. 16	:	Initiate product tag campaign.
Feb. 28	:	Initiate "Dollar-A-Day." Management/Supervisors' "goals" meetings.
March 3	:	Newsletter #5 mailed.
March 6	:	Supervisors' theme meeting.
March 7	:	Goals campaign.
March 10	:	Public relations agency meets with Task Team.
March 13	:	Customer Day.
March 14	:	First "shirtsleeve" meeting.
March 15	:	Paycheck-stuffer #2.
March 16	:	Customer Day in Reverse.
March 17	:	Initiate "Opportunity Calling."
March 18	:	Newsletter #6 mailed.
March 20	:	Public relations agency meets with Task Team.
April 3	:	Newsletter #7 mailed.
April 7	:	Supervisors' communications meeting.
April 10	:	Customer Day.
April 11	:	Paycheck-stuffer #3.
April 14	:	Customer Day in Reverse.
April 17	:	Newsletter #8 mailed.
April 25	:	Public relations agency meets with Task Team.
April 27	:	Second "shirtsleeve" meeting.
May 2	:	Newsletter #9 mailed.
May 10	:	Employee update.
May 16	:	Newsletter #10 mailed.
May 17	:	Paycheck-stuffer #3. Management/supervisors' "goals" meeting.
May 22	:	Supervisors' "theme" meeting.
May 23	:	Third "shirtsleeve" meeting.
May 29	:	Customer Day.
May 30	:	Newsletter #11 mailed.

June 1	:	Public relations agency meets with Task Team, reviews Family Day preparations.
June 6	:	Customer Day in Reverse.
June 10	:	Newsletter #12 mailed.
June 14	:	Supervisors' "communications" meeting.
June 15	:	Paycheck-stuffer #4.
June 19	:	Family Day.

9

Industrial Intrigue

How Business-to-Business Public Relations Is Changing Along with the American Work Place

One of the earliest applications of marketing public relations/publicity was in the industrial, or business-to-business area. This function, while not startingly creative (engineers and technically oriented practitioners have typed mountains of properly spiritless case histories during the past four decades), helped to pattern editorial relationships and other procedures for people working in the more flamboyant public relations specialties.

Many industrial public relations specialists continue to use traditional techniques. They develop comprehensive product stories, serve on appropriate synods of industry associations, and maintain snug liaisons with the technical press.

But business-to-business public relations is changing significantly. And, since American industry will be responding to competitive and technological challenges for the forseeable future, the function will continue to change.

Some of the most important modifications have occurred in the areas of marketing, of employee, labor, and community relations, and of dealing with the press.

One of the most productive new marketing techniques is what could be called the "Customer Confrontation"—the literal presenting of products and services to potential customers. There are several variations of this technique, all of which, understandably, receive enthusiastic support of sales forces.

THE TARGET INDUSTRY SEMINAR: HOW TO USE THE MOST POPULAR CUSTOMER CONFRONTATION TECHNIQUE EFFECTIVELY

A Target Industry Seminar is a round table conference attended by eight to fifteen people. These seminars are of a problem-solving nature. Company specialists address a specific industry problem and evaluate possible solutions. The editor of a major trade publication serves as moderator, and has exclusive rights to coverage.

If the company sponsoring the TIS manufactures a product that is marketed in several industries—for example, steel tubing for the automotive, petroleum, and chemical processing industries—trade publications representing all disciplines could participate. Companies with prominent reputations for research and engineering competence are good candidates for Target Industry Seminars.

Opportunities for Target Industry Seminars are not limited to corporations. Associations frequently have ideal messages for TIS presentations. The question that must be answered affirmatively when evaluating the possibility for TIS involvement is: "Is our message important enough to benefit an entire industry?"

Editorial slants for a TIS should be precisely documented in a proposal highlighting the professional benefits anticipated from the session. The educational aspects of a TIS usually sell the concept to an editor, and should neutralize any hesitancy concerning the fact that commercial benefits will accrue to the sponsoring company. A TIS has strong sell. Participation in a highly visible industry conference positions both editors and publications as leading authorities in their industries.

Who Should Participate and What Should They Accomplish?

The professional integrity of a TIS requires credible participants who represent a cross section of an industry. While participants' credentials would vary depending upon topics addressed, a typical panel would include:

- Trade publication editor.
- Industry economist or financial analyst.
- Government official.
- Association representative.
- Specialists from customer companies.
- Technical professionals from host company.

There are usually five objectives:

1. Develop possible solutions to an industry problem.
2. Present a corporate/association capability to industry leaders.
3. Extend this message to thousands of other professionals through the pages of the moderator's trade publication.
4. Generate sales leads and help establish attendees' professional reputations as leaders in their fields.
5. Reinforce reputations of host companies or associations as industry leaders.

A Target Industry Seminar is challenging. Not that there are inordinately difficult editorial, technical or logistic complexities, but even minor blunders can tarnish the reputation of the host organization.

Nine Steps for Orchestrating a Successful TIS

From working with the moderator to conducting practice sessions, these steps are as follows:

1. Review all parameters of the session with the moderator after receiving an editor's sanction to participate. Discuss the participative role with which the moderator would be most comfortable: a definitive "discussion script" that the host organization would prepare? his own outline, a copy of which would be shared with the host? an extemporaneous presentation? The host organization should review the material presented by the moderator in a formal dress rehearsal long enough in advance of the scheduled session to change content and/or to arrange for spokesperson training if either content or delivery is inadequate.

2. Review a list of participants that the editor/moderator should provide shortly after accepting the leadership role. Participants should be industry leaders whose professional status and reputations would lend prestige to the event. The host organization should suggest alternatives if individuals recommended by the editor/moderator do not possess the desired stature.

3. Draft a letter of invitation. Include descriptions of the topic being addressed, explanations of why the host firm selected the topic, and why the recipient was selected as a participant, plus the obvious essentials: time, place and travel arrangements.

SAMPLE INVITATIONS TO EDITORS AND PARTICIPANTS OF A TIS

Mr. Robert Osborn
Publisher
Heating/Piping/Air Conditioning
600 Summer Street
Stamford, CT 06904

Dear Bob:

Confirming our 9/14 telephone conversation, we're hoping that HEATING/ PIPING/AIR CONDITIONING will be able to host a round table conference on the state of the art of air handling systems. The conference would be sponsored by Owens-Corning Fiberglas.

The objective of such a seminar would be to examine current industry trends in air handling technology and problem areas. As we discussed, the information generated by such a conference could be the basis for a highly informational editorial piece of great interest to your readership. Examples from previous round tables are enclosed.

In organizing such a conference, while we would do the legwork, we would look forward to working closely with you in developing a detailed discussion agenda and arranging participants.

The initial thinking is to invite a maximum of 15 to 20 people, including a range of small, medium and large contractors servicing both residential and commercial construction. These contractors would be users of our Fiberglas duct system, as well as competing systems. In addition, we'd also invite a specifying or mechanical engineer and a representative of SMACNA. A spokesperson for Owens-Corning would attend. Of course, we'd value your suggestions on this.

Your specific role would be that of discussion moderator. In operating these conferences, we've found that third party leadership provides firm guidance in keeping the meeting on track, adhering to the agenda and bringing the meeting in on schedule.

Some basic details on the conference itself: The meeting would run from 9:00 A.M. to around noon, operating according to the discussion agenda—delivered to participants a week or so in advance. A sample agenda from a previous conference is enclosed. The site of the conference would be a hotel in a readily-accessible area, such as the O'Hare Hilton. Again, we'd welcome your suggestions.

The conference is recorded, and then transcribed, and the meeting is photographed. The raw transcripts are distributed to all participants for editing and approval prior to release.

After all copy is approved, we turn over to you a complete transcript and photos of the meeting. This material is for your exclusive editorial use, if you wish to publish it. It will not be released to any other publication until we have an OK from you to do so.

All meeting costs, banquets, photography, transcriptions, etc. are borne by Owens-Corning. There is no financial obligation on the part of HEATING/ PIPING/AIR CONDITIONING.

In summary, Bob, we think a conference of this type makes good sense. In addition to information value, the forum environment has proved to be extremely conductive to listening, discussion and cooperation. I look forward to discussing this further with you at your earliest convenience.

Very truly yours,

Ted Agne

Dear Mr. Little:

Confirming our conversation, we look forward to your joining us in a round-table conference to discuss "The Role of Glass Fiber Duct in Modern Air Distribution." The conference will begin at 9:00 A.M. on January 11th, at the O'Hare Hilton, O'Hare International Airport.

Enclosed is an attendance roster and agenda.

The conference room doors will be open by 8:30 A.M. for coffee and doughnuts and informal introductions. We'll sit down at the conference table at 9:00 and break for cocktails and lunch at around 12:15. Following lunch, we'll wrap up formal discussion and aim for an adjournment at around 3:00 P.M.

The conference, which is sponsored by Owens-Corning Fiberglas, will be moderated by HEATING/PIPING/AIR CONDITIONING Magazine. Bob Korte, editor of HPAC, will serve as discussion chairman. He will later publish a story on our discussion and the conclusions we reach. The conference will be recorded and all participants will receive a copy of the conference transcript for approval prior to release to HPAC.

The conference will operate according to an agenda, which includes the following subject areas:

1. Where and where not to use glass fiber duct, perhaps as a function of air velocities and as a function of ambient conditions.

2. Advantages and disadvantages of glass for given applications, or concerns.

3. Costs, initial, installation, and life cycle (embracing productivity data, etc.).

4. Proper procedures for fabrications and erections.

5. Standards for adhesives, sealants, and tapes, as well as reinforcement.

6. Available grades of material and their applications.

7. Alleged or potential hazards of glass fiber duct, both fire and nonfire.

8. Case studies, giving historical data.

Of course, this is the initial agenda. If you have other subject areas you would like to have discussed, please feel free to suggest them.

Total participants will number around 12 to 15, and will include a cross section of large-, small-, and medium-sized contractors serving both commercial and multifamily construction; consulting engineers and other top people in air handling and related fields. A final attendance roster will be mailed out prior to the actual conference.

We'll be in touch with you soon with more specifics on the meeting. In the meantime, please feel free to call me collect should you have any questions, suggestions or if we may be of assistance.

Thank you for your assistance and cooperation.

Very truly yours,

Ted Agne

Before letters of invitation are mailed, a decision should be reached concerning whether the host organization will assume hotel and travel expenses, and whether honorariums will be offered to participants. There is no standard procedure, although experience indicates that payment of travel expenses helps attract top professionals. Likewise, honorariums are normally extended to outside experts participating in a TIS.

Telephone follow-up should be made to all invitees approximately ten days after invitations are mailed. As individuals accept, a formal schedule of events should be mailed. The letters should include names of hosts that participants can contact with questions about the event.

It is important to obtain participants' up-front views of TIS topics. A backgrounder based on these conversations should be developed and disseminated to attendees. A list of questions to be addressed should be included. This material will provide all information necessary for a common understanding of the TIS topic.

4. Exercise a certain degree of creativity in the selection of a TIS location. An aircraft company once held a seminar on maintenance problems in a hangar. A steel company held a session on the capabilities of new stainless steels in a mill.

The most important criteria in the selection of a meeting location is that it be appropriate for both a conference and lunch. If it is also possible to include a demonstration that supports discussion topics, so much the better. Hotels are usually selected for TIS programs because they are centrally located and provide adjoining conference/dining facilities.

The easier a host organization makes it for TIS participants to attend, the more prominent will be the industry representatives. For this reason, conventions offer attractive meeting formats. They attract the individuals who make competent TIS participants, and they help spotlight TIS activities.

5. Make arrangements with a hotel or other meeting facility by telephone, and immediately confirm in writing. All details, regardless how minor, should be commited to paper: name of meeting room, number of ashtrays, water pitchers, writing tablets, time of coffee and danish service, break periods, menus. It is essential that a representative of the host organization evaluate the meeting facility firsthand, and meet the hotel management member with whom the host's representatives will be dealing.

6. Plan either a half-day or full-day format. Half-day formats are preferred, but some topics require a full day to arrive at meaningful conclusions.

Half-day format:

9:00 A.M. – 9:30 A.M.	Coffee and pastry
9:30 A.M. – 12:30 P.M.	Discussion
12:30 P.M. – 1:00 P.M.	Cocktails
1:00 P.M. – 2:00 P.M.	Lunch

Full-day format:

9:00 A.M. – 9:30 A.M.	Coffee and pastry
9:30 A.M. – 12:30: P.M.	Discussion
12:30 P.M. – 1:30 P.M.	Lunch
2:00 P.M. – 3:00 P.M.	Workshops
3:00 P.M. – 4:00 P.M.	Discussion
4:00 P.M. – 5:00 P.M.	Development of Conclusions
6:00 P.M. – 7:00 P.M.	Cocktails
7:00 P.M. – 8:00 P.M.	Dinner

One of the TIS highlights is the cocktail and dinner period. The informality of this period permits participants to gather in small groups to discuss items of mutual interest, and it permits the host to talk with participants interested in ongoing professional relationships.

7. Prepare the agenda to approximate the following:

I. Introduction
Editor/monitor

II. Introduction of participants
Editor/monitor

III. Broad-brush comments to guide discussion
Senior representative of host organization

IV. Discussion topics
All participants

V. Conclusions
Editor/monitor and senior representatives of host organization

VI. Cocktails/Dinner
All participants

8. Record and photograph the seminar. The editor/monitor will require a complete transcript of the session for editorial coverage; the host organization will want a complete transcript for files, and participants should be sent transcripts.

The session should be recorded for transcribing. A high-quality reel-to-reel system is not required, but some people prefer it. A cassette recorder is reliable enough. Since conference tables are usually long, figure one mike for each seven participants. Three mikes plus a mixer plugged into a cassette recorder are necessary for conferences with twenty attendees or more. It is important that batteries not be depended upon for cassette operation. Weak batteries can cause distorted recordings. Determine during conference room inspections what extension-cord lengths should be.

A host organization public relations representative, or a representative of its public relations agency, should be on hand during the entire TIS. Part of his responsibility should be to jot down the names of participants as they speak. This guarantees that comments are attributed to the correct participants. Name cards should be positioned in front of each participant. Additionally, it should be requested that, during the first thirty minutes of the session, each participant volunteer his or her name before they speak.

9. Arrange for a run-through attended by the host organization's representatives, and the editor/monitor, the evening before the TIS. All items in the conference room should be inspected at this time: recording system, name cards, water glasses, pads, and pencils.

Post-TIS Activities

Post-TIS activities are important. Follow-up procedures assure the best possible editorial coverage in the editor/monitor's publication, and they assure that participants retain a favorable impression of the host organization's professional expertise. The following procedures are typical.

1. Provide the editor/monitor with photographs (black-and-white and color), and ascertain whether product photos would enhance coverage.

2. Provide the editor/monitor with a complete transcript as soon as possible. Determine whether the editor requires other material.

3. Send letters to all participants thanking them for their attendance. Provide a complete transcript, and request critical comments.

THE TIS POSITION PAPER: AN EXAMPLE

The following position paper was developed in support of a TIS concerning the use of a plastic honeycomb sandwich construction in boat hulls to reduce weight, increase strength, and save fuel.

> (MODERATOR'S INTRODUCTION) High interest rates and fuel prices have made the average boat buyer increasingly aware of the costs of owning any type of boat, large or small, sail or motor powered. Cost-conscious consumers want improved efficiency, without sacrificing performance or comfort. Boat builders must find means of providing the best value for the buyer's dollar, whether through improved design, additional features, or reduced weight.
>
> Weight reduction, in particular, has been identified as the pivotal problem facing the boating industry today. Reducing weight is a key method of improving or maintaining product performance in all sectors of the boat building trade—power vessels as well as sailboats.
>
> Sailboat manufacturers, for example, always have looked to reduce weight in their products, since lighter boats can be made more seaworthy. Multihull designs, of course, directly improve performance with weight reduction. Increased fuel costs are winning over power boaters to sailing, and these converts, like long-time sailing enthusiasts, desire high-performance, "speedy vessels."
>
> In power boats, consumers also are looking for greater efficiency without loss of performance or comfort. This problem may be compounded as the availability of mid-sized six- and eight-cylinder engines for marine use decreases.
>
> Honeycomb sandwich construction using (name of product) as a core material is among the most promising means of accomplishing the weight reduction needed in today's boating industry. This conference will explore the benefits of honeycomb technology in applications both as a component and as a basic structural material in all types of pleasure boats.

The effectiveness of the session as far as casting the product in a positive light is concerned is evident from these transcript excerpts:

> (CORPORATE SPOKESPERSON) I would like to give an overview of the material we will be discussing today. I would like to keep it in primer form, since gathered around the table we have really the world's leading experts in this technology and its applications in the boating industry.
>
> As you know, honeycomb has been used in nature for millions of years. Today, it is used by man to solve problems where great strength and low weight are simultaneously required.
>
> (Name of product) sandwich panels, for example, are nine times stiffer per unit weight than solid steel. The strength-to-weight and rigidity-to-weight ratios of

honeycomb sandwich panels are unmatched by any other structure, as illustrated in this chart comparing (name of product) structural extrusion, sheets and stringers, and plywood. These characteristics alone make it preferable to other sandwich composites as well as more conventional materials used in boat building.

We will look at the other properties of honeycomb sandwich structures, (name of product) in particular, in a moment.

• • • • • •

(CORPORATE SPOKESPERSON) This comes to be a very tough material. For example, this is a sample of a honeycomb panel with its facings applied (indicating). It is quite a tough material. It is very lightweight, too. Compared to other honeycomb core materials, (name of product) is much tougher, as is illustrated by these plots of toughness coefficient and is also illustrated in the example that I just gave.

In fact, (name of product) offers a unique combination of characteristics which are lacking in other honeycomb cores. This unique combination really centers around lightweight strength which is the key that drives anybody to a sandwich structure to begin with.

There are other materials that have lightweight strength. Aluminum can give lightweight strength but does not provide corrosion resistance or resilience from impact. Having all of these properties simultaneously is what we mean when we say it has a unique combination of properties.

This combination of physical properties has made (name of product) the material of choice in such wide-ranging applications as these downhill racing skis, which take a brutal pounding again and again.

In the aviation industry, (name of product) is used in both exterior components and in interior panels and compartments. In fact, the plane you flew in on yesterday or today probably had well over a thousand pounds of our product, not counting the phenolic resin or facing contained within it.

Other uses include the rotor blades of this helicopter where resistance to corrosion and fatigue are critical. It is used in the bay doors of the space shuttle, where proper functioning of parts can make or break a mission. I didn't think too much of that when I heard about it because it isn't a high volume application. But those doors are sixty feet long and that is a six-story door, if you will. You are pretty far from home where they have to open and close perfectly every time. So we need lightweight to get it up and extreme rigidity to make sure it functions properly.

Closer to home, (name of product) panels are used by the Coast Guard and Navy in many interior applications. This particular Coast Guard cutter saved nine tons of topside weight by adopting our honeycomb material in bulkhead joiner panels.

In pleasure boating, honeycomb panels are being used as components and in the Stiletto, as the basic hull material.

• • • • • •

(BOAT MANUFACTURER) That is the starting point. Ultimately the true test is going out there and doing it, testing and using the product in all possible combinations and conditions.

You do have to start somewhere. With this material as any other new technology or anything else you do, you generate a starting point and you go from there.

We have learned. We have no sophisticated design or engineering staff at all. We'll take on a new project very quickly and because we have, at this point, an innate ability within our own organization, we can look at a part and see what we have to do. We know what to begin with and we have the ability. A lot of the parts are fairly exotic.

I say this on the basis of our own past experience—with the Stiletto primarily. The Stiletto has been out for six years. There are 300 of them now sailing around the world, a number of them overseas. The boat has seen every conceivable condition at this point.

This experience has given us a great deal of confidence in the structure because it has been through everything a boat can go through. We know basically how to engineer a product regardless of what it is. We are doing a number of things. I will give you one quick example that we did last week.

We built a very large part for Prairie Boat Works in St. Petersburg, Florida. It is what they call a hard top. It is essentially a sun shade that fits behind the flybridge of their trawler. The part that they have been making out of polyester and glass sheet and stringer construction weighed 800 pounds.

We built this first part out of (name of product) and it was 154 pounds. It does all of the things that their other part did. Of course what they were interested in doing was reducing the weight aloft.

This was a very simple, fast way of taking 650 pounds out of the boat at a fairly high location. Again, that was one part that we could just look at.

We talked to them for a while and got a feel for what use that part was going to see. It is not really meant to be walked on, but it has been walked on frequently. So we designed it so that six or eight people could stand on it at one time.

· · · · · ·

(MARINE ENGINEER) In our experience what we found is due to the nature of this structure you don't get traumatic damage. In the worst situation, where you have a boat broadsided by another boat, and it certainly has happened with a number of Stilletos, there are a number of factors that minimize damage. One is that the Stiletto is so light it will kind of bounce out of the way.

Normally, what we find is rather than a large traumatic damage where a chunk is knocked out of the hole or something, there will be a tear and that is all you will get. Normally it will tear in a V-shaped area. Then that area will just kind of slot back into place.

If it's below the water line it may be taking on water. But it is just kind of trickling in. To repair that then you don't have to replace anything, you merely kind of patch over.

· · · · · ·

(BOAT MANUFACTURER) We have the problem of even if we could get maybe three or four thousand pounds out of a boat, I am talking on a cruising boat, that would be terrific because all the people want less fuel consumption and faster boats. There is obviously a trawler market but we are not in the trawler market. Everything we are selling is turbo charged. People want the speed. We have got to overcome the weight and it takes fuel to run it.

Magnum is saying we will build you lighter boats with a possible savings down the road. With sport fishermen, they are like kids who want to see who is the fastest on the block. So there is a place there.

I am sure you are familiar with their development of the panel. We are looking at that for decks.

Bob is also talking with the company that we deal with in California that does the teak plywood, the coring of that. That is an increase of over 100 percent, but we are looking at that, also.

How do we justify that pricewise? If we can get ¾-inch plywood, which is quite heavy, if we can eliminate that, it would be a tremendous thing.

Conference participants, in addition to representatives of the sponsoring manufacturer and the boating trade publication, included pleasure boat manufacturers, marine engineers and architects, and a boating industry consultant.

As a direct result of the TIS, boat manufacturers learned that the economics and design practicalities of this particular material brought it into the here-and-now. The manufacturers also learned how to incorporate the material in their designs. Two manufacturers requested detailed descriptions of how to use the material in their boats.

"POINT OF PURCHASE" PUBLIC RELATIONS

The fact that corporate sales staffs willingly support programs that include customer involvement is understandable. These activities create opportunities to generate sales. And the industrial public relations function is increasingly involved in programs of this sort. Some of these efforts are fundamental, others elaborate, but all involve direct contact between company and potential customers. Here are some examples of successful consumer confrontations.

Breaking into a New Market

An engineering and construction company with a solid reputation as a constructor of office buildings and other corporate and government facilities, was seeking to enter the college construction market. However, as a virtual unknown, it received little attention.

A market evaluation by public relations personnel uncovered the knowledge that many new laws had been enacted dealing with the availability of supplementary government funds for college and university building construction. School administrators were generally unaware of this assistance.

A multi-market seminar was arranged to help create attention for the firm in the college construction market. The seminar—designed specifically for administrators charged with responsibility for the construction and maintenance of buildings—was attended by as many as 250 administrators in one eastern location. Featured on the three-hour program were representatives of the federal government, who described eligibility for funding. An executive of the construction company moderated a multimedia presentation in which architects discussed new concepts in institutional construction. The seminar concluded with a ballroom luncheon during which members of the sponsoring firm dined with the school representatives and discussed construction possibilities.

Increasing Sales in an Existing Market

A manufacturer of products for open-plan offices was experiencing sluggish market response to its durable, yet expensive, line. Public relations counsel recommended scrapping traditional promotional techniques, including direct mail and trade publicity, and substituting direct approaches to target audiences—building owners and architects. The promotion took place in office environments and demonstrated how the client's products increased productivity.

The "on-location" sessions featured a multimedia presentation, and a panel discussion moderated by company representatives, engineers, and other experts endorsing open-office concepts.

More than 1,500 potential customers were reached on the nationwide tour, and the sales of millions of dollars of the company's products were influenced by this customer-involvement technique.

Increasing Sales by Introducing the Product in the Classroom

A leading factor in the office services industry determined that its sales, while strong, lacked the vitality they were capable of because secretarial personnel were not familiar enough to use their materials with complete effectiveness. The company's public relations agency determined, following research, that the only way to solve the problem was by educating students in the nation's leading secretarial schools regarding the proper methods of office communication.

An educational program involving instruction in office communications techniques was developed. A traveling spokesperson distributed thousands of teaching kits and appeared on television and radio talk shows across the United States. The program, conducted on an annual basis, has influenced more than 20,000 secretarial students. Additionally, hundreds of the company's teaching kits have been distributed to vocational schools.

There will be increased utilization of other industrial public relations techniques during the 1980s. Plant tours, for example, will take on added importance as new facilities go on line, and as new production equipment is introduced. The trade press will also be invited to participate in educational tours involving new technologies and production methods.

PLANT CLOSINGS: HOW TO COPE WITH A PUBLIC RELATIONS NIGHTMARE

Everyone directly involved in plant closings—management, employees and their families, suppliers, customers, and the local community—suffers when this most onerous of corporate misfortunes hits. Public relations people find shut-downs especially distasteful. The spreading of negative news goes against a publicist's stripe, and deep, long-lasting hostility is often caused by what many consider to be a lack of corporate responsibility for terminated employees and for their hometowns. Also, shutdowns commonly provoke accusations that companies are walking away from union entanglements, or that facilities are being shuttered to reap tax or other financial benefits.

As a result of uncertain economic conditions, international competition, and a trend toward the construction of new, energy-efficient facilities, plant closings are widespread. Hardest hit are the steel, meatpacking, automobile, rubber and textile industries. The local and regional hardships that shutdowns have had on some parts of the United States—particularly the mature industrial states in the northeast and the midwest—have attracted the attention of unions, workers, public interest groups and legislative bodies. Unions, in particular, are applying pressure to keep plants open, and are supporting plant closure legislation that would extend severance pay, provide for lengthy periods of notification before shutdowns, and permit unions and workers to offer plans to keep plants operating.

Unions are leading advocates of plant closure legislation because the labor movement could lose considerable strength if the shutdown climate in the United States is the same at the end of the 1980s as it was at the beginning. Most termination agreements do not favor work forces, because severance pay was not traditionally bargained for vigorously. One reason for this was the fact that, up to and including the 1960s, the nation's expanding economy quickly absorbed laid-off workers. But, starting in the 1970s, shutdowns became a serious problem. America's eroding industrial base could no longer provide employment for all those seeking work. Many workers lost faith in unionization. Some took nonunion jobs. And the ability of unions to organize and to bargain in a region where shutdowns have occurred was weakened.

Pressures for plant closure legislation will make it increasingly difficult for management to close manufacturing facilities during the 1980s. Maine and Wisconsin have adopted legislation that contains severance pay formulas, and almost twenty other states have considered bills that would discourage plant closings. Additionally, there is growing support for federal legislation that would require several years' notice before shutting down, plus improved severance pay for employees, and compensatory payments for communities losing industrial facilities. Historically, the only obligation of companies in the areas of advance notification and severance pay pertained to what had previously been negotiated.

What PR People Face: Inconsistencies of Logic and Law

The most bedeviling problems that public relations people face when developing and executing plant closing programs are inconsistencies of logic and law. Attempts are being made to reconcile these inconsistencies by legal, legislative and other means. But, emotional as well as business issues are involved, and solutions will be hard-won. Some of the most challenging problems include:

1. Pending legislation that would require companies to disclose intentions to close a plant two years in advance. Management contends that protracted

shutdowns will result in cancellation of credit lines, lost customers, and poor employee morale that would translate to absenteeism, productivity losses, and poor product quality.

2. The threat of legislation that would limit the distance from an existing plant that a company could relocate to. Aimed at reducing the economic and emotional havoc wrought by corporate moves out of industrial regions such as New England, the Middle Atlantic and Great Lakes states, opponents of these proposals claim they are unconstitutional and that they restrict interstate commerce. An Ohio proposal, since defeated, would have required companies with more than 100 employees to provide two years warning of a shutdown, to give workers severance pay equal to one week's salary for each year of service, and to provide a sum equal to ten percent of the total payroll to the community the company was leaving. Industrialists believe that, if this legislation had been enacted, it could have destroyed corporate development in Ohio.

3. Tax incentives that encourage the relocation of a facility after plant, property and equipment have been fully depreciated for tax purposes. Management claims this economically viable alternative is justifiable because they must provide the best possible operating climate for the protection of their shareholders' investments, and to remain competitive. Opponents of existing tax laws claim that they encourage "runaways" that devastate entire regions of the nation, and destroy the dreams and aspirations of workers and their families.

4. Shutdowns of mature unionized facilities, then either relocating to a nonunion area, or reopening a few years later in the same location with a young work force that has not accumulated substantial fringe benefits and high wages. The textile and electronics industries have been accused of this practice. Those speaking in defense of the tactic claim it is the only way possible to break "union strangleholds," to keep prices in line, and to remain competitive in the face of strong competition from both domestic and foreign companies.

5. Sun Belt moves that threaten to provoke a North-South confrontation. With the nation's industrial base shrinking, different sectors of the nation are competing with increasing fierceness for industry. The loosely unionized Sun Belt is winning this battle. But some observers believe the South will eventually turn up a loser, too. Overseas relocations, even in advanced, politically stable nations, are frequently more economically justifiable than moves within the continental United States.

6. State and national environmental regulations requiring clean air and water. The American citizenry uniformly supports environmental regulations, but the cost of pollution control equipment—sometimes several hundreds of millions of dollars—can force a company to take plants off line and relocate them in countries such as Brazil or Japan, where environmental considerations are not as important as they are in the United States.

7. Technologically obsolete plants that have labor-intensive manufacturing processes, and skilled, dedicated work forces. Frequently, plant modifications are so costly that management makes the decision to cut loose a plant with a superior work force. This sometimes means starting from scratch in a new location.

One point that should be made emphatically is that no two closures are similar. Industrial facilities have their own personalities, their own unions and skill levels, their own management traits and union contracts. And, there are many reasons for closing plants. Individual consideration should be given to each shutdown as public relations activities are planned.

What Public Relations Should Accomplish During Shutdowns: Seven Objectives

Generally, public relations shutdown objectives include all or some of the following:

- Inform the work force of shutdown and of individual termination dates; advise workers of severance packages, and procedures for filing for unemployment and other benefits; job search assistance.

- Inform the concerned public—plant community, unions, customers, suppliers, shareholders, the press, political and legislative officials, employees in other company locations—of the shutdown and of the reasons for it.

- Attempt to retain the support of the local community and unions during shutdown procedures.

- Position the company as a fair and responsible employer with concern for the well-being and prosperity of employees, plant communities, customers and suppliers.

- Squelch rumors that would distort the magnitude of the shutdown, or the reasons for it.

- Make sure that the financial, investment and banking communities understand the reasons for the shutdown, as well as corporate strategies for future growth and profitability.

- Help apprise customers and suppliers of the status of obligations, contractual and otherwise.

Public relations activities related to plant closures should be carefully coordinated with the company's lawyers, and with the Labor Relations, Sales, Production, Personnel, Purchasing and Security Departments. Shutdown activities move most smoothly when a team consisting of representatives from each of these areas is formed, and when a schedule of events, including times and dates, is adhered to. Absolute secrecy should be maintained during the pre-announcement phase of a shutdown, or relationships with key public figures such as employees, shareholders, customers, and suppliers could be jeopardized.

Although the complexities of plant shutdowns sometimes preclude the mounting of effective public relations activities, there are several reasons why time should be made to do the job right. For example, public relations activities should not be made final until other departments have completed their work. Corporate counsel must review legal agreements and contracts between the company and its customers and suppliers. The Production Department must determine orderly phase-out schedules. The Personnel Department will be involved in intensive work, including the preparation of individual severance packages and structuring of programs (frequently with the assistance of the Chamber of Commerce and employment agencies) to assist workers in finding jobs.

Shutdown Public Relations Programs: What to Do and When to Do It

When preliminary work is done, communications personnel, working with firm dates, can prepare plant closure public relations programs. Depending upon the complexity of the shutdowns and the time parameters involved, programs will vary from fundamental to elaborate. Public relations activities included in closure programs include the following.

* *Notice of Shutdown Intent*

  Usually, work forces in vulnerable facilities are aware months, even years, in advance that a shutdown is possible. Employees know that technological obsolescence, unprofitable or marginally profitable operations, or declining orders, cannot be tolerated forever. If a shutdown is a possibility, management should do nothing—such as significant donations to local philanthropies or the installation of new equipment—to indicate anything to the contrary.

  However, if a shutdown is not expected, the work force should be informed of it in a letter from the plant manager. Frequently, and for a variety of reasons, well-placed rumors are substituted for official correspondence.

  It is important that employees receive word of a closing directly from management, and that they receive it before it is disseminated, or while it is being disseminated, to other publics.

* *The Announcement*

  Announcement of a shutdown should be in several forms: verbal, news release, and in a letter to employees' homes.

  Employees should first learn of a closing from immediate supervisors in section meetings. If the plant is a relatively small one, members of the Personnel Department should handle announcements. If supervisors break the news, however, they should provide basic information, and notify employees of the time and place of Personnel Department follow-up meetings, at which termination procedures and severance benefits will be reviewed in depth. Information concerning vacation and termination pay, stock programs, union agreements, duration of medical and life insurance plans, and arrangements for pensions, unemployment and welfare would be included.

  The news release announcing a shutdown should include the following information:

Date and time of closing

Reasons for shutdown

Number of employees involved

Number of employees being relocated to other company facilities

Disposition of plant and equipment

Assistance company is rendering the community regarding locating another enterprise interested in operating the plant, funds for industrial development, etc

Extent of employees' severance package

Assistance to employees trying to find new jobs

Name and title of company officer making announcement, and name of official to call for additional information

Quotes should be included in plant closure news releases, because they are almost always used in newspaper coverage. And quotes provide the opportunity to put the company in as favorable a light as possib.le

Additional information disseminated with disclosure material should include the text of the plant management's statement to workers, letters of notification to local government and union leaders, and other information deemed important by management.

Public relations people working on shutdowns can expect numerous telephone calls and/or press requests for interviews following dissemination of basic news releases. Shutdowns cannot be played down or underestimated.

A letter to employees' homes is important. This communication provides straight-from-the-shoulder notification about a most serious situation, and it provides an opportunity for family discussions about the future.

Efforts should be made to contact all employees by telephone who are not in the plant when the closure announcement is made. Hearing such an announcement on the radio, or reading about it in the local newspaper, is disheartening.

- *Timing*
  If legal implications are not important to a plant closure date, public relations counsel should be sought regarding this sensitive matter. The periods around holidays such as Christmas, Thanksgiving and Easter are bad times to announce shutdowns; holiday notification creates deep-seated animosity. Press deadlines should also be taken into consideration, especially for weekly newspapers. One day's difference could prevent coverage in a weekly newspaper for a week.

  Two-to-three months is considered optimum for the development of a shutdown program. While ideal as far as evaluating the situation and holding discussions with all corporate disciplines involved, this time frame also provides the possibility for news leaks. One month is adequate to prepare shutdown strategies, if necessary.

  Friday is a popular day for plant closure announcements, the assumption being that employees have the weekend to absorb the news, to discuss it with their families, to develop questions regarding severance pay and benefits, and the best methods of securing new employment. A persuasive argument for early-in-the-week notification, on the other hand, is that employees have the opportunity to obtain all severance information right away, without fretting about it over a weekend.

Control of a shutdown timing is important to all publics involved, and to management and public relations staffers, who must prepare for a barrage of questions. The following notification schedule, which a major automobile manufacturer used for the closing of one of its assembly plants in Detroit (where 2,280 workers were laid off) is a good one. Notifications are squeezed into a thirty-minute time frame, and all local publics, including government and minority groups, are included.

A SHUTDOWN NOTIFICATION SCHEDULE FOR AN AUTOMOBILE ASSEMBLY PLANT

Time	People	Responsibility
9:00 A.M.	Plant Management Staff	Plant Manager
9:15 A.M.	Union Representatives	
	International	Corporate Labor Relations
	Plant Local	Plant Personnel
	Washington Office-UAW	Washington Office
9:15 A.M.	Government	
	Governor	Civic Affairs
	Michigan Senators	
	Riegle & Levin	Washington Office
	Cong. John Conyes, Jr.	Washington Office
	State Senator	
	David S. Holmes	Civic Affairs
	Rep. Joseph F. Young	Civic Affairs
	Mayor Coleman Young	Civic Affairs
	City Council	
	Special Groups:	
	NAACP	Urban Affairs
	Urban League	Urban Affairs
9:15 A.M.	Wire to Directors	
	Company	Public Affairs
9:30 A.M.	Plant Employees	Plant Staffs
	Supervisory	
	Salaried	
	Hourly	
	Follow-up:	
	All employees	
	Shareholders	
	Field	
	Dealers	
9:30 A.M.		
	News Media	Public Affairs

A PUBLIC RELATIONS SCHEDULE FOR A PLANT SHUTDOWN

Announcement −90 Days	Announcement −60 Days	Announcement −30 Days	ANNOUNCEMENT DAY	Announcement +90 − 120 Days
Organize shutdown committee: public relations, legal, personnel, sales, purchasing, labor relations representatives.	Prepare lists of questions-answers for all publics involved.	Draft (for approval) letter to employees.	Disseminate press materials by priority.	Form community meeting groups with management and regional business, political leaders, and Chamber of Commerce.
Develop coordinated shutdown plan with each discipline providing input.	Prepare slide script about benefits, terms of separation, methods of finding employ, for Personnel Dept.	Draft news release.	Respond to queries from press, other publics.	When possible, disseminate positive news releases about employee relocations, company efforts to find new use for plant, retraining programs.
Develop integrated response plan with all disciplines providing input re methods of working with publics such as employees, customers, suppliers, financial and press communities, regional business/political communities.	Prepare employee booklet regarding claiming entitlements, and terms of separation.	Familiarize management, shutdown committee, with method of informing all concerned of the closing.	Disseminate statement via Telex to other company locations.	Publicize available manpower in regional daily, business press.
Look for another job.		Draft statement to be read to employees by supervisors.		Provide support for sales, production, investor relations functions as they inform customers, suppliers, and the investment community about the shutdown.
Develop plan to coordinate all activities with top divisional, corporate management.		Draft financial disclosure release.		Discuss shutdown with local business forums such as Rotary, Chamber of Commerce, Kiwanis.
		Prepare statement explaining shutdown for other company locations.		Arrange appropriate farewell ceremony with gift for community.
		Designate specific staffers for day/night telephone duty.		

- *Community Meetings*

    It is sometimes recommended that corporate officials hold open meetings with community political and business leaders, especially if a company maintains other facilities in the area, or if there is a possibility that the firm might want to reinstitute operations in the future. These meetings provide excellent opportunities to clear the air and to meet the citizenry more than halfway. The importance of a shutdown to the lifeblood of a community cannot be overemphasized. It is not uncommon, for example, to have the jobs of 200 or more outside suppliers and service personnel lost, for every 100 jobs lost inside the company.

- *Ongoing News Releases*

    News releases explaining shutdown procedures should be issued after the initial shutdown release. Positive information about the placement and relocation of employees, or about company attempts to find new uses for the plant, exhibit a concern for the community and for the company's employees.

    Also, news releases concerning plant security measures could help to reduce theft, vandalism, or sabotage, frequent occurrences as disgruntled employees react to shutdowns.

- *Additional Public Relations Duties*

    Public relations staffers get involved in other areas of plant closure activity, such as assisting the Personnel Department with the writing and production of materials to aid employees' job searches, in the publicizing of available manpower in regional newspapers, and in recommending and presenting gifts to communities as final goodwill gestures.

    Public relations staffers should also include in their plant closure program recommendations back-up support to the Sales, Production and Investor Relations Departments. It is the responsibility of these departments to convince important publics such as customers, suppliers, and the investment community that the company is on solid footing, and that the closing will improve future prospects for customer service and corporate viability.

    Another important duty of the Public Relations Department is preparation of comments for plant management to use when informing employees of the shutdown. Public Relations should also prepare a list of questions that plant management can anticipate from employees, the press, customers and suppliers.

During the 1980s, American management will lose some of its prerogatives in the area of plant closings, as unions, workers, public interest groups and legislative bodies attempt to soften the blow when corporate axes fall. It is doubted that the American labor movement will gain anything like the leverage its counterparts in socialistic Europe have, though. In France, for instance, the government must grant authorization for a reduction in work force. In Germany, any significant change in a production facility, including reduction of the number of workers, relocations, or new work methods, must be reviewed by a works council. And in

England, workers live in government-owned and subsidized housing, and their rents are reduced if they are laid off.

PLANT OPENINGS: HOW TO TAKE ADVANTAGE OF THE PR FUNCTION'S DREAM COME TRUE

While the onus of plant closings has stained much of America's industrial landscape with gloom and despair, the hope and promise associated with plant openings has brightened the horizon of many U.S. cities and towns. The resurgence of plant openings will continue, too, as futuristic facilities with advanced automation go on line, as Sun Belt plants are commissioned, and as foreign companies build on America's shores.

Plant openings inspire as much enthusiasm as plant closings do depression. New plants stir new hopes: hopes for jobs and careers, cars and homes; hopes for personal accomplishment and status; hopes for personal progress. Communities, too, are stirred by the possibilities that new plants offer: possibilities for new streets and schools; improved public services; the chance to grow and prosper.

The public relations opportunities fundamental to a plant opening are many. Rarely do public relations practitioners have the chance to achieve positive recognition for a company as quickly and as dramatically as they do through plant openings.

Target audiences for plant opening public relations/publicity activities include:

- Local residential and business communities
- Employees
- Regional and local governments
- State and local media
- Trade publications
- Academe
- Customers and potential customers

If the new facility is significant enough, the financial community and the national press should be added. Plant openings offer the opportunity to forcefully present a corporate strategy for viability and marketing competitiveness.

How PR People Can Capitalize on Plant Openings

Objectives of public relations programs for plant openings would vary somewhat depending upon the importance of the facilities involved and the stature of the corporation in the region where the plant is located. They should include the following:

- Assist in the positive positioning of the company in the eyes of the local and regional press and business communities

- Introduce the company to the business, professional, press, and government communities in its home area

- Present the company as a leading factor in its industry, and as a good place to work and to grow professionally

- Present the company to its hometown as a good corporate citizen that is going to stay and grow in this location

- Help instill within the company's employees the realization that their company is on the move, and that it is operating with a soundly conceived growth strategy that will provide substantially more opportunities for employees

- Introduce employees to their new community, emphasizing recreational, educational, entertainment, artistic and other attributes

The public relations strategies that prove most effective for plant openings combine publicity, special activities involving both employees and the local citizenry, and the participation of those publics that will have day-to-day professional relations: the corporate, business, and government communities. Logos especially designed for plant openings help attract attention, and themes help to achieve positive recognition from diverse audiences.

Five Public Relations/Publicity Activities to Support a New Corporate Presence

1. *Press Announcements*

Announcements disseminated to the local, regional, and trade press should precede a new plant's official opening by many months and, not unusually, by a year or two. The first press release should be distributed when arrangements to construct a new facility have been finalized. This release should be followed by others describing construction progress. These releases should also be employed to introduce management to new communities. Statements concerning construction schedules and corporate activities that will be conducted in new facilities could be attributed to individual members of the management team. Managers could also be included in site photography.

A special, reasonably elaborate press kit should be developed for the opening ceremonies. This helps assure as extensive coverage as possible, and it provides comprehensive file materials for the press.

Included in the press kit should be a news release about the opening of the facility, a specification sheet concerning the building or buildings involved, information about the products that will be produced on the site, profiles of management, an annual report and a corporate fact book, and photographs of the new facility.

2. *Speaking Platforms*

Ideally, management would start to introduce a company to a new location before the work force occupies a new facility. The most effective way to make a favorable impression on a new hometown is for management to address influential business groups, such as Kiwanis, Rotary, professional and industrial development organizations. These groups welcome business spokespersons, and engagements can normally be arranged promptly. Presentations should be about twenty minutes in length, and should address topics most interesting to business audiences:

- Reasons for selecting local area
- Description of business parent company is involved in
- Description of facility being constructed
- Expansion plans
- Discussion of environmental impact that facility will have on community
- Evaluation of economic impact new facility will have on community, including types and amounts of goods purchased locally, number of employees to be relocated to area, number of local hires, amount of payroll

If a new company does not introduce itself before start-up, it will undoubtedly be barraged with invitations for speaking engagements and press interviews upon arrival. The most positive attention is achieved when local introductory campaigns are undertaken, and when speaking engagements and press interviews are pursued.

A quality introduction is necessary to insure a good first impression. Press materials should be produced by experienced public relations people. A local public relations firm can assist with press introductions and speaking engagements.

3. *Employee Dedication*

A special employee dedication—held before the official opening day and devoted exclusively to employees and their families—is recommended. A special employee ceremony lends an element of exclusivity, and provides management with the opportunity to rehearse before outside publics are involved. Frequently, employees have already occupied a new facility, at least partially, before a building is officially dedicated. Dedication ceremonies should be held regardless. Employees expect an "official" opening day.

Typical of ceremonies conducted for employees and their families are weekend affairs that also include regional sales meetings. These events frequently include tours of new facilities, audiovisual presentations concerning a company and/or a division, and festive affairs such as barbecues (on the corporate grounds if weather permits, in the company cafeteria if not). A typical schedule of events includes:

5:00 P.M.—Employee and family office tour

5:30 P.M.—Remarks by management

5:45 P.M.—Audiovisual presentation

6:10 P.M.—Family dinner

Entertainment is also frequently included in these festivities. It can be as simple or as elaborate as deemed appropriate, and might include: Dixieland bands; mini-circuses with clowns, mimes, puppet shows, bicycle and animal acts; and visits by well-known athletes.

4. *Official Opening Day*

Official opening day ceremonies should be targeted at the regional/local business, press and academic communities, plus local residents. Dignitaries should include the governor (or a representative), the mayor, legislators representing the region, plus representatives of the regional academic and business communities. Customers and suppliers are many times included.

The agenda for commemoration ceremonies should include a ribbon cutting, a tour of the facilities, and an audiovisual presentation that explains the commercial or office activities that will be conducted at the location. A luncheon—either catered on site, or held at a location such as a nearby country club—can highlight the festivities. A management representative should serve as master of ceremonies and offer suitable remarks. The governor or other high-ranking official would present the keynote speech, and other notables, such as the mayor, would participate.

The trade press is frequently invited to opening ceremonies. Special plant tours should be provided for the trade press, preferably the day following the official ceremonies, when management representatives such as the directors of production and research can make time available for in-depth interviews.

5. *Special Events*

An official dedication ceremony, especially if a facility is futuristic or otherwise unusual, provides an excellent opportunity for a company to host a special event that will gain attention for the corporation and its products, and for its technologies and manufacturing processes. The opportunities for special events are limitless. A company could host a sales meeting, for instance, for staffers from around the nation. Seminars with economic or manufacturing themes could be conducted, and noted authorities invited to participate. Or, in the case of a pharmaceutical company, a health symposium could be hosted.

International Connections
The Latest Trends and Techniques in International Public Relations

10

The relevance of stable national economies to a stable world was never more evident than during the early 1980s. Global unemployment, persistent inflation and high interest rates, plus the indelible specter of impending protectionist trade measures, all contributed to tenuous economic and business relationships between nations. And there are no indications that conditions will improve substantially in the near future, because of the complexity of problems confronting the world business community. These dilemmas include: attempting to steer a global course of sustainable economic growth that involves creating disinflation (a decrease in the rate of price increases), while dodging deflation (falling prices for goods), that could create universal depression; attempting to encourage universal economic recovery, when any sign of renewed vigor would probably be greeted with OPEC oil price increases; and, the problem of shoring up the International Monetary Fund—the international agency that lends money to nations experiencing temporary economic problems—when many industrial nations are short of cash, and when the debt problems of countries such as Mexico, Brazil, Venezuela, Argentina, South Korea and Yugoslavia have reached alarming proportions.

There are other monetary and sociopolitical problems. There is the enigma of tight money policies, instituted to combat inflation. Should the United States, plus other major industrial nations, relax these policies in hopes of sparking global economic recovery? Or would this ignite global inflation that would, in turn, induce deep recession? Should nations such as the United States, Japan, West Germany, France and England adopt economic expansionist policies aimed at regenerating world trade, especially among the developing nations?

THE RISE OF PROTECTIONISM

Political and emotional differences are creating cleavages in the free world. Protectionism, implicit or stated, is becoming the norm as nations grapple with difficult economic times. Government policies, quotas, and discriminatory taxation muffle fair trade in many nations. Japan is the most obvious enforcer of protectionist policies. Even the Tokyo Stock Exchange will not accept foreign security firms for membership.

Protectionism and nationalism are also driving wedges into United States-European relationships. Common agreement is lacking on many issues, including NATO strategies, the Soviet pipeline, and American policies in the Caribbean and in Latin America. There is European consternation over surmised United States indifference to including traditional friends in major policy decisions. And there is the belief of many Americans that a survival-oriented western Europe could not be relied upon as a determined bastion of defense against communist aggression.

Multinational Corporations Caught in the Middle

Multinational corporations are caught in the middle of these swirling socio-economic problems. But this does not necessarily mean the imminent demise of big business internationally. Multinational involvement in worldwide investment, according to the U.S. Department of Commerce, totals $350 billion. American corporations account for a whopping $164 billion of that total. Multinationals contribute jobs and economic and political stability to their regions of operation. These corporations command respect, even though there is also the probability that, given the worldwide socioeconomic climate, some governments will increase control over foreign companies. The activities most likely affected include plant relocations, working conditions, transfer pricing, taxation, percentage of profitability permitted to be withdrawn from host nations, and corporate disclosure.

What to Expect from the European Economic Community (EEC)

The member states of the European Economic Community (EEC) are expected to exert pressure for multinational reforms. The decade of the 1980s will probably see over 15 million EEC workers out of jobs. This situation, coupled with decreasing exports, will cause problems for multinationals. Also working against the foreign business community in Europe is the fact that most governments are minorities, and political leadership is minimal. Also, the EEC is ineffectual, and apparently incapable of providing the guidance required in difficult times.

Organization for Economic Cooperation and Development (OECD)

Another organization that plays a role as far as transnational corporations are concerned is the Organization for Economic Cooperation and Development (OECD), headquartered in Paris. The OECD, through its Declaration of International Investment and Multinational Enterprises, acknowledges the economic contributions of foreign corporations, and purports that multinational corporations operating in Europe should be extended "national treatment"—the same considerations granted indiginous companies. The OECD also supports dialogue between host nations and multinationals.

General Agreement on Tariffs & Trade (GATT)

The General Agreement on Tariffs & Trade (GATT) is also experiencing nationalistic difficulties. GATT receives substantial American support for the establishment of effective trade regulations between nations. This organization, with 88 members and about 900 delegates, has been the primary hope for the perpetuation of free trade in a protectionist era.

But even GATT's members had, by the end of 1982, devised new protectionist trade restrictions. And, these restrictions are contrary to EEC and GATT rules, and OECD recommendations.

THE MOST PRESSING INTERNATIONAL ISSUES
FACING PUBLIC RELATIONS TODAY

International public relations practitioners will be called upon to assist their companies in these difficult times. In the recent past, it was their assignment to monitor issues; now it is imperative that practitioners monitor events, and also propose plans of action to assist their companies in a protectionist era. The most pressing issues they will face include:

- *Corporate disclosure.* The item of primary concern to management in Europe, disclosure has been in the limelight for several years. Disclosure pertains to both corporate and financial matters. It involves working conditions, codetermination, employment guarantees, expansion and contraction of manufacturing facilities, automation, and other matters.

  Disclosure requirements are expected to intensify as the decade moves along, with both governments and unions pressing for change.

  The Vredeling initiative, proposed by the EEC and likely to be enacted sometime in 1986-1987, would require companies to inform employees about corporate/financial strategies and activities, and to hold explanatory sessions with employee representatives. While this proposal caused alarm among Europe's American companies, none of them, according to Mr. Amadee Turner, Chairman of the EEC's Legal Affairs Committee of the European Parliament, provided information that could have resulted in changes in the proposal.

- *Corporate Governance.* This term pertains to the establishment of social responsibilities for transnational corporations' overseas operations with members of the boards of directors of parent companies. No regulations are anticipated until the end of the 1980s.

- *Working conditions.* Similar to American workers' demands for dignity, self-expression, recognition, and timely communications, Europeans want better working conditions, and more authority in matters affecting the workplace.

- *Government involvement.* European governments are more deeply involved in their communities than are their American counterparts. Government involvement remains strong, especially in the areas of consumer protection, environmental controls, and employee rights, and cries for disengagement go unheeded. Government holds are not expected to be intensified during the 1980s, though.

New Approaches to International PR:
An Absolute Necessity

International public relations has not traditionally received the concerted attention of American management. For too long, yesterday's methods were successful enough to get the job done. But now, protectionism and other problems make new public relations approaches a necessity. Practitioners believe that management's non-involvement in overseas activities generally is a major reason why international bribery has become a way of corporate life. In fact, the International Chamber of Commerce publishes guidelines entitled "Extortion & Bribery," which contain recommendations for governments and for private enterprise to help alleviate this problem. Likewise, the U.S. Congress has enacted the Foreign Corrupt Practices Act, and the United Nations has, for several years, been attempting to write a U.N. Code of Conduct for Transnational Corporations. This code, while not legally binding, would require corporations to act with propriety as far as a host nation's cultural values and political affairs are concerned, to cooperate with balance of payment objectives, to disclose operating results, and to accept several obligations for employees.

International public relations practitioners must, if they have not yet, become accustomed to dealing with "regions," rather than with specific nations. Technology is regionalizing public relations activity by beaming news without regard for national boundaries. Also, powerful business communities—such as the European Common Market, The Association of South East Asian Nations, and the Latin American Free Trade Area—likewise transcend borders.

Events also move as the wind, and can involve many continents in a matter of days. The Nestlé infant formula controversy, which started when the company marketed a product overseas which was not approved for use in the United States, provided rights activists with fodder for a case against Third World marketing practices. But the situation created more commotion in America than overseas. Then, following further exposure at the World Health Assembly in 1981, the situation became a global cause célèbre, and involved many more agribusiness, food and pharmaceutical products.

Politically, a cartel between a European nation or nations and the United States, or between Japan and the United States, could also have public relations ramifications thousands of miles away.

Advertising via Satellite

Advertising agencies are expected to take advantage of transnational marketing via satellite during the 1980s. Commercial television regulations in Europe have, for many years, impeded the placement of advertisements. Satellite-beamed television advertisements will be most appropriate for products with universal identity, such as cola drinks, automobiles, and popular foods. In these cases, commercials will have powerful graphics, but few words. In other cases, English will be used as a master language or, when television technology reaches that point, a viewer will be able to select a desired language.

INTERNATIONAL INVESTOR RELATIONS: ONE OF THE FASTEST-GROWING AREAS OF TRANSNATIONAL PUBLIC RELATIONS

During the last half of the 1970s, European investors displayed an enduring infatuation with the shares of American companies, and, according to data of the Securities Industry Association, almost 25 percent of the stock traded in America in the early 1980s was by Europeans. There are several reasons for this, including the facts that OPEC funds are invested by European firms, and that Europeans consider America to be the world's foremost bastion of capitalism. Happily for investor relations managers, European investors tend to stay with situations long-term. They are less interested in near-term successes than are Americans. An abiding faith in management is apparently all that is necessary to earn an investor's loyalty.

European companies are also coming to America to raise equity, and they are coming in numbers unknown in the past. Many nations do not possess sufficient capital-raising mechanisms to satisfy the requirements of larger corporations, and this void is filled in New York. Investment banking houses are also contributing to the "go American" trend. The houses are purchasing undervalued European shares, and selling them to institutional investors in New York.

These trends are bringing foreign executives to American shores in growing numbers. But, in their attempts to woo U.S. investors, many of them are making serious public relations blunders, as explained later in this chapter.

Your Options for Managing Overseas Investor Relations

Because of the high European interest in American stocks, the investor relations function has gained new importance in the primary investing countries of England, Holland, Scotland, France, Germany, Switzerland, and Belgium. American companies that list on European stock exchanges have several options regarding overseas investor relations activities. A company can attempt to manage these activities with its own internal staff, can handle them through public relations firms either based in Europe or with European offices, with European or American-based brokerage firms or investment banking houses, or through specialized consultants that concentrate on building European sponsorship of American shares.

There are arguments for each. Brokerage firms/investment houses are tied to the financial community. They lack public relations expertise, though, and company meetings under their sponsorship tend to become "theirs," because they invite major customers. Public relations firms usually have strong press and corporate connections, but they sometimes lack adequate financial community contacts. And the small specialized firms frequently do not have the personnel strength to conduct long-term investor relations programs.

It behooves companies that are new to European investor relations programs to experiment, to find out which arrangement is the most productive for them. Sometimes it is a combination. What works best in one nation might not be best in another. It is also increasingly important for American companies to present themselves appropriately, because of the growing numbers of corporations that are courting European investors. If approaches are not properly orchestrated, suitors will fade into the crowd. It is also important to understand that the target of American investor relations programs is a relatively small group of specialists who follow U.S. companies for European institutions. These people sometimes attend several corporate presentations each week. European analysts differ from American analysts in that they very seldom have industry specialties, and they follow as many as fifty or more situations at any given time. Because of this work load, European analysts desire as much corporate material and research from American brokerage firms as possible.

Which Companies Should Conduct Investor Relations Programs?

Not every American company is a candidate for a European investor relations program. If a company is not interested in overseas borrowing, or if a company does not have European operations, there is little reason to expend the substantial amounts of time and money necessary for a successful European investor relations program. American companies that are candidates for these programs include those at the top of the *Fortune* 500 list (perhaps the first 75), and a few others of blue chip quality. These firms are being followed in Europe anyway, and the tracking that European institutions are doing may not be completely accurate or up to date.

Other companies that should consider European investor relations programs are transnationals in approximately the *Fortune* 350. Some of these firms, especially if they are in "trendy" industries such as electronics or high-tech, are probably being followed, too. The remainder of the *Fortune* 500 companies, plus smaller firms, will have difficult, but not necessarily impossible, experiences competing for attention in the European market, unless they have unusual or exciting stories to tell.

How to Approach European Investors

When making initial approaches to European investors, it is essential that preliminary work be undertaken, especially if the company is not well-known. This includes conducting research to ascertain the degree of knowledge that the European investment community and financial centers have in a specific company. Research can also help to identify shareholders, a difficult task in Europe, where ownership is shrouded in secrecy, and where disclosure laws do not exist. But, if research is conducted properly (it should consist of both telephone and personal interviews, plus mail samples, and it should be directed squarely at U.S. company specialists) it can reveal the ownership of a majority of shares.

Ideally, an approach to European money managers is not undertaken until a positive financial relations program has been conducted in the United States. A U.S. campaign generates research reports on the part of American brokerage firms, and these reports are received enthusiastically by European money managers.

Other preliminary work includes background mailings to the European financial community. Basic material includes the annual report, plus a letter of introduction from the chairman. More complete information includes the introductory letter and annual report, a corporate fact book, plus a primer concerning international operations.

It is necessary for a company to have assistance when making its initial approach to the European investment community. American brokers/investment bankers, public relations agencies or financial consultants, or European merchant bankers understand the refinements of the European investment community. This includes methods of attracting influential people to a presentation, conducting meetings, and handling pre-and-post research.

CRUCIAL ELEMENTS FOR CONDUCTING WELL-ORGANIZED EUROPEAN INVESTOR RELATIONS PROGRAMS

Preliminary Research

The crucial preliminary research phase should contribute a knowledge of ownership of company shares, attitudes of the financial community toward a company, and a knowledge of how to target a European investor relations program for maximum benefit.

Meetings

American companies are frequently criticized for conducting poor meetings for European money managers. The ten "don'ts" most frequently voiced include:

- Don't participate exclusively in meetings sponsored by brokerage houses/investment banking firms. Invitations should always be tendered by the company involved rather than by a financial concern, and the company should exercise control over the meeting.

- Don't embark on a European tour if there is nothing positive to report, or if enlightening and candid information concerning corporate direction and operational strategies is not going to be presented.

- Don't expect to schedule a European visit during spring or fall, the busiest periods of the year, without running into conflicts. Companies are skirting this problem by scheduling midwinter meetings. Additionally, stay away from large luncheon meetings. Arrange small, personal meetings that include influentials, and are conducive to give-and-take.

- Schedule meetings only at sites that are favored by the local financial community because of their convenience.

- Don't invite European portfolio managers to a presentation unless top management is involved. Otherwise, the managers will think they are receiving second class treatment. Not infrequently, American companies include public relations or investor relations personnel in meetings. It is beneficial for European money managers to have an identity with individuals they can call with questions in the future.

- Don't include inappropriate information in European presentations. Europeans expect information very similar to what American financial analysts want: meaningful figures, elaborations regarding corporate strategies, market situations, and competitive circumstances. Too frequently, American management talks down to European audiences, probably because they are presenting in a language that is not the first language of their audience.

  European financial audiences possess reasonable knowledge of English. American presenters should take into consideration the fact that European financial managers are also probably familiar, through research, with the presenting company. Basic historical information is not necessary, and presentations should not be steeped in industrial jargon. They should be aimed at the financial generalist.

- Don't use elaborate visuals, such as pretentious slides and films, which make European financial audiences, with the exception of those in Paris, suspect. Stick to basics; if slides are used to present financial information, or to simplify technical points of a product nature, they should be straightforward. What is also appreciated, when practical, is the exhibit of a company's products.

- Don't deliver an unstructured presentation. Total time should be about two hours, including a visitor's taxi time. European money managers expect to be back in their offices in time for the opening of the American stock markets at 3:00 P.M. their time. Thus, the major address should be kept to twenty minutes or slightly longer, and adequate time should be made available for in-depth questions and answers.

- Don't be a "Good Time Joe," and provide the European investment community with a glowing report of corporate operations, only to disappear when problems are encountered.

  American companies should only initiate activity in Europe if management intends to make an appearance every twelve to fifteen months, good times and bad. Distance can create unreasonable anxiety. Also, American management should understand that European money managers are more interested in the long term—and essentials such as capitalization, cash flow, management capability, market penetration, and corporate potential—than are their American counterparts.

- Don't forget to provide corporate information as quickly as possible. Earnings releases, for example, should be telexed to a company's European consultants or public relations agency for rapid dissemination. Other important materials, such as annual and interim reports, should also be treated in an expeditious manner.

An exclusive service of KLM Royal Dutch Airlines helps in the dissemination of materials in Europe. Called Publication Distribution Service, it includes flying materials to Amsterdam's Schiphol Airport, where materials are sorted, addressed and sacked, and transferred to a terminal postal facility. There they are disseminated by air, rail and highway. Deliveries are usually made three to five days after the materials leave the United States.

The most convenient meeting time in European cities is 12:00 noon. The most popular locations for meetings include:

- London: Guild Houses
- Edinburgh: Prestonfield House, Caledonian Hotel
- Geneva: Richemond, Des Bergues, Beau Rivage
- Zurich: Zunfthaus zur Meisen, Baur au Lac
- Amsterdam: Amstel, de l'Europe
- Frankfurt: Frankfurter Hof
- Paris: Crillon, Ritz

When important corporate executives plan European visits, it is expeditious to schedule meetings with management representatives of the larger institutions. The most productive sessions are limited to a few guests, and are held either at mealtime, or in the offices of institutions.

Financial mailing lists in Europe are something of a mystery. One popular service has a master list that contains close to 875 names. However, there appears to be substantial duplication, because a major international public relations agency works with a list of fewer than 600 names which represent almost 500 institutions, compared to fewer than 370 on the other list. Most of the lists of well-known services, though, are acceptable.

The Press

The corporate, financial, and trade press offer solid opportunities for European coverage. Normally, it is not expected that European newspapers will cover a management presentation, but frequently they will interview management for future stories, if notified of executive availability in advance. Financial advertising in European newspapers is also commonplace, and is not shied away from as it is in the United States.

Post-Meeting Research

Research following a management tour, while not as important as pre-tour research, can uncover important information. For example, post-meeting research can reveal the degree of acceptance of a corporate presentation; it can reveal the purchase of shares; and it can identify areas of the presentation that require strengthening.

European Stock Exchanges

The shares of approximately 200 American companies are sold on European stock exchanges, and it is believed that listings will increase. In many cases, the success of these listings is questionable. Considerable expense is involved, and an ongoing investor relations campaign is essential if the stock is to perform properly. Also, many investor relations specialists say that Europeans do most of their buying of shares of American companies on U.S. exchanges, so overseas listings are not essential. The major reasons for listing in Europe—for additional financing, to increase investors' awareness of a company, and to create closer ties with a host nation that could also be an important manufacturer/purchaser of a company's products—are not always enough to justify listing. While the benefits of listing vary from city to city, Zurich is the only example of a listing that is economically justifiable. The Swiss government does not permit some institutions in that nation to buy the shares of companies that are not listed on the Zurich exchange. Also, the trading volume on this exchange is usually robust.

Listing requirements and expenses vary. Information concerning European stock exchange listings can be obtained from many brokers and leading commercial and merchant banks, or from the following:

LONDON

The Stock Exchange
London EC2N 1HP, England

SWITZERLAND

Credit Suisse
Paradeplatz 8
Zurich, Switzerland

Union Bank of Switzerland
Bahnhofstr. 45
Zurich, Switzerland

Swiss Bank Corp.
1 Aeschenvorstadt
Basel, Switzerland

PARIS

Chambre Syndicale des Agents de Change
4, Place de la Bourse
75002 Paris, France

BRUSSELS

Banque Bruxelles Lambert
Avenue Marnix 24
1050 Brussels, Belgium

AMSTERDAM

Algemene Bank Nederland
Kreizersgracht
573-575, Amsterdam, Holland

GERMANY

Frankfurter Wertpapierborse
Borsenplatz, 6
Frankfurt/Main, Germany

Listing in Japan is an harrassing experience for American companies. Regulations are torturous, as are requirements for maintaining a listing. Annual reports are required to be prepared in both English and Japanese, and financial statements must be prepared according to both American and Japanese accounting principles.

The Dual Program: Combining Investor Relations with Marketing

Large, multinational corporations that pursue investor relations programs usually combine them with marketing programs. Objectives of these dual programs are:

- To provide both institutions and individual shareholders with information concerning corporate activities.
- To attempt to broaden the shareholder base, and help to expedite financing.
- To help keep customers loyal.
- To inform key publics such as customers, shareholders and the press of important technological and marketing advances.
- To apprise the trade, business, and financial press of corporate progress.

To accomplish these objectives, programs are designed to: keep the press informed of corporate activities by regular mailings and by visits from communications staffers; introduce key executives to members of the press and the financial communities when their European travel schedules permit; arrange formal presentations for the chief executive officer or president before important European audiences every twelve to fifteen months; provide key European journalists with the opportunity to visit major corporate facilities in the United States approximately every three years, and vice versa for select American journalists; conduct seminars for customers, the press and financial communities on subjects of global interest.

Where overseas markets are undercapitalized, or segmented (isolated from other markets of the world), foreign companies frequently come to America for capital. In fact, several large foreign companies, such as KLM, Novo, Sony, and Ericsson, have so many shares in American hands that their major equity center is in New York, not at home.

On this side of the ocean, there is renewed interest in foreign securities. This interest, plus the need for capitalization on the part of many overseas companies, is bringing foreign executives to the United States in increasing numbers. Similar to American executives in European markets, though, many foreign businessmen are approaching the U.S. market in the wrong fashion.

Common Mistakes Foreign Companies Make When Approaching the U.S. Market

Narrow perception of American investment community. Probably because most foreign nations have so few institutions, foreign corporations tend to focus their attention on a narrow band of investment firms in this country. Usually, they approach only giants, the likes of Citibank, Morgan Stanley, Merrill Lynch, Prudential Bache, Goldman Sachs, or Salomon. Not only are many potential buyers lost this way, but knowledge of the company is not spread throughout the investment community.

Forgetting the individual investor. Non-U.S. companies also tend to ignore the retail market in this country, again because of the situations they encounter back home. Most foreign nations have only small numbers of individual buyers. But, by forgetting about the individual American investor, overseas companies are missing out on a more stable and loyal investment segment than the irresolute institution.

Not following up. Many foreign companies spend considerable time and money on introductory American investor relations campaigns, and expect their issue to flourish without assistance after that. "To most foreign companies," reasons Mary Jo Dieckhaus, a New York investor relations specialist, "no news is good news. Here, no news is bad news." The price of shares usually suffers in these instances, and corporate recognition plunges.

Providing poor information. Foreign firms also commonly provide the U.S. investment community with inadequate information. Foreign executives are almost uniformly surprised by the amount and type of disclosure that is expected in America. Questions about profitability, sales breakdowns by division and/or product line, and effects of currency valuation on profits are seldom heard in Europe, but are among the most common questions in the United States.

Not communicating across the ocean. Not communicating frequently and effectively across the Atlantic is another common mistake of European multinationals. They tend to visit America infrequently, while the domestic investment community ideally wants three to four visits from top management representatives each year.

The use of domestic public relations firms by foreign multinationals is increasing. The investment community welcomes this trend, because it provides readily accessible sources of information every business day. The favored manner of communicating, however, is through a U.S.-based company representative who is fluent in English, and who is empowered to comment on a broad range of corporate matters, including financial topics.

Poor corporate documents. Inadequate corporate documents, especially annual reports, also receive frequent complaints from the American investment community. Annual report disclosure requirements are not nearly as rigid in Europe as they are in the United States. To provide the information desired, some companies are preparing abridged annual reports for America which, while not as complete as European renditions, contain the sort of information this investment community expects.

A NETHERLANDS COMPANY GOES PUBLIC IN THE UNITED STATES

Advanced Semiconductor Materials International N.V., a Netherlands-based semiconductor equipment manufacturer, was one of the first foreign companies to offer shares in the U.S., rather than European, equity market.

After the initial flurry of investment activity, little was done to keep the company in the minds of the American investment community. One year after its over-the-counter public offering, the company suffered from negative perceptions and lack of analyst following. Additionally, because of a thin float, the potential for investment in ASMI's shares was limited. Against this negative backdrop, a decision was made to initiate an investor relations program aimed at the most influential electronics analysts specializing in the semiconductor equipment sector. Objectives of the program were to increase the investment community's recognition of ASMI, to generate immediate sell-side attention, and to help create positive retail and institutional recommendations. The various elements of the program included:

- One-to-one meetings with important financial analysts.
- One-to-one meetings with influential members of the business-financial press.
- Presentations before small institutional investor groups.
- Speaking engagements before analyst society splinter groups.
- Industry seminars.

Total management time committed to the American program by the company's Dutch officers was approximately twelve days over a twelve-month period. Three-day management tours were scheduled every three months. In between management appearances, press releases and other corporate materials were disseminated to the investment community. Significantly, an investor relations agency provided the financial community with a U.S. contact point.

Following the first year of investor relations activity, the number of analysts following the stock increased, as did market makers. And the market value of ASMI's shares rose compared to those of competitive companies. This improvement permitted the company to successfully complete a secondary offering that gave the shareholder base an institutional orientation. The larger float also provided increased recognition of the company's position in its industry. This helped to transform the corporate profile from that of an emerging growth issue to one of a quality, high-growth investment alternative.

A CONVERSATION WITH MARY JO DIECKHAUS, INTERNATIONAL INVESTOR RELATIONS EXPERT

Conversations with international investor relations experts help to crystallize trends in this specialized field. Mary Jo Dieckhaus, Vice-President, Gavin Anderson & Company, a New York public relations consultancy with many international clients, is an authority in this area. Dieckhaus, who served as a registered broker and security analyst on Wall Street before entering the public relations business, explained the back-and-forth trends in international investor relations in an exclusive interview with the author of *Secrets of Successful Public Relations*.

Is corporate financing becoming increasingly international?

Yes, where Europe is concerned. No, for Japan, but we're making progress. The internationalization of capital markets has made substantial progress in Europe, particularly on the debt side. But it will be some time before we have a one-world marketplace incorporating Far Eastern markets. Restrictive financing terms remain a major obstacle to foreign companies entering the Japanese public debt market. Only a few hundred American companies meet the issuing requirement for samurai bonds. On the equity side, only a handful of U.S. companies make investor relations trips to the Far East. This also holds in reverse, despite growing interest in Pacific Basin equities from both American and European investors.

How extensive is European investment in American companies?

Of the estimated $250 billion invested in U.S. securities by foreigners, more than half is held by Europeans. European exchanges actively trade foreign shares. Percentages of volume range from about 10 percent on the London Exchange, to 30 percent in Zurich and Geneva. In Amsterdam, there is trading in the original shares of American companies rather than depository receipts. Shortly, the program will be expanded to trade Japanese shares in the original yen-dominated form. To facilitate trading in foreign securities, the EC is investigating the possibility of an European Securities Market System. This would be similar to the National Market System in the United States.

Could you give some examples of European capital market expansion?

Some American corporations have tapped the Eurobond market as adjuncts to borrowings from private European institutions. Europe is a regular stop on "due diligence" tours of American companies. And a few small American companies have gone public on the London Unlisted Securities Market, which is similar to our over-the-counter market. New equity sources have also sprouted in Paris, with the Second Marche, in Stockholm, with the OTC Borsenin Sweden, and in Amsterdam, with the Parallel Market.

What should American companies know about European investor relations activities?

American companies must know the basics of the European investment community. It is institutionally oriented. There is increasing individual investing, but this is usually done by affluent professionals, and by wealthy expatriates and retirees. Their portfolios are largely discretionary. The universal banks, particularly in Germany and Switzerland, dominate the investment scene.

What are the basic differences between the American and the European investment communities?

There are four basic differences.

One: Europeans tend to take macro-investment approaches. They figure which world economies will grow fastest, and which currencies will be most stable.

Then, they select which industries and companies they think will perform best.

Two: European investors are less detail conscious than Americans. Communications should stress how a company relates to its industry, and prospects for the industry worldwide.

Three: Europeans invest for the long term, so quarterly fluctuations don't bother them.

Four: Europe's professional investment community is small. All major institutions in England, Scotland, France, Germany, Switzerland, and The Netherlands have only about 250 U.S. analysts.

How important is continuity in a European investor relations program?

Extremely important. Between visits by American executives, a direct mail program can help fill gaps. An initial mailing should be followed within six months by additional disclosures. Annual and interim reports, and other company literature, should be disseminated routinely.

Are management meetings important to the European investment community?

Yes. In the loan and equity markets, management rapport is vital to developing long-term credit lines. Annual visits are preferred. Sometimes, visits can be spaced eighteen months apart. Analysts say that regular visits can add several points to a stock. Group meetings should be supplemented by office visits to selected analysts and bankers. And, luncheon meetings are not the only way to meet. Other hours are perfectly fine.

The 1980s will see giant strides in the internationalization of the world's capital markets. With this trend will probably come cries to alter the outdated concept of trading shares on the floor of a stock exchange. Worldwide shareholders reside in many different time zones, and a 10:00 A.M. to 4:00 P.M. New York trading day is incredibly restrictive. A far more appealing concept is some sort of worldwide telephone market, with shares traded dealer to dealer.

MAKING HEADWAY IN EUROPEAN EMPLOYEE RELATIONS

Employee relations is another area of primary concern among international public relations specialists. European workers are demanding increased personal recognition, and some governments are pressing for codetermination. Also, groups such as the European Economic Community are focusing attention on transnational employee-employer relationships.

It will be difficult for American companies to make swift and positive headway in the employee relations area. Many American firms are in the initial phases of sorting out domestic employee relations puzzles, and if an understanding is not gained about how to achieve good employee relations at home, it is doubtful that they can be achieved overseas. The place to start is with retention of competent outside counsel skilled in the implementation of international employee relations programs. Auditing and/or research should be undertaken in overseas facilities, followed by shirtsleeve meetings with local management, where audit research results would be involved, and objectives and methods of implementation agreed upon. Although American management looks askance at European codetermination, all experiences with this relatively new phenomenon have not been negative. In Germany, for instance, management reports minimal disruption during program implementation, and positive results in the areas of employee enlightenment and concern for corporate goals.

SPEAKING PLATFORMS: CONCILIATORY VS. ISOLATIONIST

As the 1980s progress, it can be expected that corporate leaders will focus attention on the schisms that are fracturing the international business community: unemployment, inflation, and shrinking markets.

Corporate speaking programs can be expected to be perplexingly conciliatory and aggressive, depending upon the position favored by individual managements: conciliatory when corporate leaders implore other nations to join the search for mutual solutions to contemporary business problems, aggressive when executives ask Congress to assume an isolationist stance and to build America from within.

Examples of speech themes supporting these two extremes are:

CONCILIATORY

"Economic, not Political, Solutions to the Protectionist Crisis"

"Solutions for the New Wave of Isolationism"

"Economic Solutions to Global Recovery"

ISOLATIONIST

"The Critical Erosion of America's Three Basic Industries: Steel, Autos, Heavy Manufacturing"

"America's Self-Inflicted Dependency on Foreign Minerals"

"Let's Keep a Strong Dollar"

The decade of the 1980s will be both challenging and stimulating in the area of international public relations. Not only will some functions, such as investor relations, require more concerted effort than before, but public relations people's monitoring methods will have to be sharper, and program strategies more decisive and direct, than in the past.

11

The Secret Is Out

Hoopla Is In

Hoopla—big events and the use of celebrities to highlight them—is a commonly employed public relations tool. Management's early resistance to big events (they were considered beneath the corporate dignity) has largely disappeared. In its place is the realization that big events can be carefully controlled, that they can attract positive attention to a company or to a product, and that they can make the cash register ring.

The use of celebrities—screen stars, athletes, astronauts, politicians, authors, medical doctors—adds to the excitement and credibility of a big event, and creates positive recognition for a company or product.

CREATING AND ORCHESTRATING THE BIG EVENT

Creating a big event can be a challenging assignment. Only the imagination limits the scope and appeal of a big event, or of the potential benefits to the sponsoring corporation. The big event could be a hot air balloon race, a circus, a marathon, a children's competition, a scholastic contest, an international symposium, or hundreds of other spectaculars.

Meticulous planning and coordination are required for the successful execution of a big event. These are usually elaborate affairs, fraught with stiff challenges in the areas of scheduling, logistics, press relations, spectator involvement, and celebrity promotion. Objectives of a big event must be realistic, and the implementation of promotional strategies must strike a balance between appropriateness and sound commercial practice.

A theme helps drive home the reasons for staging a big event. For example, a full-blown circus could be staged for employees of a company that achieved important sales of earnings goals. The objective of the celebration would be to create a spirit of fraternalism and accomplishment, and the circus could be called "The Colossal Celebration of Mutual Accomplishment."

Big events require substantial person-power to execute, and the normal contingent of public relations staffers may not be sufficient to assure smooth implementation. In these instances, support services should be rallied. Staffers of the mayor's office are an example of available back-up support, as are the staffs of organizations such as Rotary, Kiwanis, YMCA and YWCA.

The Royal Hanneford Circus, used by some of America's leading corporations for special events, is especially good at providing support. The circus, second largest indoor show in the nation, is presented under tents or in municipal facilities. The Royal Hanneford representative who works directly with corporations is:

Mr. John McConnell
Royal Hanneford Circus
1 Skyline Drive
Morristown, NJ 07960
(201) 539-6481

Example: Schieffelin's Statue of Liberty Celebration

The large, well-known wine importer successfully publicized France's Moët champagne by hosting a fund-raising celebration for the American Museum of Immigration at the Statue of Liberty just prior to the Fourth of July.

Logically associating France with both Moët and the gift of the Statue, the event drew more than 300 celebrities, diplomats, and government officials, who consumed Moët champagne, and who contributed thousands of dollars to the museum. The gallery is housed in the statue's base. Moët was also served when Miss Liberty was dedicated in 1866.

The celebration included a water-spraying New York City fireboat, the Newport Jazz Festival All-Stars, and a re-creation of the original dedication ceremonies.

More than twenty newspaper features described the event, and radio and television highlighted it as the Fourth of July neared. Moët sales rose both regionally and nationally.

"Don't I Know You from Somewhere?"
Secrets for Selecting and Approaching Celebrities

Selection of a celebrity to represent a company should take into consideration the type of event being staged and the notable's specialty. A famous track star could present trophies at a marathon. An astronaut could serve as master of ceremonies at a balloon race. An economist of international stature could chair a prestigious business symposium.

When approaching a celebrity to participate in a big event, it is customary to explain in a letter the event, the sponsoring organization, the extent of the individual's participation, honoraria, travel arrangements, and other important details. A telephone call should follow in a few days and, if the celebrity expresses interest in participating, a meeting (usually for lunch) should be arranged.

It is expeditious to deal with a celebrity directly. Notables do not usually publish their telephone numbers, but they can frequently be contacted through their place of business (a television network, a movie production company, a book publisher), or through business associations or professional groups.

Many celebrities are represented by agents or by services that manage a stable of notables. In these situations, the agents contact the celebrities, handle all negotiations, and provide the contractual agreement. Agents can be troublesome, however, and their fees add to the cost of a celebrity's services. Sometimes, it can be difficult to locate agents—who want to be sole points of contact in dealings with the notable—and valuable time can be lost reaching the celebrity. The agent's fee is usually added to the notable's charge for services. Agents are listed in the Yellow Pages under "Celebrity Agencies," and "Theatrical Agencies." One benefit of agents is that they represent several celebrities, and can provide a selection from which to choose. The following are some major New York City agents.

Agents for the Arts Inc.
1650 Broadway
New York, NY 10019
(212) 247-3220

International Beautiful People Unlimited
330 West 56 Street
New York, NY 10019
(212) 765-7793

William Morris Agency, Inc.
1350 Avenue of the Americas
New York, NY 10019
(212) 586-5100

Sutton Artists Group
Suite #512
119 West 57 Street
New York, NY 10019

Universal Talents & Images
505 Fifth Avenue
New York, NY 10017
(212) 661-3896

Writers & Artists Agency
162 West 56 Street
New York, NY 10019
(212) 246-9029

If the celebrity will provide his or her home address and telephone number, substantial time can be saved during execution of a big event. Contrary to general expectation, notables are usually easily approachable and are not difficult to establish a relationship with. The temperamental celebrity, while not rare, is also not the norm. Celebrities are generally friendly, courteous, dependable and cooperative.

The cost of celebrities' services can be surprisingly reasonable—frequently, in the range of $1,000–$10,000 a day, depending on the time and travel required. Out-of-pocket costs are added to the fee. However, it is possible to pay as much as $25,000 per day for a well-known and currently active politician, movie star or athlete. Sometimes the notable will request an amount equal to the federal taxes he or she will be required to pay, in addition to the fee.

A SAMPLE CONTRACT FOR CELEBRITY SERVICES

Contracts are necessary, but not necessarily complicated or difficult to prepare. It is recommended that contracts be as simple as possible, in letter form, and that the document protect the sponsoring company in all areas where the corporation could be damaged if a celebrity does not perform as agreed. The following contract, which could be considered reasonably elaborate, is typical of those prepared for public relations agencies arranging the representation of celebrities for big events being conducted for client companies.

Dear (name of celebrity):

This letter confirms the agreement between you and (name of public relations agency) on behalf of its client, (name of client).

1. Term
   The initial term of this agreement shall commence on the date hereof and continue through (date). (Agency) may, if it so elects, extend the term of this agreement upon terms and conditions to be mutually agreed upon in good faith.

2. Services
   You agree to render your services as a spokesperson for (Client), including participation in a media tour. You agree to attend all meetings, interviews and personal appearances scheduled for you by (Agency) in connection therewith. It is currently anticipated that your services will be required for at least two (2) days in (year), and twenty (20) days in (year).

   You agree to render all services normally required by (Agency) of its spokespersons, including attendance at briefing sessions and (Client) meetings at the times and places designated by (Agency), subject to your bona fide professional requirements.

3. Compensation
   As full compensation for your services, use of publicity materials produced in connection with this agreement and all other rights granted and obligations assumed by you hereunder, (Agency) agrees to pay and you agree to accept the sum of one thousand dollars ($1,000) for each day (excluding travel days) you render services pursuant to Section 2 above.

4. Travel Expenses
   In the event you are required to travel in order to render your services hereunder, (Agency) shall reimburse you for the round trip transportation and reasonable living expenses you incur. All such reimbursements shall be made as soon as reasonably possible after you submit written documentation of the expenses incurred.

5. Name and Likeness
   Subject to your prior approval, which shall not be unreasonably withheld, you hereby grant to (Agency) the unlimited right to include your name and likeness along with statements made by you in all publicity, promotional and educational materials which (Agency) writes, produces and/or distributes on (Client) behalf in connection with this agreement.

6. Agency/Client
   (Agency) is acting as agent for (Client). All rights, benefits, privileges and properties vested in (Agency) pursuant to this agreement are vested in (Agency) for the benefit of (Client) and may be exercised by either (Agency) or (Client). All obligations, liabilities and duties imposed pursuant to this agreement are imposed upon (Agency) as agent for a disclosed principal and not as principal.

7. Commissions
   Neither (Agency) nor (Client) shall be obligated to pay any brokers or booking commissions which may become payable in connection with your services hereunder.

8. Ownership
   All publicity and promotional materials produced hereunder shall be and remain the sole and absolute property of (Client), and you shall have no right, title or interest of any kind in or to such materials or any component thereof.

9. Use
   Neither (Client) nor (Agency) shall have any obligation to use your services for any minimum number of days. It is understood by (Agency) and (Client) that entire liability hereunder may be discharged by the payment of the sum required pursuant to Section 3 hereof for the services you actually render. Subject to such payment, (Agency) may terminate this agreement at any time.

10. Representation
    You hereby represent that you are free to perform the provisions contained herein, and that you do not have nor shall you enter into any commitments in conflict herewith.

11. Indemnity
    You agree to indemnify and hold (Agency) and (Client) harmless from and against any claims, loss or damage resulting from the breach by you of any of the foregoing warranties and representations made by you hereunder. This indemnity shall survive the expiration or termination of this agreement.

12. Exclusivity
    During the term of this agreement, you agree that you will not render your services or authorize the use of your name, likeness or endorsement in the publicity, advertising or promotion in any medium or engage in any promotional activities on behalf of any person, firm or corporation which manufactures, distributes, uses and/or sells any product competitive with, and posed as an alternative to, that manufactured by (Client).

13. Morals
    If you should be charged with the commission of any act which is an offense involving moral turpitude under federal, state, or local laws, or should you commit any act which might bring (Agency) and/or (Client) into disrepute,

contempt, scandal, or ridicule, (Agency) shall have the immediate right to terminate this agreement and (Agency) shall be entitled to a refund equivalent to a percentage of the compensation received by you hereunder. Such percentage shall be determined by dividing the number of days remaining in the term after such termination by the total number of days in the term. In no event shall you be required to refund any compensation paid for the services you actually render.

14. Independent Contractor
   a. You have entered into this agreement as an independent contractor and not as an employee of (Agency), and therefore you will not be eligible for any of (Agency) employee benefits.

   b. You agree to discharge all obligations imposed by any applicable union code or by any orders now or hereafter in force, including without limitation, those relating to federal, state, and local income taxes, unemployment compensation or insurance, self-employment taxes and workmen's compensation, and, including the filing of all returns and reports and the payment of all assessments, taxes and other sums required of independent contractors.

   c. You agree to indemnify and hold (Agency) and (Client) harmless from and against any and all claims, actions, damages, liabilities and expenses, including attorney's fees, arising out of or in connection with your failure to discharge your responsibilities as an independent contractor pursuant to this Section 14.

15. Law Governing
   This agreement shall be governed by and construed according to the laws of the State of (name of state) as if it were to be performed wholly therein.

16. Entire Agreement
   This agreement constitutes the entire understanding between you and (Agency) with respect to the subject matter therein. Any waiver, modification, or addition to this agreement shall not be valid unless in writing and signed by you and (Agency).

17. Titles
   Titles are for reference only. In the event of a conflict between the title and the content of a section, the content of each section shall control.

Please indicate your agreement to the foregoing by signing in the space provided below and returning two signed copies of this letter to (Agency). A fully executed copy will then be returned to you.

Very truly yours,
(Agency)

_____

Accepted and Agreed:

_____   (Celebrity's name)   _____

Social Security Number: _____

It is important that all dates, times, and places be spelled out. Many celebrities travel extensively and must arrange travel schedules to accommodate extra work loads. Some public relations people retain backup notables in the event the primary celebrity is unable to appear.

All celebrities should be thoroughly coached regarding their responsibilities, and the public relations representative assigned to the notable should make sure that the celebrity's participation is as agreed upon.

It is common practice to provide amenities such as first-class air travel, first-rate hotels, and limousines when celebrities are traveling. Some notables request that these provisions be included in contracts.

12

Electronic Innovations in the Public Relations Office

Throughout history, technology has nudged those who work with words, forcing them to change their basic techniques for committing thoughts to paper. The quill yielded to the steel tip pen, which acquiesced to the fountain pen, which gave way to the ball point pen, which acceded to the felt tip pen, which assented to nylon tip writing instruments. Somewhere in the midst of all this superannuation—specifically, in 1874—the typewriter was invented by E. Remington & Sons. In 1920 the electric typewriter debuted and, in 1961, the *IBM ball*. Then there was the printing press, which came into the office in the form of the mimeograph, which was displaced by the office copier, which was rendered obsolete by computerization. Which is where we stand today.

Never has technological advance been as wide-ranging or as inclusive as that created by today's electronic technology, which is revolutionizing the manner in which the public relations business is conducted.

Stored information and the ability to use it proliferates. A single chip contains more information than the human mind. Writer Isaac Asimov claims the electronic revolution "is probably going to be the greatest change—and the most far-reaching in its implications—of anything since the invention of speech itself, simply because it is being felt so enormously all over the world."

Lawyers were the first professionals to use computers. The full-text retrieval capabilities of computers helped lawyers to reduce, and in some cases to eliminate, the requirement for extensive libraries. Public relations people were also early users. This is appropriate, since public relations is a business of words and ideas. Public relations practitioners are generating a lot of ideas regarding how to best use the electronic revolution to improve their business, and they have already put it to work easing the burden of writing, editing, storing, and disseminating the words they generate.

Entering the 1980s, public relations firms and departments were employing electronics primarily for its word processing capabilities, and to communicate with other word processing systems around the nation. These capabilities were not the sole property of the large agencies or of the larger corporate public relations staffs. Small firms were also computerizing, since basic equipment costs only about half the price of the average automobile.

The electronic revolution is so broad and touches so many facets of the public relations business, that its proper place is still unknown. Electronic tools help public relations people to save incalculable amounts of time, and they can dramatically increase the profitability, accuracy, and range of public relations activities. The electronic tools being used in the public relations business include: word processing, teleconferencing, picturephones, electronic mail, voice mail, corporate video, electronic newsletters, computer generation of graphics, paper-less news dissemination, computerized media information, and teletext and videotext.

WORD PROCESSING: A MUST FOR PR EFFICIENCY AND ECONOMY

It can be safely stated that the public relations business can no longer rely solely on the typewritten word if it is to be as efficient and as economically viable as possible, and if it is to perform as accurately and as expeditiously as possible. To accomplish this, computerization is necessary. But how much? Developing a word processing capability for those public relations operations that generate large amounts of typewritten material is the usual starting point.

The needs for word processing equipment in the public relations business are intensive, and the majority of public relations operations will have this capability by the end of the 1980s. Word processing equipment can produce any document that is "typeable" (such as letters, speeches, news releases, charts, budgets, contracts). Operators type words that appear on the electronic screen (cathode ray tube). The copy is then memorized on a diskette and typed on paper at speeds about six times faster than the average electric typewriter. Material can be stored and retrieved instantly.

Today's word processing equipment can also interface with other computers. If links are established, equipment in one location can receive entire manuscripts or changes in documents from computers in other locations. This provides users with an original plus a stored record with changes incorporated. There is no need to commit to paper or risk error by reading copy changes over the telephone. This is an especially valuable capability when important corporate documents such as annual and interim reports are being prepared. The same capability can also speed typesetting work.

Some of the glories of word processing, as far as individual public relations practitioners are concerned, include the writing process. It is faster than an electric typewriter, and you do not have to retype copy changes. You merely make changes on the video screen, touch a button, and the machine prints a new page. Spelling mistakes can also be detected by the computer.

Research can be done right on the computer, using data banks. Word processors are almost silent—all you hear is the muffled tap-tap-tap of the keys—and you are not restricted to any one work area, such as a desk or typewriter table. Many computer keyboards are detachable. You can move them to any location where you will be comfortable.

TELECONFERENCING: EXTRACTING THE REAL BENEFITS FROM ALL THE BALLYHOO

The term "teleconferencing" usually refers to the use of closed-circuit television to communicate between two or more people in two or more locations. But teleconferencing can also refer to communications involving the telephone, conference telephone hookups, electronic blackboards (whereby an individual in one location writes on a blackboard, and the words appear on a television screen at another location), and other less-utilized technologies.

Public relations people almost universally refer to closed-circuit television when discussing teleconferencing, however. While not new—it was first used in 1950 for medical and sports purposes—teleconferencing did not come into its own until satellite transmission availability made the technology commercially feasible in 1975.

Teleconferencing has been ballyhooed as the electronic marvel that will save enormous amounts of executive time and travel expense while substantially increasing managerial productivity. Believers claim a minimum of 30 percent of the routine business meetings held by the end of the 1980s will be conducted via teleconferencing. Hotel chains such as Hilton, Holiday Inn and Hyatt are investing in rooftop dishes and teleconferencing equipment to lure business trade. And airlines are studying the lost revenues they can expect as a result of this tool's utilization.

Regardless of what the ballyhooers say, video teleconferencing is viewed by responsible communications experts as a tool that will improve communications—and public relations—techniques, but which will not necessarily revolutionize them.

There is a complexity about video teleconferencing that is restrictive in itself. This sophisticated tool demands special training, rehearsal, and supervision by a knowledgeable professional technician. Complexities extend to the structure of video teleconferenced meetings. In addition, time frames are limited and must be adhered to, participants must be rehearsed to respond in a manner that will respect these time frames, and those attending must accept the psychology of a teleconferenced meeting.

Teleconferencing is not a cure-all. There are no substitutes for face-to-face meetings. But video teleconferencing can be useful. If, for example, there is a need to transmit information to a geographically separated audience, this is a practical, albeit expensive, method. You can take information to people employing this medium, rather than taking people to the source of the information.

If there were a medical symposium in Europe that would be of major interest to the professional community in the United States, it could be presented in

American hospitals. But the efforts would have to be coordinated by experts. The satellite program would originate in Europe, be transmitted via uplink (an earth station with antenna for sending television signals to a satellite) to International Atlantic satellite, then, via downlink (an earth station that receives television signals from a satellite) to domestic stations in either Maine or Virginia. Then, there would follow an uplink to a domestic communications satellite, and a downlink to the areas you are interested in reaching. Temporary TVROs (television receivers only) would have to be installed at hospitals that did not have equipment. And local connections into the hospitals would have to be accomplished through the use of AT&T land lines. Signals would be transmitted from the European point of origin to the hospitals in the United States in a matter of seconds.

Teleconferencing will become common during the 1980s. But the technique should not be overvalued, oversold, or overpraised. Teleconferencing is a specialized communications technique that will help the public relations business improve its communications when dealing with seminars, annual meetings, press conferences and the like. The fact that this technique will become an acceptable communications practice is supported by the teleconferencing equipment expenditures of American companies—approximately $200 million in 1981, and an estimated $1.5 billion in 1986 or 1987.

Points to Consider When Deciding Whether to Use Teleconferencing

When evaluating the use of teleconferencing, the public relations practitioner should consider the following points:

- The event should be important enough to justify the expenditure of a substantial amount of money.
- Companies that specialize in the field of teleconferencing should be consulted at the outset, and one should be retained to administer the project.
- The program should be live. Otherwise, tape will suffice.
- Generally, the program should be interactive, but this is not always necessary. Educational teleconferences, say, from the site of a symposium to other locations, are frequently well-received and are not interactive. And telephones can provide at least an element of "interactiveness."
- The teleconference should be structured and scheduled, and should be preceded by communications training sessions if participants are not experienced in presentation techniques.
- The teleconference should always incorporate the highest possible broadcast technical standards. The possibility of failure, or of a poor quality production, is great.

Public Satellite Services Consortium, Washington, D.C. conducts workshops about teleconferencing. The organization also publishes a text on the subject, called *Teleguide: A Handbook for Video Teleconferencing Planners.* Write: PSSC, 1660 L Street, N. W., Washington, D.C. 20036.

PICTUREPHONES: MAKING UP FOR A SLOW START

A more intimate teleconferencing technique than a television screen (although the effectiveness of large-screen, rear-projected teleconferences should not be underestimated) is provided by Picturephones, which are coming into their own after early failures. These communications tools are more specialized than straight teleconferencing methods, and are best employed for small groups, such as corporate directors located in different areas of the country. Similar to most new technologies, Picturephones are expensive. Bell Telephone has a plan for public/private corporate installations. There is a one-time fee for private room installation of almost $125,000. On top of this, there is a monthly rental and access charge of over $13,000, plus a charge of $250 per mile for connecting the private room with Bell. There is, finally, a charge for every Picturephone use, just as there is a charge for every telephone use. The charge depends upon distance and duration of calls.

HOW TO HOP ON THE ELECTRONIC MAIL BANDWAGON

This communications technology should improve dramatically during the 1980s. Electronic mail refers to the electronic transmission of messages using either land-based wires, satellite communications systems, or microwaves. And the future of electronic mail seems assured, since it is based on the assumption that business people desire their communications to get through more quickly and with more assurance than if the mails were used. Electronic mail options include facsimile, Mailgram, Telex, TWX, Videotex, communicating typewriters, and message-switching systems.

Electronic mail is common in the public relations business. Its cost-effectiveness will, to a large degree, determine its rate of growth. But, at the current level of acceptance, it appears that electronic mail devices will soon become as common as calculators and copiers in public relations offices. The establishment of satellite and fiber optics (light-wave communications) links will hasten the use of electronic mail. These technologies will permit total automation of electronic mail systems, and will render them practical for home use, too.

VOICE-MAIL: CORPORATE MESSAGES AT YOUR CONVENIENCE

Another method of electronically disseminating messages, voice-mail employs computers to store messages until a business person has time to respond to them. Voice-mail has editing capabilities, and is suitable for use during evening hours or during the day, when the receiver of the message is unavailable or busy at another task.

THE TWO FACES OF CORPORATE VIDEO

Corporate video is used as an employee information tool, and for razzle-dazzle applications such as the telecasting by satellite and by cable television of annual reports and annual meetings. While there was, early on, something of a rush to get into video for employee communications purposes, this trend has cooled, and large amounts of expensive equipment are gathering dust in dark corporate studios. Conversely, there never was a sincere rush to be among the first to participate in the production of electronic annual reports, or to provide shareholders, financial analysts and the business press with videotapes of important corporate functions.

Video for Employee Communications

Video was originally thought to be a panacea for employee communications, because of the medium's capability for instantaneous dissemination of information and because of its credibility with the American public. But the cure-all had some flaws. Fundamentally, video was an impractical communications tool for the factory, because production suffered when employees were taken off machines and marshalled into training rooms to view corporate programs. So corporate video, probably rightfully, became primarily a management communications tool. There are no indications that this will change during the 1980s.

Companies that do initiate corporate video capabilities are cautioned to keep their ventures exploratory and simple. Video can be extraordinarily expensive, both in the areas of equipment and manpower, unless concerted efforts are made to stick to basics. Elaborate equipment is not usually necessary, because equipment and human capabilities can be rented or obtained on a freelance basis.

Equipment purchase should be evaluated in comparison with rental. The latter frequently is the most practical, since equipment quickly becomes obsolete. If a corporate studio is to be built, it is usually best to stick to basics, or to what is referred to as a "box" studio. This is an unadorned studio with sets and lights; cameras and sound equipment are rented as required. If more elaborate equipment is justified, it can be added as experience is acquired.

Corporate video can cost inordinate amounts of money, and it can leave egg on the faces of public relations people. The corporate video experience must be controlled, and the best way to control it is to hold back on spending, to ease into the medium, and to continually evaluate the success, or lack of it, attributable to video.

Telecasting to External Audiences

Undoubtedly, with satellite communications circuits abounding, and with deregulation encouraging a proliferation of cable television systems, American corporations will start following the pioneering example of Emhart Corporation, and get into telecasting to external audiences. There has been no rush to do this, however.

First, corporate video candidates must have interesting stories. Many companies, such as those with commodity product lines, those suffering recessionary or inflationary problems, or those lagging competitively, would not want to create increased attention to their less-than-desirable status by airing corporate plights on the tube.

The most appropriate candidates for corporate video are companies that have grown, usually through acquisition and merger, and which have assumed new identities, new products, and new promise in the process. The drama and credibility of television can help them get their stories, and their new identities, across.

Committing annual reports and annual meetings to tape is not an easy task. These productions must be entertaining as well as educational. However, creativity is definitely restricted by much of the required content: the message from the chief executive officer (which, in many companies, could kill a show before it gets started); perhaps something from the vice president for finance (again, usually not a charismatic personality); a review of operations; and a brief presentation of a theme, usually something to do with the changed character of the corporation.

All this should be done in about twenty-five minutes or less. And, if it is not a good twenty-five minutes, if the programming is not enlightening and interesting, it could fall victim to a switched channel. For this reason, professional production houses should always be used for corporate video presentations. Overtly commercial or patronizing presentations damage corporate credibility.

Another shortcoming of corporate video is that viewers represent only a small portion of a company's shareholders, even though presentations are beamed to regions of heaviest shareholder concentration. While most companies involved in corporate video productions offer shareholders videotaped annual reports, a few, such as Emhart, telecast their meetings and reports to shareholders. International Paper Company is another of the experimenters. International telecasts its annual report to shareholders via 1,600 cable systems.

ELECTRONIC NEWSLETTERS: MAKING INSTANTANEOUS CONNECTIONS

The electronic newsletter is now available to newsletter publishers and subscribers—specifically, corporate subscribers in companies serving price-sensitive industries, and companies whose financial well-being is directly linked to pricing, legislation, commodities, availabilities of raw materials, and contracts. Rather than being subject to the caprice of mailmen and mailrooms, electronic newsletters are transmitted instantaneously by the pioneer in the field, Newsnet of Bryn Mawr, Pennsylvania. Newsnet is owned by Independent Publications Inc.

The service transmits over telephone lines to the computers of individuals or corporate subscribers. Users pay a premium fee over and above the cost of the publication. Subscribers can, for an additional fee, receive other fast-breaking information involving their markets. To do this, the subscriber's "key word profile" is added to Newsnet's computer.

COMPUTER-GENERATED GRAPHICS: SLIDING INTO THE FUTURE

Slides have become as ordinary as commas to public relations presentations. Rare is the important presentation that does not include slides to heighten impact and to enhance the narrator's delivery. Slides are used with a wide range of presentations, including analyst deliveries, annual meetings, boards of directors' meetings, management seminars, capabilities presentations for customers and prospects, and employee orientation and benefits meetings.

As slide use increases, so does concern for quality. The capabilities of art directors, artists, and slide production houses varies, as does the work they produce. The computer generation of slides has helped to fill this gap, and to substantially speed the preparation of slide presentations. The cost of this service currently remains above that of conventional mechanical preparation methods. But if slides are to be used in a presentation by the chairman, for example, quality and deadlines, not cost, are paramount.

Computer slide-making is available in most American cities. Many services work with the best known equipment, Genigraphics®, which was developed by General Electric, which then sold the technology to Genigraphics Corporation, Park 80 West, Saddle Brook, New Jersey 07662. Genigraphics Corporation is a presentation graphics organization with more than twenty service centers around the nation. The company specializes in the creation of a wide range of graphics and multimedia presentations, plus the sale of equipment such as graphic consoles and film recording machines.

One of the computer's foremost artistic capabilities is the production of organization tables, map and type slides, tabular data, bar and line graphs, pie charts, and word slides (especially for "builds").

Speed, accuracy, and productive capabilities are the primary assets of computerized slide generation. Computers operate at speeds that artists cannot, and they don't make the mistakes that artists are capable of. The quality and variety of the computer also cannot be equalled on an art board. The Genigraphics system, for instance, produces literally millions of different color combinations, and a clarity of image not possible heretofore.

Computer slide-making equipment is not economically feasible for most companies or public relations firms. The basic measures for purchase consideration are: (1) If an organization is responsible for the production of 10,000 slides annually, an image generation and recording system is economically justifiable. (2) If at least 1,000 graphic slides are produced annually, a terminal to create images is justifiable, but an outside service should be used for production. (3) Otherwise, the use of an outside service center is recommended for slide production. The cost of production equipment for slides, overheads and other visuals is being brought down, however. Less sophisticated equipment, such as that available from Centec Corp., Reston, Virginia, can produce film in less than ten minutes. This system generates graphics with as many as eight colors.

Artistic computers are also being used to create advertisements, film producers are using them to create movies, and other technicians are creating television and film animations with them. Public relations people also frequently employ this capability for the production of videotape. They are finding that computer generated graphics, in many ways, exceed the capabilities of human beings.

PAPERLESS NEWS DISSEMINATION: 1,200 WORDS PER MINUTE

Public relations operations that have a telephoning capability as part of their word-processing equipment can take advantage of another relatively new electronic resource—computerized news release preparation and dissemination.

This technology literally permits the writing, dissemination and editing of press releases without their ever touching paper. The release is not committed to paper until it appears in the newspaper. There are three steps to paperless news release technology. First, the public relations person writes the release on a video display terminal (VDT). Then, employing Direct Data Dialing (DDD), the material is transmitted directly to the computer of a service that specializes in the electronic dissemination of public relations materials to the press and financial communities. The service proofreads the material for wire-service style, and disseminates it electronically to the computers of newspapers and financial service institutions. Speed of dissemination is up to 1,200 words per minute, or 10 seconds per page. Newspaper staffers edit the material on VDTs, and send it to their production departments through computers.

The firms that specialize in computer-to-computer press release dissemination are betting that the speed and flexibility of electronics will continue to win converts in both the public relations and newspaper communities. Electronic dissemination speeds up press release work by eliminating paper work, messengers, and the mails. The press material can also be stored in computer memory at all three points for instant recall. The speed of electronic dissemination permits the use of late-breaking stories that, in the recent past, would have been tabled for later editions.

This service, similar in nature to the PR Newswire concept that deals with printed news releases, is offered by several firms, including PR Newswire and Business Wire, both of which receive material from all fifty states. These services transmit to several automated media outlets in the United States and Canada, and reach scores more through local and regional wires. Included are major dailies such as *The New York Times, The Wall Street Journal, The Boston Globe, The Washington Post, The Los Angeles Times, The Denver Post, The Phoenix Gazette, The Seattle Times, The St. Louis Globe-Democrat, The Baltimore Sun, The Louisville Courier-Journal, The Miami Herald,* and *The Toronto Globe & Mail.*

Major business and industry publishers are also automated and receive paperless news distribution, among them Fairchild Publications and McGraw-Hill Publications. Wire services such as UPI, AP, Dow Jones and Reuters also use the method, as do stock exchanges and brokerage firms, including Goldman, Sachs, Ernst & Co., Salomon Brothers, Oppenheimer, Paine Webber, and Merrill Lynch.

Advocates claim that electronic newsrooms have saved many newspapers. Detractors claim that electronics will destroy many debilitated dailies, because they will not be able to afford the new equipment.

COMPUTERIZED MEDIA INFORMATION: SAVE TIME, INCREASE ACCURACY

Some larger public relations agencies have instituted computerized media information capabilities. One of the more elaborate of these systems involves links between the public relations firm's computers and those of a major press monitoring service which continually oversees more than 100,000 domestic publicity outlets. Daily and weekly newspapers, trade and general readership magazines, television and radio stations are included in the capability.

One advantage of these systems is that they eliminate the time required to research media information in directories which are frequently outdated. Accuracy is another benefit, since computerized media lists are updated continually, although errors frequently occur. The service provides public relations people with pressure-sensitive address labels, and media information including names of publications and journalists, addresses, telephone numbers, circulation figures, and total counts.

Software is also available that lists all media by category and city, and includes journalists' names and titles.

TELETEXT AND VIDEOTEX: MANAGING THE INFO EXPLOSION

These on-line information systems help make America's information explosion manageable by providing services such as information retrieval, business transactions, messaging, advertising, and computing.

Teletext is delivered to homes and offices by either broadcast or cable television lines. Videotex has a two-way capability. It is delivered over telephone or cable lines, and requires a home or office terminal for linking with the Videotex computer.

PUBLIC RELATIONS AND THE COMPUTER: A SNEAK PEEK INTO THE FUTURE

Vast libraries of information are available to the public relations practitioner skilled in the use of computers. And during the decade of the 1980s this capability will increase to unknown proportions. "User friendliness," a term that translates to ease of operation, will be one impetus behind the ever-increasing popularity of the computer. A knowledge of computer programming is not necessary to use friendly equipment and, although problems remain, it will be possible in the foreseeable future to use verbal input to solicit information from a computer; the response will be provided either by a mechanical voice or on a display screen.

Another force behind the computer's surge in popularity will be the limitless information available when technical problems are overcome and the linking of different computers, word processors, copiers, terminals, typewriters, and printers is possible. Computer networks will evolve as problems such as the standardization of microprocessor chips and cables, and the selection of either baseband or broadband (a computer's language) are resolved.

Even so, it is now possible, by hooking a desk-top computer to a telephone line, to access approximately 1,000 data banks with both narrow and broad content. Some data banks are devoted to single subjects such as medicine or the law. Others cover extremely broad subjects, such as current events. (Several of these services are explained in more detail in Chapter 2).

From Cyberphobia to Eye Strain: Side Effects of Computers on PR People

Public relations staffers have reacted to the new world of electronics predictably. Many staffers approach the new technology hesitantly. Approximately one-third of them are "cyberphobic"—fearful of using computers. They express concern about not being able to quickly master the skills necessary to utilize the equipment satisfactorily. They appear to view computers as devices with wills of their own, rather than tools for the use of humankind. Cyberphobia can be mastered as individuals learn how to use computers.

Some department managers treat the equipment as a secretarial tool. This is damaging, because staffers respond by emotionally relegating computers to a support role. The best approach is for department managers to display keen interest in computerization, and to master the equipment early on.

As employees acquire a working knowledge of computers, they frequently become intrigued by them. This indicates acceptance is at hand, but it also frequently heralds a period when some staffers—those hooked on the novelty and intellectual challenge offered by computerization—turn into wombats and spend inordinate amounts of time learning more than they would ever need to know about the equipment. This phase gradually disappears, but it is recommended that wombats be urged to dispel their afflictions as quickly as possible.

The last phase is one of self-discipline, in which employees exhibit complete acceptance of computerization.

While the computer is making impressive penetration into the public relations business, it is also bringing complaints. Some newspaper and public relations staffers are complaining of health problems. Law suits have resulted.

Complaints about health usually center on the eyes, and sometimes on harmful effects from radiation. VDTs regenerate images at an average rate of sixty times a second. This creates an indiscernable flicker that emits low levels of microwave radiation, which is believed by some to cause radiant energy-related cataracts. Some employees have also claimed that radiation emissions might be responsible for miscarriages and birth defects.

Complaints such as these have been largely dispelled by a study requested by the National Institute for Occupational Safety and Health, a federal agency. The

National Research Council responded with research that found no valid scientific evidence to indicate that video display terminals cause serious health problems.

Eye fatigue, however, appears to be a legitimate complaint. Operators voice objections about itching, nearsightedness, watery eyes, headaches, dizziness, and cloudy vision. These conditions are usually alleviated if operators take work breaks of at least fifteen minutes every two hours.

The National Research Council panel that studied the problem believes that eye discomfort is caused by inadequately designed terminals, and by poorly designed and poorly lighted workplaces. Many terminals, the panel acknowledged, were inexpensive adaptations of components that were meant for television viewing at a distance, not for close-up work. Also, the panel reported, video equipment is frequently positioned on horizontal surfaces, rather than on vertical planes, which are optimum for computer use. It was also noted that radiation from terminals was well below what would be believed to cause birth defects.

HOW TO PURCHASE ELECTRONIC EQUIPMENT

Public relations people charged with the responsibility of purchasing electronic equipment for their agencies or departments are usually apprehensive about the assignment. They normally don't understand much about computers and other equipment, and computer sales personnel do not usually understand the requirements of the public relations business.

You can quickly educate yourself regarding computers by purchasing some of the many books on the subject. There are books on hardware, there are books on software—both general in approach and very specific. Some books are restricted to certain computer models from specific manufacturers. Some of the many books that can increase your computer smarts include:

Book	Author & Publisher
The Word Processing Book	Peter A. McWilliams, Prelude Press
The Personal Computer Book	Peter A. McWilliams, Prelude Press
The Personal Computer in Business Book	Peter A. McWilliams, Prelude Press
Questions & Answers on Word Processing	Peter A. McWilliams, Prelude Press
Data Systems and Management	Alton R. Kindred, Prentice-Hall
Buyer's Guide: Computers for Everybody	Jerry Willis and Merl Miller dilithium (sic) Press
How to Select Your Own Computer	William Constandse, Frederick Fell Publishing
Real Managers Use Personal Computers	Dick Heiser, Que Corporation

Book	Author & Publisher
Computer Insecurity	Adrian R. D. Norman, Chapman & Hall
Successful Software for Small Corporations	Graham Beech, John Wiley & Sons
Strategy of Computer Selection	Frederick Kelly and Peter Poggi, Reston
The Modern Office Series: Learning to Talk Word Processing	Dianne Galloway, Prentice-Hall
The Electronic Office	Nancy Finn, Prentice-Hall
Coping with Computers	Henry C. Lucas, Jr., Free Press
Before You Buy a Computer: A Practical Guide to Computer Shopping	Dona Z. Meilach, Crown
Are You Computer Literate?	Karen Billing and David Moursund, dilithium (sic) Press
Small Computers for the Small Businessman	Nicolan Rosa and Sharon Rosa dilithium (sic) Press
A Guide for Selecting Computers & Software for the Small Business	Paul Enockson, Reston
How to Computerize Your Small Business	Jules A. Cohen, Prentice-Hall

Manufacturers also have helpful printed materials. IBM has a fine one called *The Guide* which is printed twice a year. There are also many vertical books that concern specific products: Apple, Atari, Commodore-64, VIC-20, TI 99/4A, Timex/Sinclair, TRS-80, IBM, etc. Both hardware and software are covered in these publications.

After preparing yourself by boning up on computers, there are six steps that the public relations neophyte should follow to introduce himself to the electronics revolution.

Six Steps for Easing into the Electronic Revolution

1. *Shop Around.* Shop around for the word processing system you feel most comfortable with. Some equipment has good service records. Some equipment does not. Go to the manufacturers or their distributors; don't let them come to you. Or, visit computer stores that feature the equipment of several manufacturers. As an industry, these are smooth sellers, quite capable of producing the arguments that could result in a sale before you have an opportunity to compare competitive units or prices. They also seem to think everyone has unlimited funds to spend on electronic equipment.

2. *Inquire.* Check other public relations people regarding their experiences with maintenance. New systems almost always have bugs. Expect problems and expect breakdowns, but also expect service. And when your system is finally

operating optimally, have maintenance at least twice a year to assure continued good operation.

3. *Engage a Consultant.* If you are a poor technician, you should engage a consultant to recommend the equipment best suited to your needs. Be careful to select a consultant who represents many word processing manufacturers, though. Some consultants represent just one or two.

4. *Attend Seminars.* You can attend some of the many seminars that are held around the country that deal with the purchase of word processing equipment. Again, the seminar should not be restricted to one or two manufacturers.

5. *Investigate State Colleges.* Investigate the state college system in your region and determine if it has courses in the selection, maintenance and programming of business computers. These courses generally feature other important areas of instruction such as the proper utilization of portable units, methods of computerizing an office's accounting base in addition to doing professional work, and storage requirements.

6. *Read Computer/Software Publications.* There are many publications in this field. Some with the largest circulations include:

BYTE
70 Main Street
Peterborough, NH 03458

COMPUTE!
505 Edwardia Drive
Greensboro, NC 27409

COMPUTERS & ELECTRONICS
One Park Avenue
New York, NY 10016

P C WEEK
381 Elliott Street
Newton, MA 02164

P C WORLD
555 DeHaro Street
San Francisco, CA 94107

COMPUTER DESIGN
119 Russell Street
Littleton, MA 01460

ELECTRONIC DESIGN
Ten Mulholland Drive
Hasbrouck Heights, NJ 07604

P C
One Park Avenue
New York, NY 10016

INFORMATION MANAGEMENT
101 Crossways Park, W.
Woodbury, NY 11797

POPULAR COMPUTING
70 Main Street
Peterborough, NH 03458

COMPUTERWORLD
375 Cochituate Road
Framingham, MA 01701

CREATIVE COMPUTING
39 East Hanover Avenue
Morris Plains, NJ 07950

DATAMATION
875 Third Avenue
New York, NY 10022

BASIC COMPUTING
3838 South Warner Street
Tacoma, WA 98409

BUSINESS COMPUTER SYSTEMS
221 Columbus Avenue
Boston, MA 02116

BUSINESS COMPUTING
119 Russell Street
Littleton, MA 01460

BUSINESS SOFTWARE
3543 N. E. Broadway
Portland, OR 97232

COMPUTER USER
16704 Marquardt Avenue
Cerritos, CA 90701

INFOSYSTEMS
Hitchcock Building
Wheaton, IL 60188

INFOWORLD
1060 Marsh Road, #C-200
Menlo Park, CA 94025

COMPUTER TECHNOLOGY REVIEW   PERSONAL COMPUTING
924 Westwood Boulevard #650   10 Mulholland Drive
Los Angeles, CA 90024   Hasbrouck Heights, NJ 07604

The typewriter, teleprinter, Telex, TWX, phone facsimile, and other devices are destined for varying degrees of obsolescence during the 1980s. They will be swept aside by new technologies such as word processing, electronic mail, Data Direct Dialing (DDD), and others. And, autotypewriters and addressing machines will all but disappear. The word processor performs these tasks inestimably better and faster than old equipment.

13

Consumer Marketing
Successfully Applying the Mysteries of Public Relations

For decades, consumer marketers treated the public relations function as though it were a great mystery. They thought of public relations as publicity. Messages on printed pages were usually the only public relations tools utilized by consumer marketers and product managers to help sell products. However, progress has been made at putting it all together, or at utilizing all possible public relations tools in the marketing mix. These include:

- Publicity
- Research, primarily measurement techniques
- Sales promotion
- Spokesperson tours
- Sales training/sales meetings
- Trade shows
- Video news features
- Big events
- Monitoring of government and consumer groups
- Language simplification
- Design and production of point-of-purchase displays and literature

It would be extremely unusual for all these tools to be employed in the marketing of a product. The very nature of marketing assignments usually precludes the utilization of some of the lesser-used tools, such as the monitoring of government and consumer groups, sales training/sales meetings, and design and production of point-of-purchase materials. Additionally, specialized agencies usually win "vertical" assignments to create and execute sales promotion campaigns, which frequently require a knowledge of how to conduct contests and giveaways. Other specialized organizations, many with offices strategically located in popular convention cities, concentrate on sales meetings and sales training, while still others focus exclusively on creating a corporate or a product presence at trade shows. So-called copy-art shops, of which there are hundreds nationwide, are skilled at the production of collateral and point-of-purchase materials. And, there are also countless display houses that restrict activities to the design and construction of displays for conventions and trade shows.

Some of the largest public relations agencies possess the capability to apply all eleven public relations tools to a marketing situation, but only a few qualify—and they do not have the experience to out-perform specialized shops in areas such as the development of sales promotion strategies, and conducting sales training and sales meetings.

The decade of the 1980s, therefore, will see public relations agencies expanding their participation in the consumer marketing function from the traditional publicity role. But public relations shops will not, and should not, be looked upon to provide all services in this area. Specialized firms with specialized talents should be retained to perform specialized tasks.

SIX OBJECTIVES FOR PUBLIC RELATIONS INVOLVEMENT IN CONSUMER MARKETING

1. To complement advertising with publicity to add editorial endorsement, to extend sales messages into areas not included in advertising budgets, to provide consumers with in-depth product information, and to lengthen the period that commercial messages are before the public.

2. To provide research capabilities—primarily measurement and pre- and post-testing—to refine marketing efforts, and to measure the impact of public relations activities on a marketing campaign. The most important research capabilities would involve techniques such as: the computer-based systems VALS and PRIZM to analyze market trends, to pinpoint the most desirable markets, and to provide information concerning the socioeconomic characteristics of target audiences; store audits, purchase panels, and in-place panels to measure purchase behavior and product acceptance; and new techniques that provide insight into the most effective implementation of public relations tools in the marketing mix.

3. To provide the capability for big events that can increase product visibility, involve customers and potential customers, add drama and credibility, target promotional activities to specific audiences and regions, and create product loyalty.

4. To counsel clients regarding the most effective utilization of sales incentive and sales training experts, as well as firms that specialize in sales promotion, the design of trade show and convention exhibits, and other special activities.

5. To extend the reach and effectiveness of print publicity through the implementation of spokesperson tours and video news features.

6. To monitor governmental organizations and consumer groups regarding negatives and/or positives that could affect a product in the marketplace.

Public relations tools in the consumer marketing function should not be implemented solely during introductory campaigns. Public relations techniques are equally effective for breathing new life into mature products, and for creating new markets for products that have traditionally been positioned in restrictive ways.

Example: Church & Dwight's Arm & Hammer Baking Soda.

The market for baking soda as a leavening agent for baked goods dwindled as home baking declined, and Church & Dwight looked for large-volume applications for its product.

Since baking soda is an efficient extinguisher of fires, a program named Operation Fire Pail was introduced. Empty one-pound coffee cans were filled with baking soda. Around the cans were wrapped labels with the word "Fire" emblazoned white on red. The Arm & Hammer logo was also displayed, and there were spaces for the fire and police departments' telephone numbers.

Coordinated with National Fire Prevention Week, the program received the support of the Camp Fire Girls, Junior Fire Marshals, Girl Scouts and Brownies, Boy Scouts and Cub Scouts, Junior Grange, and 4-H Clubs. Instructional kits were distributed to elementary school teachers, and intensive publicity campaigns were conducted.

The program resulted in a significant sales jump. While spoonfuls of the product are used for baking, two pounds of baking soda are required to fill a one-pound coffee tin.

Example: Pittsburgh Brewing Company's Iron City Light Beer.

Nationally marketed beers had seriously eroded Pittsburgh Brewing's market for Iron City Beer. When it introduced a new light beer, the company embarked upon an imaginative advertising and public relations campaign that drew attention to the fact that not only the beer, but also the bottles, cans, and labeling, were manufactured locally.

The program was aimed at all of the public involved in the manufacture, distribution, and marketing of the product: employees, distributors, restaurant and tavern owners, and beer drinkers. The Mayor of Pittsburgh kicked things off by opening a giant replica of Iron City Beer, and releasing thousands of helium-filled balloons. Distributor tours, a speaker's campaign, and publicity followed. And a direct mail campaign, consisting of Iron-O-Grams, was targeted at owners of restaurants, taverns, and private clubs, as well as at beer distributors.

It was reported that Iron City Light took about thirty percent of the local market, and that it outsold nationally advertised lights in the region.

SPORTS PROMOTIONS: HOW TO WIN IN THE FASTEST GROWING SEGMENT OF CONSUMER MARKETING

Both the advertising and public relations businesses are intensifying promotional activities in sports promotion, and for the same reasons. The business justification for increased sports promotion is obvious from the bombastic growth of sports and leisure activities in the United States. Between 1965 and 1980, approximately 150 professional athletic teams were organized; there were fewer than 60 before 1965. Professional baseball attendance doubled, and professional basketball and hockey attendance increased fivefold.

Participatory sports are experiencing a similar expansion. Approximately one in every nine Americans, or twenty-five million people, runs or jogs. There are enough golf courses in the nation to put about 240 of them in each of the fifty states. About one in every eleven Americans plays tennis, five times the number that played in 1965. And emerging sports such as soccer, rugby, bicycle racing, and hang gliding, are growing with dramatic speed.

Athletics offer public relations practitioners the opportunity to target promotional activity, because each sport has distinctive followers, or "types" of sports fans. The degree of targeting afforded by sports is evident from the specialized events that companies sponsor. Moët Champagne has sponsored America's Cup racing, M & M Mars supplied snacks for the 1984 Olympics, Wrangler jeans sponsors rodeos, Valvoline sponsors auto and powerboat racing, Avon sponsors figure skating competitions, and Gillette sponsors the major league All-Star Balloting.

Targeting of a more general nature is also possible with sports promotions. Companies that market industrial products, for example, frequently sell to corporate purchasing departments. And the corporate purchasing world is staffed, generally, by males between the ages of 25 and 62 who are sports enthusiasts.

Sports promotions permit the targeting of other population segments, too. While a large number of women, for example, follow major sports such as football, baseball, and basketball, they show particular interest in sports such as tennis, golf, bowling, skating, skiing, and swimming.

The credibility of corporate sponsors receives instant and positive jolts when programs are undertaken. This is attributable to the fact that, in addition to the powerful allure of major athletic competitions, some sports require that sponsoring organizations be approved by their managing committees or associations.

Sports promotions provide the opportunity to dramatically complement existing advertising and public relations campaigns, and to add elements such as customer involvement.

Opportunities for Corporate Participation in Sports Promotions

These opportunities include:

- The Olympics
- Tier I sports (in order of attendance)
  - Horse racing
  - Auto racing
  - Baseball
  - Football
  - Basketball

- Tier II sports
  - Bicycle racing
  - Bowling
  - Boxing
  - Dog racing
  - Equestrian events
  - Fencing
  - Field hockey
  - Golf
  - Hang gliding
  - Hot-air ballooning
  - Jai-alai
  - Lacrosse
  - Motorcycle racing
  - Polo
  - Powerboat racing
  - Rodeo
  - Rugby
  - Skating
  - Skiing
  - Soccer
  - Squash
  - Swimming
  - Tennis
  - Track and field
  - Trap and target shooting
  - Wrestling
  - Yachting

How to Select Your Sport and Sponsor It

The names, addresses and telephone numbers of sports organizations, plus descriptions of their activities, can be found in a reference manual entitled *Encyclopedia of Associations,* edited by Denise S. Akey, and produced by Gale Research Company. The pertinent material will be found in a chapter entitled "Athletics & Sports Organizations."

Sponsorship or special program requests should be directed to the governing body of a sport, to the management of an individual team within a sport, or, if a player is to be highlighted, to the individual.

The dramatic increase in the popularity of sports activities translates to greater media coverage and significantly more public relations placement activity. In 1965, there were fewer than 100 sports publications, while there are almost 190 today. Daily newspapers and the electronic media have also increased their sports coverage substantially.

The primary concern when selecting a sport to sponsor is that it provide the proper audience for the product or corporate message. That is why Valvoline sponsors auto and powerboat races, and why Wrangler sponsors rodeos.

Sponsorship can be purchased for millions of dollars, or for a couple of thousand dollars, depending upon the sport and the event. For the fee, companies receive inducements such as the assistance of athletes in promotional efforts, commercial identification of the company or product, collaterals, customer entertainment, and identification on letterheads and other printed materials.

Sponsorship of an event, however, regardless of its importance or popularity, does not guarantee publicity. There must be a reason for a sponsor to be identified in press coverage of a sports event. Usually, this reason does not exist.

Special Programs vs. Sponsorship

Commonly, special programs generate more beneficial attention for a corporation than the sponsorship of an athletic event. An example is the Math Baseball program that St. Regis Paper Company conducted for several years. Cosponsored by the YMCA, the program was actively supported by many American and National League baseball teams.

St. Regis, a diversified forest products company which was acquired by Champion International in 1985, manufactures a line of educational games, one of which is called "Math Baseball." The objective of the game is to help grade schoolers understand mathematics by rewarding participants with "base hits" for responding correctly to questions about addition, subtraction, multiplication, or division. The company literally took Math Baseball out of the box, and put it on the playing field. Competitions were conducted by the YMCA in major league cities. The best two teams in each city competed in a World Series in their city's major league ballpark. A popular baseball player in each city served as the local Commissioner of Math Baseball.

The competition drew positive attention both to St. Regis, and to its line of educational games.

Sponsorship opportunities are not always available in every sport. Also, in some minor sports, no sponsorship opportunities exist. Among the most popular sponsorships are those for the Olympics. They are also among the most expensive, and they attract substantial attention. The United States Olympic Committee, Colorado Springs, Colorado, evaluates all sponsorship requests.

Who Your Spectators Are

The demographics of almost all sports are readily available. Demographic information consists of numbers of men and women participants/spectators, plus breakdowns of ages, incomes, education, and numbers of followers by individual sections of the country. VALS (Values and Lifestyle Program; see Chapter 2) is particularly effective at identifying the followers of individual sports. VALS can provide valuable information for public relations practitioners attempting to target their promotional activities within the world of sport.

Sports promotions are expected to thrive during the 1980s, as they did during the 1970s. Some major public relations firms have established departments to specialize in these promotions, and several small-to-medium agencies, most of them in New York City, specialize exclusively in sports promotions.

14

Agency-Client Relationships
Secrets of Successful Courtship

The extremes of relationships between public relations agencies and their clients are documented in the productiveness of accounts, and in the emotional stability and blood pressure readings of all involved.

Too often, corporate staffers with a total lack of experience working with agencies are assigned that very task. Ideally, individuals who understand the ramifications of this sometimes precarious relationship would be responsible for corporate liaison. A beneficial agency-client relationship requires knowledge of the procedures involved in agency selection, a comprehension of budgets and contracts, and most important, how to use a public relations consultancy for maximum benefit.

WHAT YOU SHOULD KNOW ABOUT SELECTING AN AGENCY

The most stable and rewarding agency-client relationships are built around an understanding of the responsibilities and the capabilities of both parties. When selecting an agency, it behooves corporate representatives to know the strengths of agencies under consideration, and to evaluate them candidly.

Stature is not always necessary for effective account service. Public relations is an intensely personal business—a business in which individual chemistry, trust and rapport can be important to productive and durable relationships. For this reason, small- and medium-sized public relations firms with records of solid service will continue to garner their share of business.

Don't overlook a dual agency relationship, either. Joint agreements with, say, a large, full-service shop, plus a small, specialized shop, permit multi-office availability, plus specialized support in one or more vital areas.

There is no question, though, that large, multi-office public relations consultancies, particularly those with European and Asian offices in addition to key United States addresses, will continue to attract most blue chip corporate clients. Big agencies attract big budgets because they offer full service, and because they maintain overseas representation in an era when the world's capital markets and business communities are undergoing dramatic internationalization.

Another factor favoring "bigness" is the popularity of agency mergers. Most of the largest public relations agencies have been acquired by major advertising firms: Burson-Marsteller by Young & Rubicam; Hill & Knowlton by J. Walter Thompson; Carl Byoir & Associates by Foote, Cone & Belding. But, with size and full-service capabilities so important, mergers and acquisitions are expected to continue. Most likely, these will be unions of public relations firms rather than acquisitions of public relations agencies by advertising agencies. The Carl Byoir merger with Golin/Harris Communications, a large, Chicago-based public relations consultancy, is an example. The fact that many public relations organizations were founded during the 1950s and 1960s will also influence the merger trend. The original owners of these firms are close to retirement, and buy-outs or other arrangements are necessary to purchase the equity positions of top executives.

The Top Fifteen PR Agencies in the U.S.

Discounting mergers, there should not be as many changes in the top fifteen public relations agencies as there were during the 1970s. The major firms are:

1. Burson-Marsteller
2. Hill & Knowlton
3. Carl Byoir & Associates
4. Ruder Finn & Rotman
5. Ogilvy & Mather Public Relations
6. Manning, Selvage & Lee
7. Daniel J. Edelman
8. Doremus & Company
9. Booke Communications Incorporated Group
10. The Rowland Company
11. Ketchum Public Relations
12. Rogers & Cowan
13. Fleishman-Hilliard
14. Gray and Company
15. Robert Marston and Associates

Do not expect to find many young, quick-growing public relations shops in your hunt for representation. It's becoming increasingly difficult to achieve a reputation as a hot young shop. The public relations field is saturated with over 1,200 domestic firms, compared to less than half that number in 1960. There is an abundance of agencies to absorb demand; there is also an abundance of "specialty" consultancies to respond to requests for specialized service.

Small, specialized agencies will continue to increase, however, as they did in the 1970s. These shops will concentrate on areas such as government relations, medical and sports communications, teleconferencing, and travel and leisure-time public relations—areas in which special expertise is important, and where large-staff, multinational capabilities are not necessary.

Do your homework before soliciting the interest of public relations agencies. Telephone other corporate public relations departments, the trade and business press, investment bankers, proxy solicitation firms and trade associations for recommendations.

Develop, in writing, a "to file" rationale for the selection of an agency. Evaluate such questions as: Why is the company considering outside representation? What services does the company need most from an outside consultancy? What budget is available, and is it realistic? Which individuals would provide corporate interface? Is internal staff sufficient? What does corporate management expect from outside public relations representation? Are their expectations reasonable?

Some corporations develop questionnaires for prospective agencies to complete as a part of the early evaluation process. These questionnaires ask questions concerning: size of agencies in dollars and staffs; support services available; number of offices and locations; client rosters; typical fees; corporate/trade/press/financial community references; and experience handling accounts in businesses similar to yours. They are helpful for whittling the field down early. There is an element of danger in these questionnaires, though. The information they uncover is sometimes used for the elimination of smaller, newer organizations that might be well-suited to corporate needs.

Narrowing the Field

Limit meetings with prospective agencies to no more than six, preferably fewer. It is best to meet informally at first, for about forty-five minutes. Provide a letter of invitation. Mention specifically that several agencies are being evaluated, say where the meeting is to be held and for how long, who will be attending from your company, and state that this is a get-to-know-you meeting at which formal presentations are not expected.

The purpose of these up-front meetings is to provide the opportunity for you to evaluate agency representatives, to form opinions regarding their proficiency, agency staffing arrangements, fee structures, and expertise in the areas where your company requires assistance.

Following the initial face-to-face meetings, eliminate all but two or three candidates, and request, in writing, formal presentations of one hour or a little longer. If a budget is set, inform final-round invitees. This knowledge is necessary for them to structure account recommendations realistically.

The Most Important Considerations for Evaluating the Finalists

- What was your general evaluation of the organization, and, specifically, of its creative expertise and ability to relate to your company's needs?

- What was your evaluation of the account team which would work on the account? Do they have strong experience? Writing credentials? Professional backgrounds?

- Does internal agency structure provide adequate support for your account?

- Has effective work been done for other clients?

- Was a firm grasp of working with the press, financial, professional or business communities exhibited?

- Would you be comfortable working with these people?

- Would your account be important to them?

Don't neglect the opportunity to ask questions that require revealing responses. Questions could include:

- "What are some of your agency's major accomplishments during the past two years?

- "What have been some of your failures, and why?"

- "Who are your primary press contacts?"

- "May we call some of your clients for references?"

- "What are your agency's major strengths?"

- "In what areas do you have the least experience?"

- "Could we expect reviews of your efforts on our behalf on a regular basis?"

HOW TO ESTABLISH A BUDGET FOR AGENCY SERVICES

Make sure that budget parameters are established in advance. Early disagreements about expenditures can launch agency-client relationships in a leaky boat.

The most common budget arrangements are what are called fee, retainer, time input, project, or a combination of these, such as fee plus project.

Fee accounts involve setting a budget—say $144,000 for agency time for a twelve-month period. The client is billed $12,000 per month, and agency personnel bill time against the budgeted fee just as lawyers would. Hourly time charges, depending upon the caliber and experience of the personnel working on an account, vary from about $40 to $275 per hour. Expect normal time charges, though, to be in the range of $60 to $275 per hour.

Retainers are invoiced at set amounts—say, $6,000 per month—and are intended to do just what the term suggests, to retain the consultancy for assistance when and if needed. The retainer is billed whether or not time is expended on the client's behalf, on the premise that the consultancy maintains staff to respond immediately to clients' requests for assistance.

Time input accounts are open-ended, and they are usually to be avoided. Account personnel bill time against an account, and clients usually exercise only loose budget control. Such accounts are justified only when a massive effort is required on a crash project.

Project budgets are frequently worked by public relations agencies. Clients agree to a fixed price for a project, and the agency invoices accordingly. Frequently, several projects are worked concurrently.

Out-of-pocket expenses, usually 15 to 20 percent of the fee, are always billed separately. Some agencies also have a 2 to 3 percent surcharge to cover the expense of mailing, photocopies and shipping.

CONTRACTS

Agency-clients contracts are the rule rather than the exception. And they are becoming increasingly complex.

Not many years ago, agency-client relationships were launched on a handshake. "If we can't trust you, we don't deserve to work for you," was the old agency saying.

Apparently, enough good faith was shattered through the years so that both parties now feel they require protection. Agreements are generally in letter form, and are called, perplexingly enough, Letters of Agreement. Sometimes, these agreements are massive documents, but that is the exception. A common Letter of Agreement follows.

Dear Mr.___(Client)___:

This letter will confirm the agreement entered into by and between ___(company name)___ ("Client") and___(agency name)___ ("Agency") as follows:

1. Services
   Agency will render professional services ("Basic Services") to Client as follows:
   a. preparing news releases, feature articles, background information for newspapers, periodicals, radio and television stations and other media;
   b. producing and distributing news tapes;
   c. representing Client with various publics, including the media;
   d. training spokespersons;
   e. conducting medical symposia.

2. Special Services
   In addition to the Basic Services, Agency is prepared to provide Client with such other special public relations services as Client may request, including writing and producing booklets, promotional materials, and staging and conducting meetings. Prior to the inception of such Special Services, Client and Agency will agree on supplemental compensation which Client shall pay therefore.

3. Compensation
   a. Client agrees to pay Agency for the actual time spent by account, creative, communications and other personnel in providing the Basic Services as determined, by applying the Agency's standard hourly rates.
   b. During the period January 1, 19xx, to December 31, 19xx, Agency will operate on a total budget of $360,000. Agency will not exceed this amount without the Client's prior approval.

    c. On or before December 31, 19xx, and from time to time thereafter, Client and Agency will evaluate the time input budget in light of Client's projected service requirements, and decide whether budget adjustments are appropriate.

    d. Where Agency uses the services of an outside supplier in providing services to Client, Client shall pay Agency the cost of such services, together with a 17.65 percent mark-up. Such costs shall include items such as mechanical and art costs (including typography, engraving, electrotypes, printing, photographs, artwork and comprehensive layouts), and audiovisual production costs (including talent, props, scenery, sound and lighting effects, rights, license fees, and producers' fees).

    e. Client shall reimburse Agency (without mark-up) for the out-of-pocket expenses not listed in Section 3f. Such expenses shall include long distance travel expenses of Agency personnel, calls, telexes, postage, deliveries, press clipping services, hotel accomodations, travel and entertainment of journalists and other parties whom Client has requested Agency to entertain.

    f. To cover Agency's cost of miscellaneous items, such as local telephone calls and photocopies, that are required to service Client, Agency charges three percent (3%) of the monthly hourly charge billed to Client as described in article 3a above.

4. Billing Procedures

    a. On or about the first of each month, Client will receive an invoice that presents Agency's time charges for that month, and details out-of-pocket expenses incurred during the previous billing month. Agency's billing month runs from the 16th day of one month through the 15th day of the next. Production costs shall be billed to the Client at the end of each month.

    b. Special services performed pursuant to Article 2 above will be estimated in advance and invoiced separately.

    c. All invoices shall be due thirty (30) days after the date of issue.

5. Term and Termination

    a. The term of this Agreement shall commence on January 1, 19xx, and continue until terminated by either party by giving the other 60 days prior written notice. Client shall pay all hourly charges and out-of-pocket charges incurred up to the effective date of such termination.

    b. Upon the effective date of the termination of this Agreement, all of Client's property in Agency's possession, and all contracts for services and materials entered into by Agency for Client shall be turned over and/or assigned to Client.

6. Ownership

All slogans and publicity materials submitted or developed by Agency for Client during the term of this Agreement, and which Client uses at least once prior to the termination hereof, or which Client indicates in writing to Agency during the term hereof as being specifically within the designated plans for adoption and exploitation by Client, shall be, as between Agency and Client, Client's property exclusively. All slogans, ideas or plans submitted, created or developed by Agency for Client during the term of this Agreement, and not used by Client during the term hereof, or designated by Client in writing as being specifically within designated plans for exploitation and adoption of Client thereafter, are Agency's property, and shall be dealt with by Client as such.

7. Indemnification

Client shall be responsible for the accuracy, completeness, and propriety of information concerning Client's organization, industry and products which Client furnishes to Agency in connection with the performance of this Agreement.

Client agrees to indemnify Agency, and to hold it harmless from and against any and all losses, claims, damages, expenses or liabilities which Agency may incur based on defects in goods sold, supplied, manufactured or otherwise dealt in by Client, or representations concerning Client, or its products or services, to the extent furnished or prepared by or at Client's request for use by Agency provided. Agency notifies Client within a reasonable time of Agency's receipt of any notice or claim or demand or service of legal process involving any matters for which Client has agreed to hold Agency harmless.

After material has been issued by Agency to the press or to another third party, following Client approval, its use is no longer under Agency control. Agency can therefore not assure the use of its press material by any publication, nor, if published, that it will be accurate.

8. Agency/Client

In purchasing materials or services on Client's behalf, Agency will be acting as Client's agent, and all orders placed and contracts entered into by Agency for such purpose with its suppliers and other persons may so state.

9. International Public Relations

Agency agrees to provide such services outside the United States as Client shall from time to time request, on such terms as are mutually agreed upon in advance.

10. Entire Agreement

This Agreement constitutes the entire Agreement with respect to the subject matter hereof, and may only be modified or amended in writing, and signed by the party to be charged.

11. Construction

This Agreement shall be construed in accordance with and governed by the laws of the State of New York.

12. Titles

Titles are for reference only. In the event of a conflict between a title and the content of a section, the content of the section shall control.

Agency and Client have indicated their acceptance and approval of the foregoing by signing in the spaces provided below.

Very truly yours,

(Agency name)

By:_____

(Client name)

By: _____

This agreement, which was drawn up by a public relations agency's counsel, favors the agency. Sometimes clients demand that agencies work with agreements drawn up by company lawyers. In these cases, agencies usually submit to clients' requests.

And, very often, clients say they will not sign any contract. Agencies almost always acquiesce in these situations, too.

THE BEST WAYS TO TAP AN AGENCY'S RESOURCES

A healthy, viable client-consultancy relationship requires that corporate personnel know how to utilize an agency's resources to complement those of internal staff. Corporate staffers should be aware of the several ways in which they can best tap these resources. Some important possibilities follow.

- Specialized Talents
  Call upon the diverse talents of your agency for consultation and guidance. Even though the agency may not be large, its personnel should provide more than the traditional range of public relations services. The consultancy, for instance, should strive to remain current in the state-of-the-art, and familiar with all facets of the economic community: business and industry, professional, governmental, nonprofit and other institutions.

  Full-service agencies usually offer clients a wide range of specialized services. These include media relations, spokesperson training, research, business-to-business marketing, audiovisual and graphics, financial relations, employee relations, government relations and public affairs, and sometimes even language simplification.

- Cost-Effectiveness
  Economics should be one of the most important considerations for retention of outside public relations counsel. External representation permits flexibility in the area of manpower utilization and availability. It is totally impractical, for example, for a corporation to maintain, on staff, the specialized personnel that many agencies do. When retaining outside counsel, a corporation uses as many or as few of its consultancy's services as is practical, thereby controlling costs.

- Peak-Load Assistance
  You should use your agency for assistance during peak-load periods, and for special events that demand intense effort for short periods of time. Agencies should also be called upon for long-distance assignments that may be difficult to execute from corporate headquarters. Multi-office public relations agencies, especially those with addresses in key domestic and overseas locations, excel at these assignments.

- Perspective
  Corporate staffers should also make it a practice to use outside consultancies to expand their perspectives of the public relations function. Tunnel vision is

a common affliction of corporate staffers; they are expected to react to situations involving the business or businesses their companies are involved in, and little else. Agency personnel, however, are able to provide fresh perspectives concerning business and social trends and challenges because they work with a variety of industries, and because they share evaluations routinely with members of the business, press and academic communities.

Corporate personnel should also avail themselves of the special reports that many public relations consultancies prepare. These primers cover topics such as environmental regulations, federalism, consumerism, financial reporting changes, foreign investment trends, new electronic communications techniques, employee motivation practices, and other subjects.

- Objectivity
Because of the different perspectives of internal/external staffers, corporate public relations practitioners should use their consultancies to assist in winning management confidence for, and support of, the function. For example, external counsel (with its staff specialists and broad exposure to corporate problems) can be employed to balance presentations to management, and to propose and implement sensitive projects such as researching the financial, investment, and customer communities, where anonymity is often crucial to objectivity.

- Vocational Stimulation
A well-conditioned inside/outside public relations rapport can also be expected to provide vocational stimulation for corporate staffers. Probably the best opportunity for this lies in the scheduling of occasional meetings, presided over by senior agency representatives, during which topics such as changing public relations techniques and strategies are discussed.

State-of-the-art discussions are especially valuable during periods, such as the middle-to-late 1980s, when the public relations function will be assimilating many new procedures. Not only can outside counsel help keep corporate clients apprised of new techniques and strategies, but they can also explain the proper implementation. For example, efforts to research the effectiveness of public relations activity are becoming increasingly popular. These measurements should be undertaken with extreme caution, however, because they are new, and because most practitioners are unfamiliar with the research methods involved. Industrial public relations specialists, especially, should be wary of these measurements; industrial practitioners are not as familiar with even basic research as are those who deal with consumer products.

All this is blue sky, of course. But when agency-client relationships are working reasonably well—when the egos, the unreasonable demands and expectations, and any number of other troublesome elements are in the embrace of logic—these parameters apply.

Index

I

Illinois Institute of Technology, 88
Independent, definition of, 130
Indianapolis *News, 111*
Indianapolis *Star, 111*
Indiana University/Purdue University (Indianapolis), Aerospace Research Applications Center of, 88
Information Access Corporation, 82
Interactive Market Systems, Inc., 82
Internal audit(s):
  description of, 2
  how much of a company gets an, 3
  how to conduct a face-to-face interview, 5
  objectives of, 2
  sample notification letter, 4
  sample of questions asked about the relationship between management and hourly employees, 9-11
  sample of questions asked in an, 6-8
  sample of questions asked of hourly employees for an, 8-9
  types and number of employees to interview, 4-5
  use of management consulting firms, 11-12
  use of public relations (PR) agencies, 11, 12, 14-16
  use of quotations in, 6
International Beautiful People Unlimited, 269
International Chamber of Commerce, 254
Interview(s):
  face-to-face, 5, 17, 89, 90
  length of time devoted to an, 5
  mail, 89, 90
  pre-interview analysis, 144-147
  for surveys, 89-90
  telephone, 5, 43, 44, 89, 90
  types and numbers of employees used for, 4-5
  use of recording devices, 5
Interviewers, traits of, 5-6
Interviews, marketing research, 1-2
Investor relations survey:
  excerpts from a survey of the financial community, 62-64
  objectives of a, 61-62
  sample questionnaire for, 64-66

Investors, managing overseas:
  brokerage firms/investment firms for, 255
  differences between American and European investment communities, 264-265
  elements of a program for, 257-63
  European press and, 259
  how to approach European investors, 256-257
  listing with European stock exchanges, 260-261
  marketing programs and programs for, 261-262
  meetings and, 257-259, 265
  pre- and post-meeting research for, 257, 259-260
  public relations firms for, 256
  specialized firms for, 256
  which firms should conduct European investor relations, 256
Investors Management Sciences, Inc., 82
Issues determination survey:
  objectives of an, 73
  sample questionnaire for a, 73-76
Issues stories, 100

J

Japan, stock exchange of, 261
Journalists, views of, on public relations people, 103-104

K

Kalamazoo *Gazette, 111*
K&M Publications, Inc., 83
Kansas City *Star, 112*
Kansas City *Times, 112*
Ketchum Publicity Tracking Model, 43
Ketchum Public Relations, 43, 296
Kiwanis Club of Atlanta, 184
Kiwanis Club of Houston, 184
Kiwanis International, 190
KLM Royal Dutch Airlines, 259